NEW YORK REVIEW BOOKS
CLASSICS

T0007097

RAHEL VARNHAGEN

HANNAH ARENDT (1906–1975) was born in Linden, Prussia
(now Hanover, Germany). She studied philosophy at the University
of Marburg under Martin Heidegger and at Heidelberg University
under Karl Jaspers. Arrested for researching anti-Semitism at
the Prussian State Library, she fled Germany in 1933 and lived for
eight years in Paris, where she worked for Jewish refugee organiza-
tions and completed her biography of Rahel Varnhagen—though
the book would not be published in full until 1957. Soon after
the Nazi invasion of France in 1940, Arendt immigrated to the
United States, taking part in the Commission on European
Jewish Cultural Reconstruction and teaching at Bard College,
Berkeley, Princeton, the University of Chicago, and the New
School for Social Research. She is perhaps best known for
Eichmann in Jerusalem: A Report on the Banality of Evil (1963),
The Origins of Totalitarianism (1951), and a major philosophical
work, *The Human Condition* (1958).

RICHARD WINSTON (1921–1983) and CLARA WINSTON
(1917–1979) were both born in New York City, attended Brooklyn
College, and lived most of their lives together on a farm in Vermont.
They translated more than one hundred and fifty books from the
German—including works by Kafka, Hesse, and Jung—and were
awarded the PEN Translation Prize in 1972 for their edition of
The Letters of Thomas Mann.

BARBARA HAHN is a professor emerita of German studies at
Vanderbilt University. She has written and edited a number of
books, collecting and commenting on Hannah Arendt's work
and the correspondence of Rahel Levin Varnhagen.

Rahel as a young girl. Pencil drawing by Wilhelm Hensel.

RAHEL VARNHAGEN
The Life of a Jewish Woman

HANNAH ARENDT

Translated from the German by
RICHARD WINSTON *and*
CLARA WINSTON

Introduction by
BARBARA HAHN

NEW YORK REVIEW BOOKS

New York

THIS IS A NEW YORK REVIEW BOOK
PUBLISHED BY THE NEW YORK REVIEW OF BOOKS
435 Hudson Street, New York, NY 10014
www.nyrb.com

Copyright © 1957 by the Hannah Arendt Bluecher Literary Trust
Translation copyright © by Richard Winston and Clara Winston
Introduction copyright © 2022 by Barbara Hahn
All rights reserved.

First published as a New York Review Books Classic in 2022.

Library of Congress Cataloging-in-Publication Data
Names: Arendt, Hannah, 1906–1975, author.
Title: Rahel Varnhagen : the life of a Jewish woman / by Hannah Arendt.
Description: New York : New York Review Books, 2021. | Series: New York
Review Books classics
Identifiers: LCCN 2020058368 (print) | LCCN 2020058369 (ebook) | ISBN
9781681375892 (paperback) | ISBN 9781681375908 (ebook)
Subjects: LCSH: Varnhagen, Rahel, 1771–1833. | Jewish women—Germany—
Berlin—Biography. | Jews—Germany—Berlin—Intellectual life. | Berlin
(Germany)—Intellectual life.
Classification: LCC PT2546.V22 A913 2021 (print) | LCC PT2546.V22 (ebook) |
DDC 838/.609 [B]—dc23
LC record available at https://lccn.loc.gov/2020058368
LC ebook record available at https://lccn.loc.gov/2020058369

ISBN 978-1-68137-589-2
Available as an electronic book; ISBN 978-1-68137-590-8

Printed in the United States of America on acid-free paper.
10 9 8 7 6 5 4 3 2 1

CONTENTS

INTRODUCTION
Fate and the Jewish Question

IT WAS probably Hannah Arendt's last encounter with her biography of Rahel Varnhagen. In August 1975, while vacationing in Switzerland, she received a letter from her friend Glenn Gray, who had just read the book: "It is a fascinating book, Hannah, and amazing for one who was a mere babe in arms to write.... I find it the most self-revealing of all your writings, self-revealing that is as you *then* were. Not many surely could have fathomed Rahel in all her idiosyncrasies as you do." Arendt felt "quite touched about your lines on my old Rahel." But, she insisted, "I did never identify myself with Rahel; I was interested in what she called a *Schicksal*... and the Jewish question." Looking back at her book on Rahel Varnhagen, written many decades earlier, a word of her native language came to Arendt's mind: *Schicksal*—fate. She was reminded of a key sentence the protagonist of her book had once written: "Everyone has a fate who knows what kind of fate he has." Reflections on the Jewish question and on the fate of a Jewish woman who knew so much about her own fate—this is the quintessence of Arendt's biography.

Rahel Levin, the biography's protagonist, could be introduced from different perspectives: Born in Berlin in May 1771, thrown into turbulent times—the French Revolution, Prussia's defeat in 1806, the Napoleonic Wars, the Congress of Vienna in 1815—all these historical ruptures had a deep impact on her life. In 1830, she welcomed the July Revolution as a sign of a more democratic future to come. She died in Berlin in 1833.

Or: Born the daughter of a Jewish merchant, she hoped for "civil betterment" of the Jews. In the 1790s, her salon drew young writers and intellectuals, actresses and opera singers, and even a Prussian prince to her house. They all enjoyed the art of conversation that their host practiced and promoted so masterfully. This tolerant society would soon vanish; some of her former friends converted to conservative or even openly anti-Jewish politics. In 1819, the first outbreak of modern anti-Semitism in Germany left her "endlessly sad." At the end of her life, when in 1831 the cholera struck Berlin, she wrote to one of her brothers: "We *here* were told by the domestics that two Jews had poisoned the wells *here*."

Or: A young woman with no formal education, a brilliant writer of letters and aphorisms, who created a network of correspondences that—in the end—would involve more than three hundred people. Unlike many of her addressees, she kept all the letters she received. In her papers, the Varnhagen Collection, housed today in the Jagiellonian Library in Kraków, Poland, more than six thousand letters have survived. Her first publication discussed Goethe's work; she was one of the most important writers of her time to establish his towering reputation.

Or: Goethe's daughter-in-law, Ottilie von Goethe, once wrote: "Since Rahel, we women are allowed to have thoughts." She had just read *Rahel: Ein Buch des Andenkens für ihre Freunde* (*Rahel: A Book of Commemoration for Her Friends*), published in 1834. This collection of Rahel Varnhagen's letters, edited by her husband, Karl August Varnhagen, would become one of the nineteenth century's most famous books by a woman. The three volumes, filled to the brim with the most unusual thoughts and reflections, found enthusiastic readers not only in Germany but also in the English-speaking world: Thomas Carlyle reviewed them in his essay "Varnhagen von Ense's Memoirs" (1838); with *Rahel: Her Life and Letters* (1876), Kate Vaughan-Jennings published the first English monograph on this exceptional woman and dedicated it to Carlyle.

In the last years of the Weimar Republic, Arendt turned her

attention to this fascinating figure and began writing a biography of Rahel Varnhagen. Soon, history would intervene. In the spring of 1933, Arendt was arrested by the Gestapo. After her fortuitous release from prison and before her flight from Germany, she managed to get the completed chapters of her book typed up by professional typists. In the greatest haste she added twenty more pages before she sent copies of the typescript to friends. Obviously, she had no time even to correct typos; some words contain numbers in the place of letters. One copy of this typescript survived the intervening disasters; it was published only in 2021. In Parisian exile Arendt managed to bring the book to a more satisfactory conclusion. Before she fled occupied France, she was able to mail a copy of this version to Palestine, where it survived the war. Another copy traveled across the Atlantic and landed in New York. Arendt's ex-husband, Günther Stern, was supposed to take care of that one. Within days of her arrival in May 1941 in the United States, when Arendt tried to locate this copy—"I need the Rahel typescript. It's urgent!" she wrote—it turned out this copy of the typescript had disappeared, and has never resurfaced.

Only as the war was ending did Arendt again hear of her book: "I am so proud to have saved your manuscript on Rahel Varnhagen. Where is the book's final resting place? At a publisher's? On your desk?" Gershom Scholem wrote from Jerusalem in the spring of 1945. This was the version Arendt had finished in Paris and had hoped to get from Stern, but even having recovered it, many more years would have to pass before she could get the book to the desk of a publisher who was willing to print it. Time and again, Arendt contacted publishing houses, first in Switzerland, later in Germany. All this while she earned a living in a new world, began to write in English, and composed a major book, *The Origins of Totalitarianism* (1951). Only in 1955 did Arendt return to her biography of Varnhagen. The occasion was that the recently established Leo Baeck Institute in New York wanted to publish the book. Arendt assumed they would bring it out in German; the institute, though, insisted on an English translation. In the end, the book appeared in England, not in the United States, which turned out to be a considerable disadvantage.

Despite the fact that Arendt already enjoyed a reputation as an internationally known author, her biography of Rahel Varnhagen did not find many reviewers and readers. "*Rahel Varnhagen* is an unusual biography. We are warned in the preface," Sybille Bedford began her review for the *Reconstructionist*. She read "a relentlessly abstract book—slow, cluttered, static, curiously oppressive; reading it feels like sitting in a hothouse with no watch." Many years later, in January 1965, Jacob Neusner reviewed the book. For him, Arendt's biography had gained new importance after the publication and controversy concerning *Eichmann in Jerusalem* (1963):

> [Arendt] has been much maligned, and perhaps she has erred in some of her historical judgments. I for one will always read her writings with respect and admiration, respect for integrity and admiration for her rich insights. I have every certainty that she will be regarded, in time to come, as one of our generation's great lights, for she has given us— and this book is yet another part of her intellectual legacy—a heritage of understanding and painful honesty about our situation as Jews. Only she could have written at once so usefully and so sensitively of Rahel Varnhagen; of both mass movements and isolated individuals; and told us, in all, so much about ourselves, even when we do not want to listen.

Arendt's American friends did want to listen, and some of them tried to help find a publisher in the United States. We know of at least three attempts; all failed. It was only in 1974, a year before Arendt died, that Harcourt Brace Jovanovich finally brought out the book. This prompted a review in *The New York Times*, a rather critical one: "To present this book to the American public more or less as it was written 40 years ago is a disservice. The book alludes to the political events and historical figures of Rahel's time as if they were familiar, accessible landmarks; they may be in Germany, but they are not well known to the general American audience," Lore Dickstein remarked. The translation "adheres too closely to the author's original German formulations." This might not reduce "the impact and fascination of Rahel Varnhagen's story," but it prevents "the book from being a major work. The material is all there; it needs only to be fleshed out."

By this time, all the reviewers treated the book as the work of a highly respected author. But critical remarks predominate. Some reviewers felt that Arendt overlooked the fact that her protagonist had been a woman: "What was not, perhaps, so easy for the distinguished historian to 'see' (that is, to consciously attend to) was the fact that Rahel's destiny was so unalterably that of an outsider every bit as much because she was a woman as because she was a Jew," Vivian Gornick wrote, while Lilly Rivlin concluded her review by stating that "one wishes at times for some kind of sympathy for Rahel's life as a woman."

It was only after Arendt's death that the biography found more empathic readers. Sometimes a book is so ahead of its time that it takes decades to build its audience.

THE JEWISH QUESTION

Arendt first encountered Rahel Varnhagen as a teenager. Sometime around 1920, Anne Weil, "the friend of my youth," gave her a copy of *Rahel: Ein Buch des Andenkens für ihre Freunde*. Arendt read the letters immediately "and reflected on them but left all that alone when I went to study philosophy." Having finished her dissertation, "it occurred to me that I should go back to this unfinished Rahel-business," as she wrote to a friend. Initially, she called her project "On the Problem of German-Jewish Assimilation, Exemplified with Rahel Varnhagen's Life." She later shifted the focus, and "Rahel Varnhagen" moved into the center of her attention. "The Life of a Jewess," as the subtitle of the first English edition reads, which became "The Life of a Jewish Woman" in the United States, tells the story of a "bankruptcy," as Arendt called it—in the sense not of a personal failure but rather of a historically necessary one. Assimilation in Germany around 1800 came at a high price: it meant being forced to assimilate with a people who only accepted Jewish individuals who had left their roots behind. Jews were supposed to forget who they were, and yet in return the Gentiles never forgot that they were Jews. Rahel Varnhagen always tried to be honest and not accept these lies that held contemporary societies together; she was among the very first fully to understand this dilemma. As Arendt shows, she decided against becoming a "parvenue," choosing rather to remain "a Jew and a pariah." Endowed with a "rebellious heart," she accepted her fate.

FATE

When it was published, *Rahel Varnhagen: The Life of a Jewish Woman* was—as we have seen—difficult to read. This is at least in part due to the fact that the book breaks with almost all of the genre conventions of biography. Arendt wrote hers in the mode of "as if." As if Rahel Varnhagen herself had written her autobiography. But this was an enterprise the historical Rahel Varnhagen—as we know—had never embarked upon. Her genre of writing was the letter, or more precisely, correspondence. Autobiographies are written after the fact, when we look back on our lives. Rahel Varnhagen, though, wrote to friends and family; she even corresponded with her cook. The first letters that came down to us date back to the 1790s; the last one she penned a couple of days before she passed away. Her writing was constant and, as Arendt phrased it, "not reflective or retrospective" but, rather, in "a mode of 'experiencing,' of learning." In the midst of experiencing, exposed to life and committed to always telling the truth—this was Rahel Varnhagen's *Schicksal*, her fate. Because she had no "umbrella" to shelter her from "letting life rain upon" her, she knew what it meant to have a *Schicksal*. Being a Jew, a Jewish woman, cut off from Jewish tradition, cast her into a singular and lonely existence.

But who could write the biography of a woman who represents nothing but her own fate? A woman who never had the privilege of belonging?

Arendt decided to write as if she could "re-whistle with variations...the melody of an offended heart," as she once explained in a letter. She composed a book together *with* the voice of her protagonist and not *on* her; "interpretation" of Rahel Varnhagen's thinking, so Arendt remarked, had "to take the path of repetition." For Arendt, repetition meant literally to repeat and not just to quote Rahel Varnhagen's letters. In her biography, hundreds of words, sentences, and passages taken from these letters are to be found, sometimes with quotation marks, sometimes without. In some places, these words or phrases meander through a couple of paragraphs; in others, we come upon a longer passage. And Arendt almost never gives her readers any information on the addressee or where and when the letters were written. By incorporating all these quotes, she creates a conversation, a dialogue with her protagonist. Accompanied by many, many citations from letters, poems, novels, books, and pamphlets written by Rahel Varnhagen's contemporaries, a choir of very different ways of writing the German of the eighteenth and early nineteenth century can be heard. In the translation, this dimension of Arendt's book vanishes.

A BOOK IN ENGLISH

Arendt herself decided to work with translators who had experience rendering contemporary German literature, rather than nonfiction, into English. She approached Clara and Richard Winston, whose translations she knew and liked. After having received the typescript, Richard Winston wrote back to Arendt:

> Now I have read it, and I am overwhelmed with admiration and scared stiff about the translation. It is the most extraordinary kind of biography, so complete in its psychological and philosophical identification that it comes close to Rahel's autobiography. Extraordinary, too, your basic view of what is the human person. So supple and undoctrinaire. This is something I sense fiction is just beginning to give us, but you have done it already. And the prophetic quality is there throughout; amazing, for example, that you should have written in the thirties that discussion of the subjectivity of history.

The Winstons produced a very elegant translation. Even quotations from canonical authors such as Herder, Mendelssohn, Goethe, and Schleiermacher do not appear in their nineteenth-century translations but are rendered into twentieth-century American English. Rahel Varnhagen, who wrote a most idiosyncratic German and often peppered her texts with French words, now sounded almost like the biography's author, Arendt herself.

Older translations offered more literal versions of her letters. In Ellen Key's *Rahel Varnhagen: A Portrait* (1913), a passage that is extremely important for Arendt's book reads:

> "I imagine that just as I was being thrust into this world, a supernatural being plunged a dagger into my heart, with these words: 'Now, have feeling, see the world as only a few see it, be great and noble; nor can I deprive you of restless, incessant thought. But with one reservation: be a Jewess!' And now my whole life is one long bleeding. By keeping calm I can prolong it; every movement to staunch the bleeding is to die anew, and immobility is only possible to me in death itself."

This the Winstons rendered:

> "I have a strange fancy: it is as if some supramundane being, just as I was thrust into this world, plunged these words with a dagger into my heart: 'Yes, have sensibility, see the world as few see it, be great and noble, nor can I take from you the faculty of eternally thinking. But I add one thing more: be a Jewess!' And now my life is a slow bleeding to death. By keeping still I can delay it. Every movement is an attempt to staunch it—new death; and immobility is possible for me only in death itself.... I can, if you will, derive every evil, every misfortune, every vexation from *that*."

Even more striking is the difference between Kate Vaughan-Jennings's *Rahel: Her Life and Letters* (1876) and the Winstons' translation. Vaughan-Jennings found grandiose expressions for

Rahel Varnhagen's last words, spoken on her deathbed, the words with which Arendt opens her biography:

> "What a history is mine. I, a fugitive from Egypt and Palestine, find with you help, love, and tender care! It was God's will, dear August, to send me to you, and you to me. With delighted exaltation I look back upon my origin, upon the link which my history forms between the oldest memories of the human race and the interest of to-day, between the broadest interval of time and space. That which was, during the early part of my life, the greatest ignominy, the cause of bitterest sorrow, to have been born a Jewess, I would not now have otherwise at any price."

The Winstons toned this down considerably:

> "What a history!—A fugitive from Egypt and Palestine, here I am and find help, love, fostering in you people. With real rapture I think of these origins of mine and this whole nexus of destiny, through which the oldest memories of the human race stand by side with the latest developments. The greatest distances in time and space are bridged. The thing which all my life seemed to me the greatest shame, which was the misery and misfortune of my life—having been born a Jewess—this I should on no account now wish to have missed."

As a prelude to her biography, Arendt chose the last two stanzas from Edwin Arlington Robinson's poem "Eros Turannos." The first four tell of a woman and man living together long after their love has disappeared. "She fears him, and will always ask / What fated her to choose him; / She meets in this engaging mask / All reason to refuse him," the poem begins. It continues in tones of quiet desperation: "And home, where passion lived and died, /

Becomes a place where she can hide." None of this appears in Arendt's quotation. No longer the voice of an omniscient narrator, it is rather a "we": "We tell you, tapping on our brows, / The story as it should be." "We"—as the opening of a biography that from the outset plays with multiple perspectives. A biography, written in different voices. A biography, waiting for readers who appreciate its fascinating and utterly unusual way of writing.

—BARBARA HAHN

PREFACE

THE manuscript of this book, except for the last two chapters, was completed when I left Germany in 1933, and the last two chapters were also written more than twenty years ago. I intended originally to add a lengthy appendix and extensive notes presenting in part the unprinted letters and diaries contained in the Varnhagen Collection of the Manuscript Division of the Prussian State Library. The Varnhagen Collection, which in addition to Rahel's papers contained a great wealth of material from the Romanticists' circle,[1] was stored during the war in one of the eastern provinces of Germany and was never brought to Berlin; what happened to it remains a mystery, so far as I know. I am therefore unable to carry out my original plan; I have had to rest content with quoting from my old excerpts, photostats and copies of those documents which, it seems to me, do not need to be checked once more against the originals. It is particularly regrettable that once again the complete text of Gentz's letters to Rahel cannot be published. Passages of great interest, with all they show of the age's freedom from prejudice, were sacrificed to Biedermeier morality. Unfortunately, my copies contain only such additional material as I needed for my portrait.

The greatest loss to this book is the extensive correspon-

[1] In this collection were a portion of the papers of Clemens Brentano which his sister, Bettina von Arnim, had given to Varnhagen for preservation. It also included the originals of Friedrich Gentz's letters, extracts of which were published by G. Schlesier (*Briefe und vertraute Blätter von Friedrich von Gentz*, 1838) and by Wittichen (*Briefe von und an Gentz*, 1909). There were also letters of Hegel, Wilhelm and Caroline von Humboldt, Henriette Herz, the Mendelssohn-Bartholdys, Adam Müller, Leopold von Ranke, Prince Louis Ferdinand, Friedrich and Dorothea Schlegel, Ludwig Tieck—to mention only the most famous names. See Ludwig Stern, *Die Varnhagen von Ensesche Sammlung in der Königlichen Bibliothek zu Berlin*, 1911.

dence between Rahel and Pauline Wiesel, Prince Louis Ferdinand's mistress, the collection having included one hundred and seventy-six letters from Pauline to Rahel, and one hundred letters from Rahel to Pauline. These letters constituted the most important source material on Rahel's life after her marriage, and upon them are primarily based the sometimes radical revisions I have made in the conventional literary portrait of Rahel. This correspondence has scarcely ever been used because Varnhagen, who copied most of Rahel's letters in his extremely legible handwriting (these copies forming an important part of his Collection), prepared only sixteen of the letters to Pauline for the press in this way; later students and editors of the papers apparently made little use of this material because the handwritings and the spelling of both ladies made them hard to read. Some of this correspondence has been published by Carl Atzenbeck.

Aside from the known publications of Rahel's letters, which are listed in the bibliography, my account is based on a large amount of unpublished material. To the extent I have been able, I have indicated these sources in footnotes. There are numerous corrections and additions to the letters and diary entries which Varnhagen published in his three-volume *Buch des Andenkens*, 1834.[2] Varnhagen's arbitrariness in the publication or preparation of Rahel's papers has been commented on frequently.[3] In some cases he did not stop at interpolations and mutilations are frequent.[4] He made wholesale corrections, expunged essential portions and coded personal names in such a

[2] My personal copy of this book, corrected by comparison with the manuscripts, as well as all other copies and excerpts, are now in the Archives of the Leo Baeck Institute.

[3] See the introduction by Heinrich Meisner to his edition of the correspondence with Alexander von der Marwitz, 1925, and Augusta Weldler-Steinberg's Afterword in *Rahel Varnhagen, Ein Frauenleben in Briefen*, 1917.

[4] The best known of these interpolations consists of a few sentences in a letter of Rahel to Varnhagen which is designed to pretend a close acquaintance with Beethoven. The intention is obvious: Varnhagen wanted to show one more "famous man" as part of Rahel's circle of friends. (The most recent "discovery" in this field, naming Rahel as Beethoven's *ferne Geliebte*, scarcely needs to be mentioned, since the author himself makes no claim to having documentary evidence for this thesis. Not only in the published correspondences, but in all the unpublished material as well, there is not a single line which might support this conjecture. In Rahel's day it was not customary to make a secret of such matters; to suspect her, of all persons, of harboring such a secret, indicates an extraordinary ig-

manner that the reader was deliberately led astray. But for all that these practices have been exposed, Varnhagen's conception of Rahel, his stereotyping and embellishing of her portrait, and his deliberate falsifications of her life, became established and have remained almost uncontested. The significant fact is that almost all his omissions and misleading codings of names were intended to make Rahel's associations and circle of friends appear less Jewish and more aristocratic, and to show Rahel herself in a more conventional light, one more in keeping with the taste of the times. Typical of the former effort is the fact that Henriette Herz always appears as Frau von B. or Frau von Bl. even where there was no need to disguise the name on grounds of the remarks being unfavorable; that Rebecca Friedländer, who as a writer used the pen name of Regina Frohberg, is always denoted by Frau *von* F. Typical of the latter is that the few letters and extracts from letters to Pauline Wiesel are dressed up as diary notes, or appear as addressed to a Frau *von* V., so that the part this friendship played in Rahel's life has been completely eradicated from the documents.

There is always a certain awkwardness in an author's speaking of his book, even one written half a lifetime ago. But since this book was conceived and written from an angle unusual in biographical literature, I shall nevertheless venture a few explanatory remarks. It was never my intention to write a book *about* Rahel; about her personality, which might lend itself to various interpretations according to the psychological standards and categories that the author introduces from outside; nor about her position in Romanticism and the effect of the Goethe cult in Berlin, of which she was actually the originator; nor about the significance of her salon for the social history of the period; nor about her ideas and her "weltanschauung," in so far as these can be reconstructed from her letters. What interested me solely was to narrate the story of Rahel's life as she herself might have told it. She considered herself extraordinary, but her view of the source of that quality differed from that of others. She attempted to explain this

norance of her personality.) On the mutilation of the letters, and the motives, see the episodes with Clemens Brentano, pp. 187–88, and Pauline Wiesel, pp. 206–07.

feeling in innumerable phrases and images which retain a curious similarity throughout her life as they strive to formulate the meaning of what she called Destiny. Her whole effort was to expose herself to life so that it could strike her "like a storm without an umbrella." ("What am I doing? Nothing. I am letting life rain upon me.")[5] She preferred not to use characteristics or opinions on persons she encountered, on the circumstances and conditions of the world, on life itself, for purposes of shelter. Following this principle, she could neither choose nor act, because choice and action in themselves would anticipate life and falsify the purity of life's happenstance. All that remained for her to do was to become a "mouthpiece" for experience, to verbalize whatever happened. This could be accomplished by introspection, by relating one's own story again and again to oneself and to others; thereby one's story became one's Destiny: "Everyone has a Destiny who knows what kind of destiny he has." To this end, the particular traits one had to have or to marshal within oneself were an unflagging alertness and capacity for pain; one had to remain susceptible and conscious.

Rahel herself once very clearly characterized the romantic element in such an undertaking when she compared herself to the "greatest artists" and commented: "But to me life itself was the assignment." To live life as if it were a work of art, to believe that by "cultivation" one can make a work of art of one's own life, was the great error that Rahel shared with her contemporaries; or rather, it was the misconception of self which was inevitable so long as she wished to understand and express within the categories of her time her sense of life: the resolve to consider life and the history it imposes upon the individual as more important and more serious than her own person.

My portrait therefore follows as closely as possible the course of Rahel's own reflections upon herself, although it is naturally couched in different language and does not consist solely of variations upon quotations. It does not venture beyond this frame even when Rahel is apparently being examined critically. The criticism corresponds to Rahel's self-criticism, and since she—unburdened by modern inferiority feelings—could rightly say of herself that she did not "vainly seek applause I would not record myself" she also had no need

[5] Unpublished diary entry dated March 11, 1810.

"to pay flattering visits to myself." It is, of course, only of my intentions that I speak; I may not always carry them out successfully and at such times may appear to be passing judgment upon Rahel from some higher vantage point. If so, I have simply failed in what I set out to do.

The same is true for the various persons discussed and the literature of the period. These are seen entirely from her point of view; scarcely a writer is mentioned whom Rahel did not certainly or most probably know and whose writings were not of importance for her own introspections. The same principle has been applied, though here with more difficulty, to the Jewish question, which in Rahel's own opinion exerted a crucial influence upon her destiny. For in this case her conduct and her reactions became determinants for the conduct and attitudes of a part of cultivated German Jewry, thereby acquiring a limited historical importance of which, however, this book does not treat.

The German-speaking Jews and their history are an altogether unique phenomenon; nothing comparable to it is to be found even in the other areas of Jewish assimilation. To investigate this phenomenon, which among other things found expression in a literally astonishing wealth of talent and of scientific and intellectual productivity, constitutes a historical task of the first rank, and one which, of course, can be attacked only now, after the history of the German Jews has come to an end. The present biography was written with an awareness of the doom of German Judaism (although, naturally, without any premonition of how far the physical annihilation of the Jewish people in Europe would be carried); but at that time, shortly before Hitler's coming to power, I did not have the perspective from which to view the phenomenon as a whole. If this book is considered as a contribution to the history of the German Jews, it must be remembered that in it only one aspect of the complex problems of assimilation is treated: namely, the manner in which assimilation to the intellectual and social life of the environment works out concretely in the history of an individual's life, thus shaping a personal destiny. On the other hand, it must not be forgotten that the subject matter is altogether historical, and that nowadays not only the history of the German Jews, but also their specific complex of problems, are a matter of the past.

It is inherent in the nature of the method I have selected that certain psychological observations which appear to thrust themselves forward are scarcely mentioned and not commented on at all. The modern reader will scarcely fail to observe at once that Rahel was neither beautiful nor attractive; that all the men with whom she had any kind of love relationship were younger than she herself; that she possessed no talents with which to employ her extraordinary intelligence and passionate originality; and finally, that she was a typically "romantic" personality, and that the Woman Problem, that is the discrepancy between what men expected of women "in general" and what women could give or wanted in their turn, was already established by the conditions of the era and represented a gap that virtually could not be closed. I could touch upon such matters only in so far as they were absolutely essential to the facts of Rahel's biography and could not consider them in any general way, since the point was not to assume to know more than Rahel herself knew, not to impose upon her a fictional destiny derived from observations presumed to be superior to those she consciously had. That is to say, I have deliberately avoided that modern form of indiscretion in which the writer attempts to penetrate his subject's tricks and aspires to know more than the subject knew about himself or was willing to reveal; what I would call the pseudo-scientific apparatuses of depth-psychology, psychoanalysis, graphology, etc., fall into this category of curiosity-seeking.

The bibliography at the end of this book lists only the printed source material I have used, in so far as I have been able to collate it again from my old notes and to recheck it. Secondary works on Rahel, which for the most part consist of magazine articles and essays in more comprehensive works, I have been unable to re-examine after so long a time and outside of Germany. All quotations whose authorship is not expressly noted or obvious from the context are taken from Rahel Varnhagen's letters and diaries.

I am grateful to the Leo Baeck Institute for the sponsorship of this book, for the opportunity to go over the manuscript once more in preparing it for the press and for generous aid in securing the translation, as well as secretarial and scholarly assistance. I wish also to thank Dr. Lotte Köhler for her help in final preparation of the manuscript, the bibliography and the chronological table.

HANNAH ARENDT

NEW YORK
Summer 1956

PREFACE
TO THE REVISED EDITION

THE first English edition of this book appeared in 1957 in England and was published by East and West Library in London. It was sponsored by the Leo Baeck Institute. This is the first American edition, slightly revised textually and containing a few additions to the original bibliography.

Since the research for this book, originally written in German, was completed more than forty years ago, the German manuscript had to be checked before it could be translated. Additional changes in the present American edition have been based on the published German version (München 1959). Once again, the text was prepared for publication by Dr. Lotte Köhler.

HANNAH ARENDT

March 1974

RAHEL VARNHAGEN

To Anne
since 1921

WE tell you, tapping on our brows,
  The story as it should be,—
As if the story of a house
  Were told or ever could be;
We'll have no kindly veil between
  Her visions and those we have seen,—
As if we guessed what hers have been
  Or what they are or would be.

Meanwhile we do no harm; for they
  That with a god have striven,
Not hearing much of what we say,
  Take what the god has given;
Though like waves breaking it may be,
  Or like a changed familiar tree,
Or like a stairway to the sea
  Where down the blind are driven.

Edwin Arlington Robinson

1

JEWESS AND SHLEMIHL
(1771–1795)

"WHAT a history!— A fugitive from Egypt and Palestine, here I am and find help, love, fostering in you people. With real rapture I think of these origins of mine and this whole nexus of destiny, through which the oldest memories of the human race stand by side with the latest developments. The greatest distances in time and space are bridged. The thing which all my life seemed to me the greatest shame, which was the misery and misfortune of my life—having been born a Jewess—this I should on no account now wish to have missed." These are the words Karl August Varnhagen von Ense reports Rahel to have said on her deathbed. It had taken her sixty-three years to come to terms with a problem which had its beginnings seventeen hundred years before her birth, which underwent a crucial upheaval during her life, and which one hundred years after her death—she died on March 7, 1833—was slated to come to an end.

It may well be difficult for us to understand our own history when we are born in 1771 in Berlin and that history has already begun seventeen hundred years earlier in Jerusalem. But if we do not understand it, and if we are not outright opportunists who always accept the here-and-now, who circumvent unpleasantness by lies and forget the good, our history will take its revenge, will exert its superiority and become our personal destiny. And that is never any pleasure for the person affected. Rahel's history would not be curtailed because she had forgotten it, nor would it turn out to be any more original because she, in utter innocence, experienced the whole of it as if it were happening for the first time. But history becomes more definitive when (and how rarely this happens) it concen-

3

trates its whole force upon an individual's destiny; when it encounters a person who has no way of barricading herself behind character traits and talents, who cannot hide under moralities and conventions as if these were an umbrella for rainy weather; when it can impress something of its significance upon the hapless human being, the *shlemihl*, who has anticipated nothing.

"What is man without his history? Product of nature—not personality." The history of any given personality is far older than the individual as product of nature, begins long before the individual's life, and can foster or destroy the elements of nature in his heritage. Whoever wants aid and protection from History, in which our insignificant birth is almost lost, must be able to know and understand it. History bashes the "product of nature" on the head, stifles its most useful qualities, makes it degenerate—"like a plant that grows downward into the earth: the finest characteristics become the most repulsive."

If we feel at home in this world, we can see our lives as the development of the "product of nature," as the unfolding and realization of what we already were. The world in that case becomes a school in the broadest sense, and other people are cast in the roles of either educators or misleaders. The great trouble is that human nature, which might otherwise develop smoothly, is as dependent upon luck as seed is upon good weather. For should anyone's life fail in the few most important things that are naturally expected of him, his development is stopped—development which is the sole continuity in time that nature recognizes. Then the pain, the grief, is overwhelming. And the person who has no recourse but nature is destroyed by his own inexperience, by his inability to comprehend more than himself.

German literature offers only a single example of real identity between nature and history. "When I was eighteen years old, Germany had also just turned eighteen" (Goethe). In case of such an identity, indeed, the purity of a person's beginnings may immediately be transformed, materialized as it were, and "stand for" something impersonal, not to be sure for some definite notion or concept, but for a world and history in general. It is his singularity not to need experience to know a world and a history which he contains in himself. Confronted with this kind of identity, with so great, well-known and deeply loved an exemplar, persons wiser and more gifted than Rahel could find themselves losing their hold on standards; those even more sensible and cultivated than she could be deluded into excessive demands upon life, excessive susceptibility to disappointment. In such a fortunate case, to be sure, the person's initial purity is transformed; his function becomes to "stand for"—not for anything particular, anything different, but for himself. And then the person in whom history is embodied can know the world even without experience.

In those days Jews in Berlin could grow up like the children of savage tribes. Rahel was one of these. She learned nothing, neither her own history nor that of the country in which her family dwelt. The earning of money and the study of the Law—these were the vital concerns of the ghetto. Wealth and culture helped to throw open the gates of the ghetto—court Jews on the one hand and Moses Mendelssohn on the other. Nineteenth-century Jews mastered the trick of obtaining both wealth and culture. Rich Jewish parents sought an extra measure of security by having their sons attend the university. In the brief and highly tempestuous interval between ghetto and assimilation, however, this practice had not yet developed. The rich were not cultured and the cultured not rich. Rahel's father was a dealer in precious stones who had made a fortune. That fact alone decided the complexion of her education. All her life she remained "the greatest ignoramus."

Unfortunately, she did not remain rich. When the father died, the sons took over his business, settled a lifetime allowance upon the mother, and determined to marry off the two sisters as quickly as possible. With the younger sister they succeeded; with Rahel they failed. Left without any portion of her own, she was dependent upon her mother's allowance, and after her mother's death upon the dubious generosity of her brothers. Poverty, it seemed, would condemn her to remain a Jew, stranded within a society that was rapidly disintegrating, that scarcely existed any longer as an environment with a specific self-awareness, with its own customs and judgments. The only ties among German Jews of the period seemed to be that questionable solidarity which survives among people who all want the same thing: to save themselves as individuals. Only failures and "shlemihls," it would seem, were left behind within this German-Jewish society.

Beauty in a woman can mean power, and Jewish girls were frequently not married for their dowries alone. With Rahel, however, nature went to no great trouble. She had about her something "unpleasantly unprepossessing, without there being immediately apparent any striking deformities." Small in body, with hands and feet too small, a disproportion between the upper and lower parts of her face, she had, below a clear brow and fine, translucent eyes, a chin too long and too limp, as though it were only appended to the face. In this chin, she thought, her "worst trait" was expressed, an "excessive gratitude and excess of consideration for others." These same qualities struck others as a lack of standards or taste. This, too, she was aware of. "I have no grace, not even the grace to see what the cause of that is; in addition to not being pretty, I also have no inner grace. . . . I am unprepossessing rather than ugly. . . . Some people have not a single good-looking feature, not a single praiseworthy proportion, and yet they make a pleasing impression. . . . With me it is just the opposite." So she wrote in her diary when she had occasion to think back upon a succession of unhappy love affairs. Although this was written fairly late in life, she adds in explanation: "I have thought this for a long time."

In a woman beauty creates a perspective from which she can judge and choose. Neither intelligence nor experience can make up for the lack of that natural perspective. Not rich, not cultivated and not beautiful—that meant that she was entirely without weapons with which to begin the great struggle for recognition in society, for social existence, for a morsel of happiness, for security and an established position in the bourgeois world.

A political struggle for equal rights might have taken the place of the personal struggle. But that was wholly unknown to this generation of Jews whose representatives even offered to accept mass baptism (David Friedländer). Jews did not even want to be emancipated as a whole; all they wanted was to escape from Jewishness, as individuals if possible. Their urge was secretly and silently to settle what seemed to them a personal problem, a personal misfortune. In Frederick the Second's Berlin a personal solution of the Jewish problem, an individual escape into society, was difficult but not flatly impossible. Anyone who did not convert his personal gifts into weapons to achieve that end, who failed to concentrate these gifts toward this single goal, might as well give up all hope of happiness in this world. Thus Rahel wrote to David Veit, the friend of her youth: "I have a strange fancy: it is as if some supramundane being, just as I was thrust into this world, plunged these words with a dagger into my heart: 'Yes, have sensibility, see the world as few see it, be great and noble, nor can I take from you the faculty of eternally thinking. But I add one thing more: be a Jewess!' And now my life is a slow bleeding to death. By keeping still I can delay it. Every movement in an attempt to staunch it—new death; and immobility is possible for me only in death itself. . . . I can, if you will, derive every evil, every misfortune, every vexation from *that.*"

Under the influence of the Enlightenment the demand for "civil betterment of the Jews" began to advance toward realization in Prussia. It was spelled out in detail by the Prussian official Christian Wilhelm Dohm. Excluded for centuries from the culture and history of the lands they lived in, the Jews had in the eyes of their host peoples remained on a lower stage of civilization. Their social and political situation had been unchanged during those same centuries: everywhere they were in the rarest and best case only tolerated but usually oppressed and persecuted. Dohm was appealing to the conscience of humanity to take up the cause of the oppressed; he was not appealing for fellow citizens, nor even for a people with whom anyone felt any ties. To the keener consciences of men of the Enlightenment, it had become intolerable to know that there were among them people without rights. The cause of humanity thus became the cause of the Jews. "It is fortunate for us that no one can insist on the rights of man without at the same time espousing our own rights" (Moses Mendelssohn). The Jews, an accidental and embarrassing hangover of the Middle Ages, no longer thought of themselves as the chosen people of God; equally, the others no longer viewed them as suffering condign punishment for resisting Christianity. The Old Testament, their ancient possession, had in part become so remote, in part entered so completely into the body of European culture, that the Jews, the contemporary Jews, were no longer recognized as the people who had been its authors. The Old Testament was an element of culture, perhaps "one of the oldest documents of the human race" (Herder), but the Jews were merely members of an oppressed, uncultured, backward people who must be brought into the fold of humanity. What was wanted was to make human beings out of the Jews. Of course it was unfortunate that Jews existed at all; but since they did, there was nothing for it but to make people of them, that is to say, people of the Enlightenment.

The Jews concurred in this and similar emancipation theories of the Enlightenment. Fervently, they confessed their own inferiority; after all, were not the others to blame for it? Wicked Christianity and its sinister history had corrupted them; their own dark history was completely forgotten. It was as if they saw the whole of European history as nothing but one long era of Inquisition in which the poor good Jews had had no part, thank God, and for which they must now be recompensed. Naturally one was not going to cling to Judaism—why should one, since the whole of Jewish history and tradition was now revealed as a sordid product of the ghetto —for which, moreover, one was not to blame at all? Aside from the question of guilt, the fact of inferiority secretly hung on.

Rahel's life was bound by this inferiority, by her "infamous birth," from youth on up. Everything that followed was only confirmation, "bleeding to death." Therefore she must avoid everything that might give rise to further confirmation, must not act, not love, not become involved with the world. Given such absolute renunciation, all that seemed left was *thought*. The handicaps imposed upon her by nature and society would be neutralized by the mania "for examining everything and asking questions with inhuman persistence." Objective and impersonal thought was able to minimize the purely human, purely accidental quality of unhappiness. Drawing up the balance sheet of life, one needed only to think "in order to know how one must feel and what is or is not left to one." Thinking amounted to an enlightened kind of magic which could substitute for, evoke and predict experience, the world, people and society. The power of Reason lent posited possibilities a tinge of reality, breathed a kind of illusory life into rational desires, fended off ungraspable actuality and refused to recognize it. The twenty-year-old Rahel wrote: "I shall never be convinced that I am a Schlemihl and a Jewess; since in all these years and after so much thinking about it, it has not dawned upon me, I shall never really grasp it. That is why 'the clang of the murderous axe does not nibble at my root'; that is why I am still living."

The Enlightenment raised Reason to the status of an authority. It declared thought and what Lessing called "self-thinking," which anyone can engage in alone and of his own accord, the supreme capacities of man. "Everything depends on self-thinking," Rahel remarked to Gustav von Brinckmann in conversation. She promptly added a thought that would hardly have occurred to the men of the Enlightenment: "The objects often matter very little, just as the beloved often matters far less than loving." Self-thinking brings liberation from objects and their reality, creates a sphere of pure ideas and a world which is accessible to any rational being without benefit of knowledge or experience. It brings liberation from the object just as romantic love liberates the lover from the reality of his beloved. Romantic love produces the "great lovers" whose love cannot be disturbed by the specific qualities of their sweethearts, whose feelings can no longer be rubbed raw by any contact with actuality. Similarly, self-thinking in this sense provides a foundation for cultivated ignoramuses. Being by birth exempt from obligation to any object in their alien cultural environment, they need merely, in order to become contemporaries, peel off old prejudices and free themselves for the business of thinking.

Reason can liberate from the prejudices of the past and it can guide the future. Unfortunately, however, it appears that it can free isolated individuals only, can direct the future only of Crusoes. The individual who has been liberated by reason is always running head-on into a world, a society, whose past in the shape of "prejudices" has a great deal of power; he is forced to learn that past reality is also a reality. Although being born a Jewess might seem to Rahel a mere reference to something out of the remote past, and although she may have entirely eradicated the fact from her thinking, it remained a nasty present reality as a prejudice in the minds of others.

How can the present be rendered ineffective? How can human freedom be so enormously extended that it no longer collides with limits; how can introspection be so isolated that the thinking individual no longer need smash his head against the wall of "irrational" reality? How can you peel off the disgrace of unhappiness, the infamy of birth? How can you—a second creator of the world—transform reality back into its potentialities and so escape the "murderous axe"?

If thinking rebounds back upon itself and finds its solitary object within the soul—if, that is, it becomes introspection—it distinctly produces (so long as it remains rational) a semblance of unlimited power by the very act of isolation from the world; by ceasing to be interested in the world it also sets up a bastion in front of the one "interesting" object: the inner self. In the isolation achieved by introspection thinking becomes limitless because it is no longer molested by anything exterior; because there is no longer any demand for action, the consequences of which necessarily impose limits even upon the freest spirit. Man's autonomy becomes hegemony over all possibilities; reality merely impinges and rebounds. Reality can offer nothing new; introspection has already anticipated everything. Even the blows of fate can be escaped by flight into the self if every single misfortune has already been generalized beforehand as an inevitable concomitant of the bad outside world, so that there is no reason to feel shock at having been struck this one particular time. The one unpleasant feature is that memory itself perpetuates the present, which otherwise would only touch the soul fleetingly. As a consequence of memory, therefore, one subsequently discovers that outer events have a degree of reality that is highly disturbing.

Rousseau is the greatest example of the mania for introspection because he succeeded even in getting the best of memory; in fact, he converted it in a truly ingenious fashion into the most dependable guard against the outside world. By sentimentalizing memory he obliterated the contours of the remembered event. What remained were the feelings experienced in the course of those events—in other words, once more nothing but reflections within the psyche. Sentimental remembering is the best method for completely forgetting one's own destiny. It presupposes that the present itself is instantly converted into a "sentimental" past. For Rousseau (*Confessions*) the present always first rises up out of memory, and it is immediately drawn into the inner self, where everything is eternally present and converted back into potentiality. Thus the power and autonomy of the soul are secured. Secured at the price of truth, it must be recognized, for without reality shared with other human beings, truth loses all meaning. Introspection and its hybrids engender *mendacity*.

"Facts mean nothing at all to me," she writes to Veit, and signs this letter: "Confessions de J. J. Rahel"—"for whether true or not, facts can be denied; if I have done something, I did it because I wanted to; and if someone wants to blame me or lie to me, there's nothing for me to do but say 'No,' and I do." Every fact can be undone, can be wiped out by a lie. Lying can obliterate the outside event which introspection has already converted into a purely psychic factor. Lying takes up the heritage of introspection, sums it up, and makes a reality of the freedom that introspection has won. "Lying is lovely if we choose it, and is an important component of our freedom." How can a fact mean anything if the person himself refuses to corroborate it? For example: Jews may not go driving on the Sabbath; Rahel went driving with the actress Marchetti "in broad daylight on the Sabbath; nobody saw me; I would have and would and shall deny it to anyone's face." If she denies it, nothing remains of the fact except one opinion against other opinions. Facts can be disintegrated into opinions as soon as one refuses to consent to them and withdraws from their context. They have their own peculiar way of being true: their truth must always be recognized, testified to. Perhaps reality consists only in the agreement of everybody, is perhaps only a social phenomenon, would perhaps collapse as soon as someone had the courage forthrightly and consistently to deny its existence. Every event passes—who may claim to know tomorrow whether it really took place? Whatever is not proved by thinking is not provable—therefore, make your denials, falsify by lies, make use of your freedom to change and render reality ineffective at will. Only truths discovered by reason are irrefutable; only these can always be made plain to everyone. Poor reality, dependent upon human beings who believe in it and confirm it. For it as well as their confirmation are transitory and not even always presentable.

That facts (or history) are not acceptable to reason, no matter how well confirmed they are, because both their factuality and their confirmation are accidental; that only "rational truths" (Lessing), the products of pure thought, can lay claim to validity, truth, cogency—this was (for the sophistries of the Assimilation) the most important element of the German Enlightenment that Mendelssohn adopted from Lessing. Adopted and falsified. For to Lessing history is the teacher of mankind and the mature individual recognizes "historical truths" by virtue of his reason. The freedom of reason, too, is a product of history, a higher stage of historical development. It is only in Mendelssohn's version that "historical and rational truths" are separated so finally and completely that the truth-seeking man himself withdraws from history. Mendelssohn expressly opposes Lessing's philosophy of history, referring slightingly to "the Education of the Human Race, of which my late friend Lessing allowed himself to be persuaded by I do not know what historian." Mendelssohn held that all realities such as environment, history and society could not—thank God—be warranted by Reason.

Rahel's struggle against the facts, above all against the fact of having been born a Jew, very rapidly became a struggle against herself. She herself refused to consent to herself; she, born to so many disadvantages, had to deny, change, reshape by lies this self of hers, since she could not very well deny her existence out of hand.

As long as Don Quixote continues to ride forth to conjure a possible, imagined, illusory world out of the real one, he is only a fool, and perhaps a happy fool, perhaps even a noble fool when he undertakes to conjure up within the real world a definite ideal. But if without a definite ideal, without aiming at a definite imaginary revision of the world, he attempts only to transform himself into some sort of empty possibility which he *might* be, he becomes merely a "foolish dreamer," and an opportunist one in addition, who is seeking to destroy his existence for the sake of certain advantages.

For the possibilities of being different from what one is are infinite. Once one has negated oneself, however, there are no longer any particular choices. There is only one aim: always, at any given moment, to be different from what one is; never to assert oneself, but with infinite pliancy to become anything else, so long as it is not oneself. It requires an inhuman alertness not to betray oneself, to conceal everything and yet have no definite secret to cling to. Thus, at the age of twenty-one, Rahel wrote to Veit: "For do what I will, I shall be ill, out of *gêne*, as long as I live; I live against my inclinations. I dissemble, I am courteous . . . but I am too *small* to stand it, too *small*. . . . My eternal dissembling, my being reasonable, my yielding which I myself no longer notice, swallowing my own insights—I can no longer stand it; and nothing, no one, can help me."

Omnipotent as opinion and mendacity are, they have, however, a limit beyond which alteration cannot go; one cannot change one's face; neither thought nor liberty, neither lies nor nausea nor disgust can lift one out of one's own skin. That same winter she wrote: "I wish nothing more ardently now than to change myself, outwardly and inwardly. I . . . am sick of myself; but I can do nothing about it and will remain the way I am, just as my face will; we can both grow older, but nothing more. . . ." At best, then, there remains time which makes everyone older and carries every human being along, from the moment of birth on, into constant change. The only drawback is that this change is useless because it leads to no dream paradise, to no New World of unlimited possibilities. No human being can isolate himself completely; he will always be thrown back upon the world again if he has any hopes at all for the things that only the world can give: "ordinary things, but things one must have." In the end the world always has the last word because one can introspect only into one's own self, but not out of it again. "Ah yes, if I could live out of the world, without conventions, without relationships, live an honest, hard-working life in a village." But that, too, is only possible if the world has so arranged matters, whereas: "But I have nothing to live on."

Relationships and conventions, in their general aspects, are as irrevocable as nature. A person probably can defy a single fact by denying it, but not that totality of facts which we call the world. In the world one can live if one has a station, a place on which one stands, a position to which one belongs. If one has been so little provided for by the world as Rahel, one is nothing because one is not defined from outside. Details, customs, relationships, conventions, cannot be surveyed and grasped; they become a part of the indefinite world in general which in its totality is only a hindrance. "Also, I fear *every* change!" Here insight no longer helps; insight can only foresee and predict, can only "consume" the hope. "Nothing, no one can help me."

Nothing foreseeable, and no one whom she knows can help her, at any rate. Therefore, perhaps the absolutely unforeseeable, chance, luck, will do it. It is senseless to attempt to *do* anything in this disordered, indefinite world. Therefore, perhaps the answer is simply to wait, to wait for life itself. "And yet, wherever I can get the opportunity to meet her, I shall kiss the dust from the feet of Fortune, out of gratitude and wonder." Chance is a glorious cause for hope, which so resembles despair that the two can easily be confounded. Hope seduces one into peering about in the world for a tiny, infinitesimally tiny crack which circumstances may have overlooked, for a crack, be it ever so narrow, which nevertheless would help to define, to organize, to provide a center for the indefinite world—because the longed-for unexpected something might ultimately emerge through it in the form of a definite happiness. Hope leads to despair when all one's searching discovers no such crack, no chance for happiness: "It seems to me I am so glad not to be unhappy that a blind man could not fail to see that I cannot really be happy at all."

Such was the inner landscape of this twenty-four-year-old girl who as yet had not actually experienced anything, whose life was still without any personal content. "I am unhappy; I won't let anyone reason me out of it; and that always has a disturbing effect." This insight rapidly became a final one, unaffected by the fact that Rahel went on hoping for happiness almost all her life; secretly, no matter what happened to her, Rahel always knew that the insight of her youth was only waiting to be confirmed. Suffering disadvantages from birth on, unhappy without having been struck down by destiny, without being compelled to endure any specific misfortune, her sorrow was "greater than its cause . . . more ripely prepared," as Wilhelm von Burgsdorff, the close friend of Caroline von Humboldt, wrote to her during those years. By renouncing—without having had anything definite to renounce —she had already anticipated all experiences, seemed to know suffering without having suffered. "A long sorrow has 'educated' you; . . . it is true that a trace of suffered destiny is visible in you, that one sees in you silence and reticence early learned."

In waiting for the concrete confirmation, which for the present did not come, she converted her vagueness about the world and life into a generalization. She saw herself as blocked not by individual and therefore removable obstacles, but by everything, by *the* world. Out of her hopeless struggle with indefiniteness arose her "inclination to generalize." Reason grasped conceptually what could not be specifically defined, thereby saving her a second time. By abstraction reason diverted attention from the concrete; it transformed the yearning to be happy into a "passion for truth"; it taught "pleasures" which had no connection with the personal self. Rahel loved no other human being, but she loved encounters with others in the realm of truth. Reason met its counterpart in all people, and these encounters remained "pleasurable" so long as she kept her distance and sold her soul to no one. "How happy is the man who loves his friends and can live without them without restiveness." Generalities cannot be lost; they can be found again or reproduced at any time. She was not happy, could not be happy, but she was also not unhappy. She could love no one, but in many people she could love a variety of qualities.

She made the acquaintance of many people. The "garret" on Jägerstrasse became a meeting place for her friends. The oldest of these, and for many years the closest, was David Veit, a young Jewish student of Berlin. In the mid-nineties he was studying medicine at Göttingen University. They wrote frequently to one another, their letters constituting journals, diary entries. He knew her and her milieu because he came from a similar one himself. He knew the conditions in her household; she told him everything without reticence, showed him, giving a thousand details as proof, the incompatibility between herself and her domestic environment; she demonstrated it, provided circumstantial evidence for it, adduced petty incidents. Veit did not understand the strength of her despair. The solution, as he saw it, was to get out of Judaism, to be baptized (this he did a few years later); it was possible to escape these surroundings and these experiences, and later they could be forgotten. She became aware that her complaint lacked content. Single obstacles could be removed; how well she knew that specific things or events could be denied. But she could not yet express the essence to which she was referring; only experience could explain that, only experiences serve as examples of it.

More important for her than his comprehension of these

matters was the fact that Veit became her first correspondent from the contemporary world. She prized his accurate, reliable reports, always remembered him for having suppressed not a word, not a detail, in describing his visit with Goethe. Her letters were equally precise, equally reliable answers. Never did he write a word into a void; she unfailingly took up, commented on, answered everything. Letters served as a substitute for conversations; she used them to talk about people and things. Excluded from society, deprived of any normal social intercourse, she had a tremendous hunger for people, was greedy for every smallest event, tensely awaited every utterance. The world was unknown and hostile to her; she had no education, tradition or convention with which to make order out of it; and hence orientation was impossible to her. Therefore she devoured mere details with indiscriminate curiosity. No aristocratic elegance, no exclusiveness, no innate taste restrained her craving for the new and the unknown; no knowledge of people, no social instinct and no tact limited her indiscriminateness or prescribed for her any particular, well-founded, proper conduct toward acquaintances. "You are," wrote Veit, "*candid* toward acquaintances who understand not a syllable of what you say and who misinterpret this candor. These acquaintances ask candor of you where you are reticent, and do not thank you for the truth." Instead of saying little to a few, Rahel talked with everybody about everything. She was maligned as malicious—and was made a confidant. Her curiosity operated like a hidden magnet; her passionate tension drew people's secrets out of them. In her absence, however, she struck people as equivocal. You never knew what she thought of you, what your relationship to her was; when you went away, you knew nothing about her. Not that she had anything specific to conceal or to confess; it was her general condition that she hid. And precisely that engendered the atmosphere of equivocation and uncertainty.

This faulty relationship to people pursued her all her life. Not until twenty years later did she realize what her reputation, good and bad, her equivocation despite her innocent intent, was based on. "Although in one penetrating look I form an undeviating opinion of people, I can find myself involved in crude errors without being mistaken in those whom I have, so to speak, right before me. Because I do not decide on the madly arbitrary assumption that any one particular individual would be capable of carrying out any one crude, ugly action. I won't say I cannot decide; I do not like to decide. If I did, I would be shaming, sullying myself." Essentially, she expected the same thing from everybody, could deal with people only in generalizations, could not recognize the accidental character of individuals' physiognomies, the "crude and common" chanciness of a particular person, a particular juxtaposition of traits. Details were so important to her because she immediately saw them as typical; they communicated much more, contributed far more information to her hungry curiosity, revealed far more to her mind, which depended on deduction in its attempts at orientation, than anyone could guess or possibly understand. "Since, for me, very small traits . . . decide the whole inner value of a person for all eternity, it obviously becomes impossible for me to show him what I think of him, what are my ideas about the particular circumstances in which we happen to be. They must think me mad. . . . Therefore there remains for me only keeping silent, withholding myself, annoying, avoiding, observing, distracting and using people, being clumsily angry, and on top of all suffering criticism all the time from stupid vulgarians!" She could not admit that a person may be no more than his qualities, since she herself started out with none but the most formal qualities, such as intelligence, alertness, passionateness. To make any such assertion would be, for her, an offense against the dignity of man. But at the same time she could not be consistent in treating people as though they were different from themselves, as though they were more than the accidental sum of their qualities. For "what a person is capable of, no one knows *better* than I; *no one* grasps more quickly." Her equivocation resulted from this attitude and this knowledge of people which she owed to an extreme sensitivity. Moreover, her sensitivity was constantly sharpened by repression. "This penetration, then, and that lack of decisiveness produce a dichotomy in my treatment of people: full of consideration and respect outwardly; and inwardly a stern, judging, contemptuous or worshipful attitude. Anyone can easily find me inconsistent, cowardly, pliable and timid . . . and believe that my better judgment operates only before or after the event, while in the course of it passion throws my good sense to the winds." The discrepancy between treatment and judgment, "before and after," the decision taken behind the back of the person concerned, was naïve and not malicious. If she was to associate with people, she could only treat them as if they were as independent of their good and bad qualities as she herself; but when she wished to judge them, she could not blind her keen insight. After all, no one was too likely to ask her opinion of himself to her face. And even if someone did, she had the defense that, after all, she did not judge on the basis of particular actions; she passed no moral condemnations upon this person or that; and she had no standard of value and no prejudices, no matter how useful these might be; she availed herself only of "very small traits," nothing tangible; her judgment was, so to speak, based upon the very substance of which a person was made, upon the consistency of his soul, the level he attained or did not attain.

She acquired insight into these matters quite late, and paid disproportionately dear for them. No one, she rightly commented in her youth, was more candid than she; no one wanted more to be known. She repeatedly told Veit he was free to show all of her letters to others; she had no secrets, she wrote. On the contrary, she believed people would know her better from her letters, would be more just toward her. The world and people were so boundless, and whatever happened to her seemed so little directed toward her in particular, that discretion was incomprehensible to her. "Why won't you show anyone a whole letter of mine? It would not matter to me; nothing I have written need be hidden. If only I could throw myself open to people as a cupboard is opened, and with one gesture show the things arranged in order in their compartments. They would certainly be content, and as soon as they saw, would understand."

The true joy of conversation consisted in being understood. The more imaginary a life is, the more imaginary its sufferings, the greater is the craving for an audience, for confirmation. Precisely because Rahel's despair was visible, but its cause unknown and incomprehensible to herself, it would become pure hypochondria unless it were talked about, exposed. A morsel of reality lay hidden in other people's intelligent replies. She needed the experience of others to supplement her own. For that purpose, the particular qualifications of the individuals were a matter of indifference. The more people there were who understood her, the more real she would become. Silence was only a shield against being misunderstood, a shutting oneself off in order not to be touched. But silence out of fear of being understood was unknown to her. She was indiscreet toward herself.

Indiscretion and shamelessness were phenomena of the age, of Romanticism. But the first great model of indiscretion toward oneself had been provided by Rousseau's confessions, in which the self was exposed to its farthermost corners before the anonymous future reader, posterity. Posterity would no longer have any power over the life of the strange confessor; it could neither judge nor forgive; posterity was only the fantasied *foil* of the perceiving inner self. With the loss of the priest and his judgment, the solitude of the would-be confessor had become boundless. The singularity of the person, the uniqueness of the individual character, stood out against a background of indefinite anonymity. Everything was equally important and nothing forbidden. In complete isolation, shame was extinguished. The importance of emotions existed independently of possible consequences, independently of actions or motives. Rousseau related neither his life story nor his experiences. He merely confessed what he had felt, desired, wished, sensed in the course of his life. In the course of such a ruthless confessional the individual is isolated not only from the events of public life, but also from the events of his private life. His own life acquires reality only in the course of confessing it, only in recollections of emotions which he had at some time. Not the emotions, but *narrated* emotions alone can convince and overwhelm the hypochondriac. The utter absence of inhibition, so that no residue of silence is left, formed —according to Rousseau's own judgment—the uniqueness of his confessions. Such absence of inhibition is possible only within an absolute solitude which no human being and no objective force is capable of piercing.

Uninhibited utterance becomes open indiscretion if it is not addressed to posterity, but to a real listener who is merely treated as if he were anonymous, as if he could not reply, as if he existed simply and solely to listen. We find only too ample evidence of such indiscretion among Rahel's closest associates; its "classic" representation may be found in Friedrich Schlegel's *Lucinde*, which will serve for an example.

Lucinde is no more the story of a life than Rousseau's *Confessions*. All that we learn about the hero's life in the novel is couched in terms so general that only a mood, no real events, can be represented. Every situation is wrenched out of its context, introspected, and dressed up as a specially interesting chance occurrence. Life is without any continuity, a "mass of fragments without connection" (Schlegel). Since each of these fragments is enormously intensified by the endless introspection, life itself is shown as a fragment in the Romantic sense, "a small work of art entirely separated from the surrounding world and as complete in itself as a hedgehog" (Schlegel).

Introspection accomplishes two feats: it annihilates the actual existing situation by dissolving it in mood, and at the same time it lends everything subjective an aura of objectivity, publicity, extreme interest. In mood the boundaries between what is intimate and what is public become blurred; intimacies are made public, and public matters can be experienced and expressed only in the realm of the intimate—ultimately, in gossip. The shamelessness of *Lucinde*, which aroused a storm of indignation when it was published, is supposed to be justified by the magic of its mood. This mood supposedly possesses the power to convert reality back into potentiality and to confer, for the moment, the appearance of reality upon mere potentialities. The mood thus embodies the "fearful omnipotence of the imagination" (Schlegel). The imagination need hold no limit sacred, since it is limitless in itself. In the enchantment of mood, which expands a detail to infinity, the infinite appears as the most precious aspect of intimacy. In the flimsiness of a society which, as it were, exists only in a twilight state, communication is interesting only at the cost of unmasking; no limits may be placed upon revelation if it is to do justice to the claim that mood has no limits. But the less anything definite and objective may be communicated, the more it becomes necessary to relate intimate, unknown, curiosity-arousing details. It is precisely the ultimate intimacy which is intended to denote, in its uniqueness and un-generality, the breakthrough of the infinite which has withdrawn from everything real, tangible, understandable. If the infinite was revealed to earlier centuries, if its mystery was beginning to unfold to the Reason of a generation not yet dead, this generation now insisted that it betray its secrets privately. That alone is what Schlegel was really concerned with in all the shamelessness of his confessions—namely, with the "objectivity of his love" (Schlegel).

What the novel fails to do because mood, fascination, cannot survive when divorced from the personality, can be done in conversation. Young Schlegel must have possessed the magic of personality just as strongly as Rahel, of whom Gentz once said that she had been Romantic before the word was invented. In the limitlessness of conversation, in personal fascination, reality could be excluded just as effectively as in introspection or pure self-thinking. Rahel's friendships during this period were all, so to speak, tête-à-têtes. "You are never really with a person unless you are alone with him." Every chance additional person could disturb the intimacy. Even the interlocutor in the mood-drenched conversation was almost superfluous. "I will go still further—you are never more actually with a person than when you think of him in his absence and imagine what you will say to him," and—it might be added—when he is cheated of any chance to reply and you yourself are free of any risk of being rejected.

In such converse Rahel withdrew from the society which had excluded her; in it she could confirm her own situation and neutralize the bitterness of being involuntarily at a disadvantage. Confirmation must always be renewed, just as the sense of being wronged must repeatedly be revived. All praise was an inspiration: "Blame has little power over me, but I can be caught with praise." Only in an atmosphere of praise could she prove her uniqueness; she consumed more and more flatterers. Even listening to reproof would be tantamount to admitting that she was "nothing." But by never attempting to defend herself against blame, she rendered it powerless. Toward Wilhelm von Humboldt, who could not endure her and her indiscriminateness, she was curiously hard of hearing —and yet she attempted to captivate him anyway. Indiscriminately, she tried to win everyone over. If in spite of this she was rejected, she saw the rejection only as an insult that frightened her and thought she could prevent such insults by intriguing. Thus she wrote "the most *servile* letters to wholly unimportant people, in the vain hope of changing the only relationship really possible between us: bad feeling."

This misunderstanding seemed to be inescapable. Other people were never the "mirror images which reflected her inner self"—a specific, unalterable inner self—whose existence could help make her "inner self more distinct" (Goethe). For she did not possess herself; the purpose of her introspection was merely to know what could happen to her, in order to be armed against it; in introspection she must never let herself know who she was, for that might possibly be a "shlemihl or a Jew." She was so little mistress of her inner self that even her consciousness of reality was dependent upon confirmation by others. Only because she was in no sense sure of herself did condemnation have little power over her; and her words are remote indeed from the proud serenity with which Goethe could say: "Antagonists are out of the question . . . ; they reject the purposes toward which my actions are directed. . . . Therefore I wave them away and refuse to know them. . . ."

Among the "praisers" the most important, for a time, were Gustav von Brinckmann and Wilhelm von Burgsdorff. Brinckmann, the Swedish ambassador in Berlin, is known for his letters to Schleiermacher and Gentz, letters full of pen portraits of acquaintances, of gossip and affairs with women. This extremely commonplace and highly typical child of his time was never heavily committed to anything; he was pliant and had the gift of politeness; he moved from one person to another, was a cultivated man without any center to his personality. Prince Louis Ferdinand, writing to Pauline Wiesel, commented: "Brinckmann is really so sweet. Lovers write letters for the sake of love, but he loves for the sake of letters." He also indulged in philosophical speculations—leaning heavily on Schleiermacher, whose disciple he called himself; his *point d'appui* was always in the realm of psychology, and his ponderings were without consistency. Women as the most important because least explored psychological territory were by no means his discovery. Interest in man, during this period, degenerated on the whole to psychological interest in a newly discovered type of man. Brinckmann was merely one "brooder on humanity" among many "for whom women are the principal study" (Brinckmann). Rahel was splendidly suited to be a "friend without adjectives or connotations" (Brinckmann); psychologically she was the hardest of women to understand, while for her part she affected to be able to understand everything. She was a brilliant interlocutor: "She came, *talked* and *conquered*" (Brinckmann).

Burgsdorff met Rahel at Bad Teplitz in the summer of 1795, through Brinckmann's introduction. She was spending the summer with Countess Pachta and was happy to have a companion who was an indefatigable talker and a cultivated person; she delighted in the extraordinary "receptivity of his mind" (Varnhagen). In spite of his pretended rejection of the world, Brinckmann nevertheless possessed ambition; her friend Veit was endeavoring with every means at his disposal to force his way into society, precisely because he had been originally excluded from it; in Burgsdorff, on the other hand, Rahel saw a nobleman's unstrained repudiation of offices, dignities and effectiveness in the world.

These few names are intended only as examples of the nature of her friendships: neither Brinckmann nor Burgsdorff nor Veit loved her. With all these men it is difficult to imagine how they could possibly become involved in a love situation.

Brinckmann was driven by restless curiosity from one woman to another; Burgsdorff's love for Caroline von Humboldt is a familiar tale. The decay of that love was no less fearful for being peculiarly unmotivated: Caroline's love became burdensome to him; he fled from Paris to escape it when it began to involve more than "grasping the most individual character traits, the faintest nuances."

Veit, as Rahel's first friend and her ally in the struggle with the alien world, occupied a special position. He was the first to whom Rahel said: "Only galley slaves know one another." He was the first to discover everything praiseworthy in her: her understanding, her precision, her intelligence. He was the first person who knew how "to use" her, who knew that she was good for more than "helping to consume the sugar." But in this relationship, too, there was never any talk of love.

Alongside this life with her friends she lived another, unofficial life whose details she concealed from these friends; she candidly admitted the wretchedness of it only to her brothers. In this other life she kept alive the reality of her first setbacks. In fact she noted carefully, with a "cruel joy," every confirmation of her being a shlemihl: not rich, not beautiful and Jewish. She told her friends about this only in generalities. Thus she wrote to Brinckmann from Teplitz, where she had by chance encountered Goethe, and briefly became acquainted with him: "I don't know—it is as though many years ago something was shattered inside me and I take a cruel pleasure in knowing that henceforth it can no longer be broken, pulled at and beaten—although now it has become a place to which I myself can no longer reach. (And if there is *such* a place inside one, all possibility of happiness is ruled out.) I can no longer remember what it was; and if I do not succeed in minor things, I must at once provide so many rationalizations for my bunglings, that no one else will believe me and I myself become frightened. . . . For it is frightful to be forced to consider oneself the only creature that makes *everything* come to grief . . . for that, as far as I know, is my only accomplishment."

2

INTO THE WORLD
(1795-1799)

I. By Marriage

In the winter of 1795 Rahel glimpsed from her box at the theater Count Karl von Finckenstein. A few months before she had written to Brinckmann: "I am now fully convinced that I am going to marry." She made the acquaintance of Finckenstein and soon afterwards was engaged to him.

Rahel wanted to escape from Judaism. "Everything is topsy-turvy; no Jew stays put; but, alas, I alone wretchedly stay where I am,"[1] she wrote to Brinckmann again a few years later, when all her prospects for marriage had been shattered. If she married the count, the son of the Prussian minister, she would become Countess Finckenstein. He had fallen in love with her, was "blond as yellow brick" and the first man, *le premier qui a voulu que je l'aime,* as she wrote to Alexander von der Marwitz sixteen years later. She said yes at once, snatched at the chance as though she had been only waiting for such an event, never for any particular person. As though she longed only to be taken away from what and where she was. Once she became a countess, her disadvantages could be forgotten overnight; nothing would remain of Jewishness but a natural solidarity with all those who likewise wanted to escape from Judaism.

Rahel longed to depart from Judaism; there did not seem to be any other way to assimilate. In spite of mixed social groups, in spite of the illusory disappearance of hatred for

---

[1] Both remarks excised by Varnhagen in his published edition of the letters. Supplemented from the manuscript: the first from the letter of September 4, 1795, *Buch des Andenkens,* I, 156; the second from the letter of February 11, 1799, ibid., p. 178.

Jews among cultured people, the situation was already growing worse in the nineties. As long as it had been possible for
Jews to assimilate to the Enlightenment, and to it alone, because it fully represented the intellectual life of Germany, a
social rise for the Jews was not absolutely necessary. The
possibility of acceptance, the chance for culture, existed, and
was in fact easy as long as the potency of reason remained
complete, because innocent of history. Thus Moses Mendelssohn had been able to assimilate to his alien surroundings
without abandoning his Judaism. He needed only to lay aside
old "prejudices" in a highly deceptive present and learn thinking. It was still possible for him to believe that his course
should serve as a model, that it was not the accidental destiny
of an individual. He had arrived in Berlin fifty years ago;
thirty years ago, after only two decades of residence, he was
already being spoken of in the same breath as the other
"learned men of Berlin," Rammler, Nikolai and Lessing. He
was included as one of the representative figures of the German Enlightenment, for all that everyone knew that he was
a Jew and that he expressly clung to Jewish tradition. His lack
of civil rights hardly troubled him; the idea of political emancipation was first urged upon him by Dohm who saw in him
(as did later Mirabeau and all those who supported the "civil
betterment of the Jews") the guarantee that the Jews were
worthy. Mendelssohn himself took only a very incidental interest in social inclusion. He was content with the enlightened
absolutism of Frederick the Second under which "the Jews
enjoy the most honorable liberty in the exercise of their religion," under which "the flourishing of arts and sciences and
reasonable freedom to think has been made so general that the
effects extend down to the least inhabitant of his state" (Mendelssohn). He was satisfied to be that "least inhabitant." For
as such he had "found opportunity and cause to acquire culture, to meditate upon the destinies of himself and his fellow
citizens, and to make observations on people, fate and provi-
dence according to the measure of his strength" (Mendelssohn). Since he adhered to Judaism, since he did not recognize history, he maintained a dignified composure toward

society which had banished him to the lowest step of its ladder. At most he wanted to defend Judaism; he desired for all Jews the respect which Lessing and the rest of intellectual Germany paid to him; but he was absolutely unwilling to decide for or against Christianity "as a Socrates would have done" (Lavater). For "as long as we cannot demonstrate any authentic liberation from the Law, all our sophistries cannot free us from the strict obedience which we owe to the Law" (Mendelssohn).

This "strict obedience" was something already unknown even to his disciples. They felt themselves to be Jews only because as Jews they tried to throw off the Jewish religion. With dubious justification they considered their assimilation as already achieved because they had borrowed the blindness of the Enlightenment, for which the Jews were no more than an oppressed people. They blamed whatever was alien in them upon their history; they saw whatever was peculiar to them as Jews merely as an obstacle to citizenship. Their study of the Jewish religion became admittedly one means among others for "changing the political constitution of the Jews" (David Friedländer). Out of this spirit arose Friedländer's *Epistle by some Jewish patresfamilias,* which in the name of the Enlightenment, Reason and moral feeling volunteered mass acceptance of baptism so that the Jews might "publicly become part of society." This embarrassing offer was made by Friedländer at a time when Rahel, and her whole generation with her, had already discovered that escape from Judaism was possible only for individuals and that appealing to the spirit of the Enlightenment was no longer of any use. Nor was it of any use to Friedländer. Provost Teller, a liberal and enlightened theologian to whom the epistle had been addressed, answered coolly, while Schleiermacher energetically fended off the unwelcome guests. Characteristically, he assigned the *Epistle* to a place in the "older school of our literature," and against the appeal to Reason and moral feeling stressed the distinctive character of Christianity which, he said, could only be watered down by such proselytes. Reason, he went on, had nothing to do with religion, but only with citizenship; Reason

could only bring about a partial integration. Hence Schleiermacher favored the swiftest possible naturalization of the
Jews—but this was far from being the beginning of complete
assimilation, of the disappearance of the Jews' separate existence—which was what they were offering. As a Jewish citizen
the Jew would continue to exist in all his peculiarity. In other
words, there could be no thought of ending the Jewish question. "The Enlightenment manner" had become "contemptible," Schleiermacher averred. Friedländer wished to perpetu-
ate the Mendelssohnian Enlightenment because it enabled
him to forget his own origins. It had escaped him that he no
longer lived in those days, and that Johann Gottfried Herder's
insight into the power of history had also cast a new light upon
the Jewish question at least for the non-Jews; that the question
could no longer be settled by a "religious controversy"
(Herder).

Herder was the first writer in Germany expressly to identify
his Jewish contemporaries with their history and with the Old
Testament; that is to say, he endeavored to understand their
history as they themselves had once interpreted it: as the history of the Chosen People. He regarded their dispersion as
the first step and the reason for their influence upon humanity.
He called attention to their peculiar attitude of clinging to
the past and attempting to fix the past in the present. Their
lament over Jerusalem, destroyed so many years ago, and their
hope for the Messiah, were to him not superstition but a sign
that "the ruins of Jerusalem . . . are as it were . . . founded
in the heart of time." Their religion was to him neither a well-
spring of prejudices nor the Mendelssohnian rational creed;
rather it was the "inalienable heritage of their race." At the
same time Herder held that their history, which derived from
the law of Moses, could not be separated from that law; they
stood or fell according to whether they obeyed the law. Jewish
history in the Diaspora was essentially an adherence to the
religion of Palestine; in keeping to their own history the Jews
had remained aliens everywhere, a people of Palestine and
therefore "in Europe an Asiatic folk foreign to our continent."
Herder emphasized not their equality as individuals with all

other human beings, but their collective, historical alienation. This did not exclude assimilation; in fact Herder was all the more fervent for assimilation. Lessing's and Dohm's discussion of the Jewish question had been primarily guided by the call for tolerance, by outrage against the offense to human dignity represented by an oppressed people, by shame at the injustices Christian Europe had committed so continuously. But for Herder the emancipation of the Jews became a political question. He saw the problem not as one of tolerating another religion—as, after all, so many prejudices of various kinds had to be tolerated—nor of improving a socially undesirable situation, but of incorporating a different nation into the German people and into Europe. "To what extent this law (of Moses) and the way of life and thought arising out of it has a place in our political institutions, is no longer a religious controversy, in which opinions and faith may be discussed, but simply a *political question*" (Herder).

The Jews had but the poorest understanding of the new era and the new generation on which Herder had had a crucial influence. This incomprehension was manifest not only in the few official "Jewish fathers," but in almost every individual Jew, with few exceptions. They understood only one thing: that the past clung inexorably to them as a collective group; that they could only shake it off as individuals. The tricks employed by individuals became subtler, individual ways out more numerous, as the personal problem grew more intense; the Jews became psychologically more sophisticated and socially more ingenious. The history of the German Jews evaporated for a brief spell—until the first Emancipation Decree of 1812—into the history of individuals who succeeded in escaping.

One such individual case was that of Henriette Herz. At first glance her situation was the same as Rahel's. It is no accident that the two names are generally coupled. Henriette Herz's *Jugenderinnerungen* ("Memories of Youth") are quite typical. From them it is evident that the last physical (figuratively speaking) obstacle to assimilation, Jewish tradition, had already been overcome in youth. While still very young Henriette married Marcus Herz, a scientist and disciple of Kant who enjoyed equal prestige in Berlin as a physician and a scholar. His pupils, who came to their house for seminars, became her friends; they formed one of the first Jewish salons. From them Henriette learned: Latin, Greek, some Sanskrit, mathematics and physics. Christianity, in Schleiermacher's version of it, became for her another element of culture. Nevertheless, she underwent baptism relatively late, having to wait first for the death of her husband and then of her mother. She was respected because she was very virtuous, much loved because she was very beautiful. She was called cold because nothing penetrated her reserve, because she remained unaffected. When some man fell in love with her, she wrote with laughable solemnity: "The corruptest gift of the gods has blinded him." But at bottom she was merely inexperienced. Subsequently she tried to strike roots by learning, but was incapable of understanding "any general ideas, or their application." With sound instinct she fended off all passion, all serious entrance into the world; she could not "distinguish an error about things from the still nature of things . . . she succumbs immediately to the approbation or opinion of people." [2] She believed that the world could be learned and society bribed by virtue. And her suppositions would seem to have been right, for the world responded by according her respect.

But, "gods of the world! How can anyone stay alive living so little," Rahel commented. How ridiculous even virtue would be when she grew old at last, when life had passed by this "colossal figure" without having given her anything, frightened away by so much virtue. In old age virtue no longer has much meaning; what remains is a "miracle of triviality," and "in mockery of those who think themselves virtuous the eternal gods doom this being; it is injustice to use a soul, that is after all alive, for such purposes." She would have learned

[2] See *Buch des Andenkens*, III, 18, where Varnhagen used the code "Frau von B." for "Hofrätin Herz."

nothing, experienced nothing, had no life: "the wind has passed around her high-held head as it would around a church steeple." [3]

Another such individual case was Dorothea Schlegel. As the youngest daughter of Moses Mendelssohn she could with some justice and without too great malice be considered the perfect product of her father's naïvely ambiguous orthodoxy. For he allowed her the advantages of a modern European education —and then married her off in good old Jewish fashion, without her having a word to say in the matter, to a respected Jewish businessman of Berlin. The result: she ran off from her husband and two children, ran to Friedrich Schlegel like a moth to a candle. Her sons by her first marriage became the most devout Christian painters of the epoch, the so-called "Nazarenes."

Dorothea did not learn to know the world, but only Schlegel; she did not belong to Romanticism, but to Schlegel; she was not converted to Catholicism, but to Schlegel's religion. She wanted to "build a temple" to him. Her love was completely unreflecting, only the reflected expression of her fascination. Even her nasty gossip about Caroline Schlegel, who was absolutely her superior, expressed such naïve spite, such childish partisanship and lack of insight, that one prefers simply to forget it. The crucial fact is that she succeeded in freeing herself, in attaching herself to a man and being dragged by him through the world. The world was nothing but the passing foil for her emotions, for all the churned-up passion within her. When, in her old age, the passion withered, she became bigoted.

Dorothea Schlegel encountered life just once, when she met Schlegel and he loved her. But she at once abandoned life again by immortalizing this one moment. There was nothing in her life to narrate, because it had no story, because it stubbornly took its stand upon the experience of a single, swiftly passing moment. She simply threw her life away upon a moment.

[3] Excised sentences from a letter to Wilhelm von Humboldt dated June 28, 1809, *Buch des Andenkens*, I, 426 ff.

Other individual cases were the sisters Marianne and Sarah Meier. They came from a wealthy family which had already provided them with a "genteel rearing and cultivated education" (Varnhagen). Their cleverness and their culture were merely worldliness. Marianne married Prince Reuss and after his death bore the title Frau von Eybenberg. Sarah had a long and happy marriage with a Livonian baron named Grotthus. Both ladies lived in high society, surrounded by sycophants. Their relationship to Goethe is well known. Frau von Grotthus succumbed to mental illness; she suffered from a pathological vanity. Frau von Eybenberg lived in high society in Vienna until her death. In that city her rise was not so astonishing; besides her, the Itzig sisters, Frau von Eskeles and Frau von Arnstein, had salons. The Austrian State needed money almost more urgently than Prussia, and the moneyed men, Austrian Court Jews or state bankers, were in consequence highly respected people. In the salons the men played a secondary role, just as Marcus Herz did in his wife's salon. In those days the women were actually the agents of social assimilation; the men were too busy with the economic side of the matter. "Among the Jews . . . the women are . . . one hundred per cent better than the men" (Gentz). At any rate, they were accepted in society, though here and there they might suddenly be rebuffed, although there always remained houses to which they were refused admittance, although Gentz thought that their sociality "always borders on *mauvaise société*," and although all of Vienna repeated the Prince de Ligne's bon mot: that Baron Arnstein was *le premier baron du vieux testament*. Minor insults, which every Jewess must be prepared to meet at all times, engendered in Frau von Grotthus her immoderate vanity and in Frau von Eybenberg her "animosity-colored knowledge of mankind" (Varnhagen). But they also engendered cleverness, alertness and the art of "making even boredom entertaining" (Varnhagen).

As for Rahel, she could not "learn answers" like Henriette Herz. She must remain all her life an "ignoramus" who would have to be taken as she was. No tradition had transmitted anything to her; her existence was not foreseen in any nation's history. Without ties because she had not been born into any cultural world; without prejudices because, apparently, no one had done any prejudging before she came into the world; in the paradoxical situation of the first human being, as it were —she was compelled to grasp everything for herself as if encountering it for the first time. She was dependent upon originality. Herder once expressly demanded open-mindedness on the part of the "cultivated Jew." In Henriette Herz freedom from all bias was translated into receptivity to virtually everything; everything became learnable. Her freedom from ties was expressed in a senseless, objectless talent. Since Rahel insisted upon her ignorance, she provided an example of liberation and lack of fixation upon a particular historically conditioned world.

From this freedom was derived her striking manner of describing things, people and situations. Her wit, which had made her redoubtable even as a young girl, was merely her completely untrammeled manner of looking at things. She dwelt in no particular order of the world, and she refused to learn any such order. She could bring together in a witticism things that appeared to be utterly remote from one another; she could discover in the most intimately related matters the essential incoherence. This her friends praised as her "great originality"—which struck even Goethe about her when she was a girl; this her enemies felt to be lack of style, disorder, wanton delight in paradox. She wrote letters, Gentz declared, "in which the flowers and fruit lie together with the roots and the earth lifted right out of the ground." Having neither models nor tradition, she consequently had no real consciousness of what words belonged together and what did not. But she was really original; she could never blur a matter for the sake of a customary expression. In her originality, in her mania for thinking, Rahel evinced not only the open-mindedness but also the emptiness of the person who is utterly dependent upon experiences, who needs a whole life to form every opinion. She was too young to have experiences, too isolated to know where life could strike her.

She was presumably too clever to attach herself to a so-called genius; "for that very reason," she wrote to Veit immediately after meeting Goethe, "I cannot be blindly captivated by any person, so that I don't go in for worship . . . because otherwise I would certainly have fallen in love with Goethe, and, you know, I only worship him." Certainly, moreover, she was too curious; for she had begun too early to settle with herself and the world without relying upon anyone. There remained for her, therefore, only social assimilation through marriage— a course very frequently adopted in those days. Rahel's engagement to Finckenstein was, in the beginning, hardly anything but just such an attempt.

The Finckensteins were one of the oldest noble families of Prussia. Karl Finckenstein and his three sisters had grown up in the ancestral house at Madlitz in Brandenburg. His parents, himself and his sisters formed a small unit in themselves, each bound to each by ties of love and a sense of natural belongingness. To be sure, Karl felt a special love for his eldest sister, whose happiness was "the most sacred thing" in his life. But even this love was only special in appearance; it, too, was merely the expression of his sense of the cohesiveness of the whole family. "As soon as you enter this house you become a member of the most delightful family; on the other hand, you lose all your freedom; you cease entirely to be an individual person existing for yourself and really no longer have a will of your own" (Burgsdorff).

Count Finckenstein's family belonged to the Kurmärkischer Kreis, the group which, under the leadership of old Finckenstein and Ludwig August von der Marwitz, fought the reforms of Hardenberg and Stein with all the means at their command. The nobility had "for more than a hundred years ceased to be of any significance politically" (Hardenberg); the Enlightenment and the bourgeoisie had made deep intellectual inroads among the nobility and had destroyed that class's ideological foundations. The landed nobles, however, continued to live on their estates, relatively secure and unassailed by the spirit of the times. Consequently "the patriarchal and family setup was still so firmly established that mere reading could make no impression upon it" (Ludwig von der

Marwitz). The conservative element was the family in which the individual member, as a specific person with a personal destiny, played scarcely any part. Nevertheless, the individual was indispensably important as the representative of the class and as the perpetuator of the house. That this individual might have a right to his own personal life, that he could demand the right "to be happy," was considered that "basically false premise" of modern times, from which followed "the whole devilry which has since stood Europe on its head" (Marwitz). The individual represents merely one moment as against the memory of the family stock and the need for its continuance into the future. The individual is therefore only the representative of the "lasting and immutable interest of a class as a moral and consequently immortal being" (Marwitz). The family cannot be represented by deputies (as can the corporations of the middle class), but only by a person. Hence the person is everything, but the individual nothing. How little the individual may be considered the representative of the nobility is clearly evident in the "reform of the nobility" proposed by Marwitz. He suggested that the younger sons who did not inherit the landed property—which in the interests of the family ought to remain undivided—should retire into the middle class and enjoy no privileges above those of the other classes of the population. The dissolution of the Estates which permitted every individual to leave his place, unleashing "a wild pushing up from below" because "every peasant's son would and could become an artisan, every artisan's son a clerk, every clerk's son a bureau chief, every schoolmaster a scholar, and every merchant or scholar a great lord"—this unbinding of the individual's ties to a specific place in the social framework meant to Marwitz nothing more nor less than "the war of the present moment against the past and future, of the individual against the family."

When Marwitz spoke of the bourgeoisie, he meant the tradesmen and the artisans. The rising mercantile entrepreneurs who fought for freedom of trade and for the right to acquire landed property, who were ultimately carrying out the "revolutionization of the country," were to him only objects of hatred and contempt. This type of bourgeois was only "what he had" (Wilhelm Meister) and therefore cared only for his own life and his chances of success. He belonged to no Estate in the old sense; he represented nothing. All he had to show was what he had; if he made any attempt to "seem," he at once became "ridiculous and absurd." In being unable to represent anything he was not a "public person," but a private individual. If by some chance he nevertheless entered the public eye or public life, there remained alongside this public self an essentially private self with a specific occupation which had nothing to do with himself as a public person. Out of this, Marwitz held, there arose the "great confusion of this era . . . that people think one and the same person can hold and proclaim a twofold point of view, the one as a private person and the other as a citizen of the state." Characteristic of the duality of the bourgeois existence is the distinction made by the liberal writer Friedrich Buchholz between having and being. "To the question, who is so and so?" he writes, "there is no more unsuitable answer than that he is a minister, president . . . or something of the sort. This answer would be appropriate only if having were being discussed, for then it would mean that someone holds the position of minister or president, which permits him to represent so and so much. . . . Being, in its richness, seeks only for occasions to manifest itself and instinctively hates every kind of representation because that is always merely appearance." When a man has achieved representative status, he is visible as what he is. Among the bourgeois, who had to renounce representational status, there arose after the dissolution of the Estates the fear of no longer being visible, no longer being secure in their own reality. Wilhelm Meister attempts by acquiring education in the broadest sense to learn how to represent himself. If he succeeds in this he will become a "public person" and no longer one who merely is and has. But a private path leads to this acquisition of public personality. Meister receives his education from those who stand outside both bourgeois and noble society and who therefore can "seem" anything and everything. "On the stage the cultivated person makes as good an appearance as in the upper classes; mind and body must go in step in every endeavor, and I shall be able to be and seem there just as well as anywhere else" (Wilhelm Meister).

The salons were the meeting places of those who had learned how to represent themselves through conversation. The actor can always be the "seeming" of himself; the bourgeois as an individual had learned to show himself—not something beyond himself, but nothing but himself. The nobleman was, in the Enlightenment, gradually losing the thing he represented; he was being thrown back upon himself, "reduced to the bourgeoisie." The world of the aristocracy remained intact in the landed gentry in which the closeness of the family still survived. Where an individual did leave from such a family, the only circles he could enter with impunity were those of the aristocracy, where nothing was asked of him but to be "a member of the family," where he was accepted and esteemed simply for being what he was.

Finckenstein came to Berlin for professional reasons. For him it was like going into exile. In bourgeois Berlin where even the princes "would have despised themselves if they had lived differently and sought for anything different from the small-town citizen" (Marwitz), in this city of individuals, he was forced to be an individual. That was all the more so when he came to Rahel's salon, a socially neutral place where all classes met and where it was taken for granted that each person would be an individual. But as an individual Finckenstein was nothing; stripped of his title of nobleman he had nothing he could represent. And this title of his was of little account among Rahel's friends.

Rahel was engaged to Finckenstein; in marrying him she would become a countess. But she did not leave her circle for him; on the contrary, she drew him into her circle, where he immediately ceased to be a count and was exposed in all his nullity. Now, suddenly, she was the superior, the magnanimous woman who condescended to be engaged to him who amounted to nothing.

Rahel misunderstood his nullity as a psychologically understandable inferiority feeling. She tried to put this to flight by showing him what he meant to her. But it was precisely this that he did not understand. In the atmosphere of the salon his being a count had evaporated like a phantasm. And as for himself, who was he? She could not love him for himself—then why was she pursuing him? And on the other hand, as a count he could not marry a Jewish girl without a dowry, could he?

Confused, he fled back to Madlitz, back to considerations of class and family; from here he let her know of the disapproval of his sisters and his parents. She began to fight against them.

What a hopeless fight it was. Considerations of class seemed to her merely fetters from which she must free him, from which he ought to free himself. Did she seriously think she could draw him wholly over to her, compensate him for all he would be losing, be his family and his ancestry, be so close to him that he would no longer be anything but a part of her? Perhaps he did want that; he even seemed ready to give up everything for her, since it was part of his nobility to recognize the claims of love. Rahel, however, fought for her vacillating fiancé only so long as he did not lay his cards on the table; he kept evading, but in his evasions he always came closer to her, returned to her. Finally he confided in her, uncovered the cards, explained what the family and its objections meant to him; then he waited for her to help him, to pull him to her. But she suddenly gave ground, abandoned the struggle, declared that he must decide for himself; she would do no more. At the moment of half-victory she threw all her own cards away. He realized, when she confronted him with the alternative and abandoned him to it, that she would never really want to have him, that it was all merely a game intended to educate him, to make him worthy of her. And at this realization he made his final retreat, did nothing, said nothing, let his own specific gravity operate—and that drew him of its own accord back into the life most natural to him.

Rahel had lost the game. For the first time the world was denying her explicitly, for all to see. She could have achieved everything, forced everything to come her way. And undoubtedly she had wanted this marriage. But she had not realized the price she would have to pay. She had required her lover to be an individual, to amount to something, to be a man—and had misunderstood everything. In trying to draw him to herself she had committed the fatal error. In her last letter she wrote: *"Be* something, and I will recognize you. You cannot take any pleasure in me. I overawe you, and therefore I too cannot find any happiness with you." These sentences were only the summing up; and it was as if the four-year history of their engagement had been protracted only in order to make this one fact ultimately clear to her and to him.

II. *Through Love*

"Yesterday morning, May 20, 1811, Finckenstein came to see me. He asked after no one. Nor asked how I was. He seemed to me the same as always, only that all his qualities and opinions have become very compact; he is also so calm and gentle and contented about it, as though he really had entered the temple of wisdom and happiness. . . . Suddenly he said: 'I wish very much you would see my wife and see whether you liked her.' I remained seated; the sun shone gently. So it is not for me to think anything horrible which does not come true. . . . My whole soul was as outraged, as much in upheaval, my heart just as affected as twelve years ago, as though nothing had happened in all the interval. 'Your murderer!' I thought, and remained seated. Tears came into my throat and to my eyes; . . . I felt like a creature that he owned; he once consumed me. *He—me,* God forgive him; may he forgive himself. This vow I shall certainly keep: I will never avenge myself, but I cannot forgive him for that! . . . Perhaps there are people whose hearts can change; much has happened to me, I have had to experience much: but still, from every flame, I take out with me an unharmed and also an indignant heart that goes on living entirely for itself. . . . Finck had entirely vanished from my mind; I summoned up accusations against him only when I thought over the course of my life; . . . and now, seeing and scrutinizing him, I felt, I knew, that I had remained faithful to him, as he is, in spite of my knowledge of him. I would have remained faithful to him if he had permitted it, if he had wanted it. If yesterday, by twisting a magic ring, he had been able to abolish all that has taken place in these twelve years, he could once again have drawn my whole life to him, if he had wanted to!"

Only a magic ring was needed, and everything could have started from the beginning again. What then was he, who was nevertheless a nullity? Did she really mean this man when she said she had remained faithful to him as he was, in spite of her knowledge of him? Or was he merely accidental, simply *le premier qui a voulu que je l'aime*? And was she so happy when he died a few months after this renewed meeting (*rayé de ce globe, enfin dessous, lui avec sa fausse ambition et ses perfidies, mensonges, bassesses et orgueils*, as she wrote to Marwitz immediately after receiving news of his death) because she knew that at any time he could have drawn her whole life again, if only he had wanted to?

So then she had loved him—he who was nothing; she who, as Veit had said, could find no object of love. And Finckenstein was not even merely the chance object that made her catch fire. She was in no wise seeking Romantic love which "often is more than the object of it"; otherwise she could have calmly dropped him and still have had her love intact. But in fact she had let Finckenstein go at last only after years of fighting for him, for him in particular.

In her innocence and inexperience she saw in him a person who represented nothing specific and unequivocal. Since she herself was attached to nothing specific, she had no possibility of choice. Excluded from society, she could only allow herself to be "drawn" when something chanced to encounter her. He was the first man who wanted her to love him. If this demand had come from someone else who had, in her sense, particular gifts, a specific physiognomy of the psyche, she would have had to decide for or against this person. But as it was, she was not becoming involved with an individual; rather, through the man she was becoming involved with the whole world. Here was double reason to be cautious. She must not, like Dorothea Schlegel, see the whole world and the foundation of all truth in her beloved. For that would mean fabricating, in

altogether absurd fashion, an object out of a function. Finckenstein had come to her as the representative of everything
from which she was excluded. Because he was personally nothing, it was possible for him to represent everything.

Given this complicated state of affairs, everyone was
prompted to ask how the two had "hit upon" one another. The
verdicts of their friends are undoubtedly just. Caroline von
Humboldt said of Finckenstein that he was a person who
"for all his sensitivity possesses no complexity or versatility."
Genelli, who had known him at Madlitz, and called himself
his friend, asserted that the whole affair was "a woeful mistake," for Finckenstein possessed nothing but his "slavish in-
adequacy." Josephine von Pachta put the matter more clearly
and precisely: "Too weak to create any true personal happiness
for himself; too weak to endure misfortune." Rahel was perfectly familiar with these opinions, since all these quotations
are taken exclusively from letters to her. Certainly they told
her nothing new, and probably they made scarcely any impression upon her. Such criticisms are meaningless when opposed to the fact of loving and being loved. What was
happening to her was simply incommensurate with what
Finckenstein, from a psychological point of view, was or was
not.

His coming to her and loving her was a matter of chance,
for he did not know her. He was very slow in learning to know
her, and as this knowledge grew, his love slackened. No
amount of knowledge could frighten Rahel off, however.
What she loved about him was the very chanciness of him.
How else was the world going to come to her, except in the
form of chance? There were no other opportunities for her,
no other ways in which life might pay attention to her. This
seemed more important to her than winning by intrigue a place
in the world for herself, which she tried desperately and with
some justification to do even now and certainly later on. For
the sake of a chance to experience something, anything, to be
a human being, she threw up everything, "ventured to yield
to chance when everything might have been calculated,"
translated what might have been a career into a love affair,

took his little infatuation, took her love seriously, assumed that the typical marital story of her generation was indeed a matter of chance, obtained for herself by lies and freedom ("by the noblest, loveliest sort of lying"), the good that crude and malicious reality, unintelligible necessity, had denied to her.

When he came to her, he was not nothing, but Count von Finckenstein, a specific person whose life was predetermined by birth to a degree that she could scarcely even guess. She might have been able to enter into this particular life of his; instead of that, she drew him out of his own situation and converted him to a nullity, so that she would be able to love him. Only when he was no one in particular could she successfully silence the question in herself: Why this man in particular?

But he, when he chanced upon her, fell in love with her, with her in particular, and in so doing made her a specific person. It is hard to say whether he seriously loved her. She, at any rate, did not believe that he did. He wrote to her in such stereotyped phrases as "if you had only been able to see how . . . if you only knew how . . . ," etc. Which did not seem very convincing. She demanded a binding, definite acknowledgment, and took offense when he put her off with hopes of the future. He was accustomed to having his life predetermined for him, and hope was for him only the sweet surrogate for specific planning. He knew in advance what his life in this world was going to be like; he had every assurance that the world would not deny itself to him. But Rahel was distrustful, because there was no place in the world for her, and she considered hope foolish. Hard to say whether he loved her. He was overwhelmed by the consequences that had resulted from his first small stab at love. True, he had wanted her to love him, but he had not known what he was asking. Now he felt inexplicably entangled. He had never meant anything quite so serious. By returning love, she cut off all his retreats. Thus she who had been conquered, slowly conquered him. "I wanted to love him into love." Faced with such resolution, everything, whether he wished it or not, inevitably became a dodge: so his well-founded hopefulness and his sense of being inferior to her. His love lost its "incisiveness"; it could not cope with hers, "destroyed itself in and through itself."

Finckenstein fled. His first refuge was a little flirtation with the actress Unzelmann, who was no real threat to Rahel. But then he fled in earnest. He went back home to Madlitz. There he lived once more in what he called his "own conditions," which, for all that they oppressed him, possessed a reality which was nevertheless a comfort. He took refuge from her letters, from her reproaches, in the "frivolity" of daily life. Since he did not want to take any steps, he waited for the day when everything would collapse of its own accord. At the same time he was really longing for her and wanted to see her again. But not as she was in actuality; rather he wanted to see her in fancied situations: "Oh, if I were sick, then you would be with me." He knew that this period of waiting was merely a "reprieve," but he was resolved "to be happy as long as it is still possible" (Finckenstein).

His flight to Madlitz, therefore, did not signify the final break. Everything remained *sans conséquence*. He had merely abandoned the struggle to be an individual and had taken shelter behind those obstacles which traditionally stood in the way of a marriage. "Such a silly bugbear is this fate which has interposed itself between me and you, and is thrusting me back, thrusting me back into my misery; it is so omnipotent, and yet it is so ridiculous" (Finckenstein). Unhappy he might be, but he was going to sink back into the comfortable role of being nothing but the member of his family. Once again Rahel was being opposed by *the* world, society prejudices, and not any individual, not any individual's particular will. She tried to force him to a decision by provoking an open breach. This way she might be able to extract something from the misfortune by showing that the generalized "fate" he chose to hide behind was in fact expressly her own individual destiny. On one occasion, when he was passing through Berlin, she refused to see him. He intended to give her up passively, slowly, but he was beside himself that she should dare to anticipate him—although this was her only way to preserve a remnant of freedom for herself. After all, it was of no help to her that he was "gently submissive to his destiny" (Finckenstein). Passionately, angrily, she was constantly inventing new alternatives—and yet she could achieve neither a break nor a definitive bond. He simply could not be induced into any action. She kept away from him, thereby plunging him into a solitude in which he was no longer capable of any decisions at all because he was no longer anything at all. She herself deprived him of the shelter of her love, after having shaken him loose from the shelter of his family. Inexorably, she cut off all his chances for flight, even the possibility of flight to her, even the fancied flight with her away from other human beings; ultimately she blocked even escape into the present from "the voices of the future." She conjured up everything that might be going to happen before it happened, not out of mad whimsy, but because she knew that some day these things would really be, and because she had a craving for any kind of reality, even the harshest.

But what, then, is reality? Did she seriously want the break? Those four years of loving and being loved, of suffering and uncertainty—were they not also reality? To be sure, Finckenstein bent every effort to people the present with illusory images and to make any definite decisions impossible; thus breaking with him would at least constitute an assurance that life would not stand still, that something would be happening. It was as though the break were the only reality still possible. But later, in her old age, the break would have entered so completely into the story of her love that she would have difficulty differentiating among the various types of reality.

"Supposing that we could, it would be a mad decision, by means of a *single* action, willfully separate ourselves forever from someone whom we love and know perfectly." She tried to provoke the break because she did not really believe it would come off. "For what if we knew that we were going to go on living, always knowing that everything we encounter for all eternity will separate us from this object for all eternity?" She saw it as monstrous to conclude something by a merely negative action; after all, one had at one's disposal an infinity of future possibilities which could never all be present to the mind in the midst of action. To kill another ought to be impossible, since no one could bring another back to life. No man ought to be so free, for no matter how free he appeared, he remained nevertheless the slave of his own actions. "To think that no communication, no meeting, no exchange of any sort is possible; like two ships sailing in eternally opposite directions, or two stars." Namely, two products of nature which once, in a delirium of freedom had resolved to transform themselves into "bodies driven only by necessity."[4]

Finckenstein did not accept the break because he did not understand it. Had it not been Rahel who "had freed his soul from the oppressive feeling of nullity to which it had previously succumbed" (Finckenstein), who drew him "out of this dreary meaningless state by being the first to hold out to him sympathy and love" (Finckenstein)? She recognized "the better part of his nature"; she had "eyes for the noble qualities" which he had previously "kept locked within himself and cruelly suppressed because they appeared merely ridiculous to the others around him" (Finckenstein). But Rahel was "unconvertible." She did not believe that he loved her. And so he gave up; he did not break with her, but he stopped writing.

"I merely want to ask you how it is possible for you no longer to write to me (don't you understand the point that it would not be the same thing if I stopped writing to *you*? You are supposed to be the active one; you are worshipped)—you cannot have forgotten my existence, but you have forgotten what I am like." Was he then the "active one"? Had she not hitherto acted alone—when she confronted him with alternatives, when she turned him away, when she did not let him see her, when she opposed to his love her wariness? What was this sudden appeal of hers, what did it refer to? "You are worshipped" meant: you have attained what you wanted. As against this first decisive action, everything which she undertook was only pursuing matters to their logical conclusion. And this pursuit, moreover, followed directly from her despair over her lover's passivity. He *qui m'a séduite par son amour*

[4] From an unpublished diary entry, 1799.

had once had the power to move her to love; that is to say, what he did affected her, whereas all that she did had no effect whatsoever upon him. She continued her letter: "I am engaged in a fine business here; what I am actually doing is writing a desolated love letter; I am finally reduced to this! But be calm; I am writing it only for myself, not for you. I am showing you what I am suffering . . . what you have made me suffer without your intending it." Showing was not acting, but suffering unseen, without either witnesses or spectators was the ultimate in nonacting. If she were to lose the visibility, the recognition of her suffering, she would be robbed of the last reality of her grief. If now he again did not reply, if he continued in his dreary passivity, she would have no more of him than the unendurable nonrelationship of pure yearning. "Please tell me what I should think of in order not to despair. You are the one who is always speaking of yearning. I tell you, I am dying of yearning, of pure yearning. I would willingly bear all this suffering once more (which, as true as God lives, I thought impossible to bear) only to see you." But now he began to be alarmed by the passion of her outbursts, which to him were only incomprehensible, and he tried, if possible, not to see her at all when he was in Berlin. "If you are here, you are not here for me, and will soon be gone again. And then . . . then . . . kill me. That is the only thing you can do for me." This absolute nothingness in which all that had happened was disavowed was worse than the most horrible things he might have done to her. Any malice would have represented something, a reality she could understand, a certainty to which she could cling. "I beg you, write to me that I must not speak to you in this manner. Tell me coldly that you cannot endure this tone; drive me away from you, and that will be *something*. I shall then *have to* stay away from you. Do something altogether mean to me." Ah, but he would do nothing at all; the end could not have been more terrible. "Oh, dear Karl, what shall I think or do in the long life to come. I love you more than ever, and it will always be thus."

Still this was not the end. Finckenstein replied "in the very hour that I have received your letter." He excused himself simply on grounds of the "stale bustle" around here, of the "dull, unfeeling state" into which her absence had cast him, the "absence of everything that I love and of all love." This was supposed to make up for everything. What was still worse, it was the end and he did not even take the trouble to notice it. This was the break, accomplished at last so thoroughly that there was no longer any reversing of the matter. He was the victor and had attained what he wished: namely, mastery over his own life and his own destiny, in spite of those claims of hers which to him appeared immoderate and mad; and he had achieved this mastery *as* he wished, without committing himself to evil or to good, without taking any stand at all. He went on picturing to her fantastic situations which would make him happy, as for example if she and his sisters were to meet and love one another. But she had taken from him his naïve optimism, his ability calmly to delude himself. And losing that, he had also lost the naïveté of incomprehension. Secretly, behind her back, he began to toy with plans for marriage which his family desired and had probably already broached. Here, too, however, he did nothing; he let things drift once more—this time, in all probability, out of despair.

"May eternal justice grant me that I tell the truth as audibly and strongly as I feel it in my soul." That is to say, Rahel would do nothing more, would merely tell the truth, testify to the truth, so that she, at least, would not be buried in the mass of evasions, illusions, half lies, and whole vulgarities with which their relationship had become encumbered. Since no one besides Rahel had any interest in such belated and desperate truths, she gathered up all her breath and blew upon the trumpet of "eternal justice"; she hoped that she might be the mouthpiece of justice, since, after all, upon this rather inhuman earth no human ear is fond of hearing human lamentation. She cried out at his original, careless disregard of her first proposal that they break. Even the freedom of will and the courage "to be the first to have broken with you," to make herself into a willing victim—even this freedom had been struck from her hand. "Once, for what I saw to be necessary I made the most terrible sacrifice human beings are capable of making. Only I can judge it, and I wish there were a god at my side who could judge it also: human beings know nothing about one another. I did not succeed in making it: apparently fate itself was not pleased with it, did not accept it, and hurled me right back to the place whence I had summoned up the strength within myself to make this sacrifice."

If one merely accepts fate, if one does not act at all, one attains a security which enables one to offer the same passive resistance to all misfortune. When Rahel tries to act, she would find she had no starting point from which she could meaningfully begin. She could not do anything specifically individual, but since Finckenstein's love had made her a specific person without a specific world and without specific patterns, outlined only by love; since she had entered upon the adventure of particularity without having been taken in by any particular society, the sole stake she could offer for any action was her own self. When fate did not accept her sacrifice, when she became aware that she could not succeed in converting her lover into a specific person, after having first deprived him of his support, stripped him of his social being, she was thrown back into the despair and hopelessness out of which she had come.

"Never shall I do anything like this again; I vow that to you by whatever you may hold most sacred!—as I have vowed it to myself. To destroy oneself out of respect for what is most sacred can please the gods only once; they cannot demand it a second time. I shall *never* do it a second time! As truly as I cannot deny my existence, as truly as I have done it once! I shall never again be the first to break with you, not if heaven and hell, the world and you yourself, are ranged against me. Never again will I take the active part; rather do I wish to suffer everything. This letter is the last *act* of mine your eyes will ever see, or your mind detect."

She kept her word. Henceforth she only waited to see how he would pull away from her; she gave him no encouragement to do so, took it as quite in order when in the process of breaking free he chanced to insult her. She did not destroy herself a second time; she accepted what was given her, the good as well as the bad. For a time her life had threatened to turn into a personally differentiated destiny; the world and life had been dangerously on the point of becoming specific; for a short time she had seemed no longer exposed to generality—but by and by she had reverted to character, that is, her life was only the theater of "life" in general, and her history only whatever happened to her. This most confined of spheres was her natural home, and now she asked him to leave her there, not to rouse her into doing useless things, things whose end she already knew in advance.

"You have said that Fräulein von Berg loves you. If she does, it must be because she has some hopes. . . . To that I have no way of objecting, and I am silent. If you feel, if you know there to be in some depth of your soul the desire, the intention, the thought, of wanting to unite with her, then bring it out, and do so right away. This is still one thing you can do for me. I call upon you for the last time to do it. In one, in two, in three years it would be base and bad. Then—I should consider myself one spewed forth by destiny, and would not be able to answer for myself, which a person always ought to be able to do. Then—I should no longer be a person. Examine your heart. Have courage! Do not stand with one foot on either shore. Cross over. I can no longer act for you. Once I was able to do so. . . . Do not think this any threat. If only you knew my soul! I desire to empty the cup which my God has given to me; only, of my own volition I shall not take it up again."

This, now was really the end. All that still followed were repetitions, misunderstandings, insults, "the last chords of a bad concert." He destroyed her letters (the quotations here are from copies or drafts); his were found complete among her papers after her death.

3

ALL OVER
HOW CAN ONE GO ON LIVING?
(1799–1800)

"WHAT I have not received, I can forget; but what has happened to me I cannot forget. May God protect others from understanding this."

Desires which are not marked out beforehand by destiny, which are only the expressions, converted into fantasies, of half-childish pretensions to happiness; dreams of youth, no matter to what degree they may be characteristic complements of frustration and discontent, or legitimate protests against obstacles to development or lack of joys, dissolve, blow away, under the first impact of life, the impact which comes with real experience, with passion linked to something specific. On the other hand, any real reply to passionate appeal coming straight to us out of the great wide world, which is directed toward us in particular, confirms us—this reply absorbs and concentrates all the phantasmagoria of wishes into one of the three wishes of the fairy tale, which must be fulfilled if we are not to think ourselves forever unhappy.

Rahel had not believed that a blow could strike her, of all persons; she had been struck, and now only this one fact existed. She had not known what reality was, or how she could prove her own reality to herself; for there was no way she could have known beforehand that grief can be a confirmation, that unhappiness, loss, snatching away, could provide evidence after the event that one had held something in one's hands. What had happened to her she could not forget; it possessed an inviolable actuality. Forgetting, concealing, falsifying, applied only to what one had "*not* received," to exaltations of one's own inner self, which left no trace behind in the world. Over what actually happened, over the happenings that chance produced, even introspection had no power. Rahel carried with her a burden of disadvantages—that, she had forgotten; she had been rejected—that, she could not forget. This rejection and this grief were what she was.

Rahel had become a specific person; but she had not acquired any specific qualities. Her reality manifested itself only in what she had suffered in what was now past. There was an inexorability about the past which no future, no hope, no possibilities, no matter how deeply longed for, could outweigh. Rahel had dared "to yield to chance"; chance was mightier than she, its reality stronger than any "calculable" fulfillment of natural, necessary hope. What had happened to her was irrevocable, had happened to her "for ever." Passion's insistence upon absoluteness causes her capacity for novelty to perish, its organ to atrophy. Where hope does not wait expectantly, it is difficult for anything unexpected to occur. Her future would now be prolongation of the past; if the future were some day "going to appear as the present," all it could do would be to "repeat the past." This was "the truest unhappiness," for she had arrived at a point when she could no longer "wish to be happy by force."

Only complete happiness and complete unhappiness permit life to be seen as a whole, because in both hope is canceled out. "Anyone who was ever really unhappy can never again be happy; anyone who was ever completely happy ought not to be able to be unhappy again. Otherwise he would lack a clear consciousness in being so. That is why we find a cruelty in unhappiness; and that is why it is such a great good fortune to be happy." [1] Life, then, was really done, had nothing more to say. Hopeless despair understands itself; no false expectations cause it to waver. In hopeless despair—and this is the sole profit to be gained from it—the whole course of life is laid bare before one; in despair we speak "as we speak upon our deathbeds"—namely, the truth.

Because everything was over, because life no longer seemed to have any future, the suffering which had made Rahel a specific person did not go on existing in its specific and par-

[1] Unpublished diary entry of March 1799.

ticular form; she was persuaded she had experienced *life*, life in general, as it was. She would not revert back to her former personality, which had been a nothingness. Life had trodden roughshod over her desires. It had treated her as if human pretensions did not exist at all. It had equipped her with no gifts and developed no talents in her. Experience had taken the place of her nonbeing; she now knew: *this is the way life is.*

Those who harbor hopes and have some prospects for a next day can go on hoping that life will deny itself, that it may still show another face. Rahel no longer had any hope. Her love had been refused, her desire to fit into the world expressly rejected. She had known all along the world's hostility in general, and now she had proved it in particular, as it affected her. Now her inferiority, her "lucklessness" was confirmed; what she had always known was corroborated: "Since my earliest childhood, since my infamous birth, everything had to turn out this way, you know."[2]

It was as though fate had only touched her in order to hammer in with a single blow everything that affected her, everything that she could comprehend; as though it had made contact with her only in order to disgrace her, to humiliate her, to force upon her the perception that inferiority could only be confirmed, that safety could be found only off in some quiet corner, disgrace avoided only by avoiding all life, by renunciation. "Disgraced by destiny, but no longer susceptible to disgrace."

Everything was over; only life, stupid, insensitive life, went on. One did not die of grief, of unhappiness. Day after day, one awoke, behaved like other people, went to sleep. In these "absurd regularities" greater misfortunes than being jilted had faded away to nothing.

No life was conceivable without the certain alternation of day and night, of waking and sleeping; without the day's hope of the night, which brought sleep whose eternal sameness blanked out the diurnal event. "Tiredness is a protection from madness"; "we must know that we are going to sleep; that

[2] From an unprinted letter to Rebecca Friedländer, dated June 25, 1806.

protects us." Because life went on, as though unaware that all was over; because Rahel could again and again sink back into the sameness of the night, she succumbed neither to madness nor to death, but inescapably to recovery which she could not allow herself to want because she did not want to forget. For was not recovery retrogression, escape from the grief which vouched for her existence?

What had happened to her was more than merely the grief, which she might perhaps have been able to cling to daily and hourly, in order to prevent the natural continuance of life, the natural joy in the new day. Regularity is not so "absurd" as youth is inclined to believe. It alone guards one against confusing the grief with the bad experience. It alleviates the pure and unqualified lament—everything is over—and stops one from reviving the past again and again and experiencing it as present; keeps one from wiping out the attributes of reality and perpetuating what is transitory. Life itself, by going on, by refusing to show any consideration for the person who claims that everything is over, thrusts the past further back into the past with every passing day, thrusts it back but does not obliterate it. In continuance the consequences of the past continue to be experienced. The consequences of the flow of time are independent of deliberate forgetting or sentimental remembering. Continuance fulfills a person's fate, which is left with its consequences, its reality unimpaired, only when the person does not become ensnared in its memories. Rahel had no home in the world to which she could retreat from fate; she had nothing to oppose to her destiny; hence there remained nothing for her but to "tell the truth," to bear witness, to gather in "the splendid harvest of despair." And as formerly she had had to be flexible in order to be touched at all, to be noticed at all by life; as formerly every gift and every talent had served only to shut out destiny—so now, when everything was over, she had to make herself "into a wall, into something impenetrable," in order to be able to fight her battle with everything that opposed her in the world, "with causes and with people who set themselves up as causes."

Thus, turned to stone, she was ready to go on living, to

reconcile herself to the fact that "life continues on its course, though we may bear within us what we will." Nothing must, nothing could ever change again, neither she nor circumstances. Consolation was not to be thought of. Consolation would only be a veil obscuring the truth—"it would be utterly abominable for me to console myself, to throw away the best thing I possess—for nothing! Out of the hollow hope of obtaining something better; out of hollow, mean, mechanical hope; and nothing better would come along; this is obvious beforehand. . . . I ought to console myself? God forbid—I do not *want* to. That would be the worst of abominations." She, who was utterly changeable, who had been made into what she was only by life, who was in herself nothing—she believed she could be unchangeable, "above" everything that life and time could possibly do to her. "I am the way I was," she wrote to Veit, "and never, never, are you going to find me changed; even if you were to find me in the madhouse, with a paper crown upon my head, you would have no need to be alarmed; you would find again the friend you know. . . . Rather would you find me totally disintegrated, destroyed, before you would find me any different."

Only now, when everything was over, did she realize "what everyone feels and what everyone lacks." "I do not want to be respected for any particular gifts, I do not want to enjoy any particular advantage; everything is talent, but this one is self-acquired, a *unique* gift. This is what I should be distinguished, honored for." Life itself had distinguished her by marking her lucklessness with the stigma of unhappiness, by imprinting upon her the "deficiency" and the eternal "deficit" from which "the thing that everyone lacked" could be derived.

During those years Rahel's attic room on Jägerstrasse received visitors from all the social circles of contemporary Berlin. Her "unique gift" became a kind of attraction, and her friendship with Prince Louis Ferdinand a kind of advertisement. At this time she was still conscious of the chance offered her by her being a social outsider; for a brief moment she was even proud of being a Jewess: "Such a one as me he should not yet have met. He is going to hear a good dose of garret verities. Up to now he has known only Marianne, but she is baptized, and Princess and Frau von Eybenberg—and what does *that* amount to?" Since she was Jewish, everyone could come to her; she could form a circle "into which everyone, royal princes, foreign ambassadors, artists, scholars or businessmen of every rank, countesses and actresses . . . strove for admission with equal eagerness; and in which each person was worth neither more nor less than he himself was able to validate by his cultivated personality" (Brinckmann).

This "cultivated personality" was what Brinckmann—more than three decades later, after Rahel's death—believed to be the common element which held together the extraordinarily variegated and disparate existences of the visitors to the garret flat. The phrase was even then, at the time Brinckmann used it in this letter to Varnhagen, a cliché, and scarcely gives any idea of how wide apart the personalities were and to what extent all who came were held together only by Rahel herself, by her originality, her wit, and her lively freshness. To the flat on Jägerstrasse came the princes of the ruling house. There was Prince Louis Ferdinand who said of Rahel that she was "a moral midwife who provided one with so gentle and painless a confinement that a tender emotion remained from even the most tormenting ideas." He came accompanied by his mistress, Pauline Wiesel, and by his brother-in-law, Prince Radziwill. Ministers and diplomats came, among them Privy State Councilor Stägemann (who twenty years later refused to receive Rahel, though she was then Frau von Varnhagen). There were the Swedish ambassador, Brinckmann; Peter von Gualtieri, who belonged to court society, had never written anything, and whom Rahel counted one of the "four vain men" and thought very well of, for "he was capable of a higher degree of suffering than anyone I know; he simply could nor bear it"; Count Tilly, who spoke "tremendously well": "I am an auditorium for him, he a kind of stage director of life for me." Besides these there were her old friends David Veit, a Jewish doctor, and Wilhelm von Burgsdorff, who spent his time in that aristocratic dilettantism which had always been the pastime of the nobility, but which now was acquiring new value and status as self-cultivation; there were the famous actor Fleck and the actress Unzelmann, whom all the men were in love with; there was Christel Eigensatz, Gentz's mistress, and the famous singer Marchetti; there was the Bohemian "original," Countess Pachta, who ran away from her husband and was living with some bourgeois; and there was Countess Schlabrendorf, who occasionally wore men's clothes and who had to go to Paris with Rahel because she was expecting an illegitimate child. Far more conventional was the attendance of all the well-known writers and publicists of the period in her room: the Humboldt brothers, although neither liked her; Friedrich Schlegel, Clemens von Brentano, Friedrich de la Motte Fouqué, Ludwig and Friedrich Tieck, Adalbert von Chamisso, Friedrich von Gentz, Friedrich Schleiermacher, the classical philologist Friedrich August Wolf, Jean Paul— who complimented her handsomely and justly: "You treat life poetically, and consequently life does the same for you." The list could be expanded indefinitely, for Varnhagen dutifully collected everything, the persons and the compliments they paid to Rahel, and incorporated them into his *Denkwürdigkeiten* (Memorabilia) and *Galerie von Bildnissen* (Gallery of Portraits). One thing is clear: for a brief time everyone who counted in society had turned their backs on the social rigors and conventions, had taken flight from them. The Jewish salons in Berlin provided a social area outside of society, and Rahel's garret room in its turn stood outside the conventions and customs of even the Jewish salons.

The exceptional Berlin Jews, in their pursuit of culture and wealth, had good luck for three decades. The Jewish salon, the recurrently dreamed idyll of a mixed society, was the product of a chance constellation in an era of social transition. The Jews became stopgaps between a declining and an as yet unstabilized social group: the nobility and the actors; both stood outside of bourgeois society—like the Jews—and both were accustomed to playing a part, to representing something, to expressing themselves, to displaying "what they were" rather than "showing what they had," as Goethe put it in *Wilhelm Meister*; in the Jewish houses of homeless middle-class intellectuals they found solid ground and an echo which they could not hope to find anywhere else. In the loosened framework of conventions of this period Jews were socially acceptable in the same way as actors: the nobility reassured both that they were socially acceptable.

German culture was not grounded in any particular social class; neither was it to be inferred from the Jewish salons, for all that they formed centers of cultivated sociability, that the German Jews had attained to social rootedness. The truth of the matter was exactly opposite: precisely because the Jews stood outside of society they became, for a short time, a kind of neutral zone where people of culture met. And just as Jewish influence upon political life faded as soon as the bourgeoisie had taken political control, so (only much sooner) the Jewish element was expelled from society as soon as the first signs of cultivated middle-class society began to dawn.

In the vague, idyllic chaos which the Jewish salon of those days represented, there could not exist any principle of social selectivity. Beyond the limits of society and of any particular social class there prevailed an incredible freedom from all conventions. Among the visitors, Rahel had very few real friends; she was fundamentally indifferent toward all of them and yet terrified of losing a single one. "If I should lose you," she wrote to Brinckmann, "I should lose a great part of myself. For you know one side of me that nobody else knows . . . and that side must be recognized; otherwise it is dead." She believed herself superior to, beyond the game of life, and shielded herself against being dead by contact with many people.

The suspicion people had felt for her was distinctly lessening. She had become impenetrable and was concealing something specific, a definite shame which she might have confided. With each passing day, as the past receded further into the past, her need for speaking out grew. She was afraid that it might vanish away; the thing of which she was a symbol might lose its reality. She would have liked to show herself like a "spectacle." For as yet she did not know what she ought to do with herself, with the ruin that was left of her. Certainly, she could not go on like this, merely mutely insisting upon what had been in the past and mutely waiting until death at last carried her away. "I must die, but I don't intend to become dead." How, then, could one go on living when everything was over?

Schleiermacher

Perhaps what happens to a person takes place only for the purpose of developing his idiosyncratic nature. Can it not be said that the individual, in the "sublime moment" in which the shock of the infinite strikes him, has already "perfected" himself, formed himself into a "consolidated whole," already learned everything he is capable of learning? Is it not proper to petrify thereafter, to become a living token of one's idiosyncratic nature which remains immutably fixed until death? What can one desire more than to be one's "perpetuated ego," to enter as a part into the "universe" whose infinite perfection has been revealed to one? Henceforth such a person will stand above "idle hope" and the "common lament." He has only to succeed in holding fast to the moment which is itself "no longer a part of temporal life." Perhaps the compulsion to go on living, with the attendant trivialities, can be beaten by reiterating again and again the first "sublime moment" which has marked one out as an individual; by holding on to the "territory of eternity" which was guaranteed at that moment and to which the "perpetuated ego" can at any moment return because it can "at any time check and cut across the stream of temporal life." The moment, thus, has stopped life and time. Any perfection is always a matter of the past; anything perfect must necessarily decline. All past must become new creation, all future a passing, a disintegration of perfection in aging and death. Just as man in isolation from all futurity becomes a thing of nature, "part of the universe," so, when his singularity is fixed in perfection, he is raised out of time; time has ceased to form the connecting element of things, the nexus of life.

In the light of these thoughts it seems quite in order for

life and reality to be stripped of any further power over a person; they condition only the past, the temporal existence, to the point of its perfection. Thus, at any rate, Schleiermacher thought to settle matters with life. He played his highest trump against life—himself, the perfected person, who had "never lost himself since." Such arguments were of little help to Rahel. She had not become an "individual," had experienced neither herself nor infinity in the things that had happened to her. And even if she had believed that her rigidity, her indifference, her muteness, were signs of her "idiosyncratic nature," or even of the "perfection of her idiosyncratic existence," how would such belief help her?

What did one have when one had nothing but oneself? What had been gained if life was eliminated—life which, after all, proved to have the last word in the end when age and death ensued? What if one had to "wither away" anyhow—like Schleiermacher himself, who thus expressly confirmed Schlegel's phrase about him? Man's life is stripped of its meaning if it remains fixed to the "sublime moment"; man's history is destroyed if he becomes indifferent to his own destiny.

In order to go on living one must try to escape the death involved in perfection. Schleiermacher had declared that man's potentialities became fixed in perfection; but perhaps this perfection could be dissolved, perhaps the fixed potentialities could be modified without a person's losing his "idiosyncratic nature," his "interestingness." Perhaps it was possible to oppose a different reality to life which tramples over a person; perhaps a new reality could be magically conjured up by variation of potentialities, and life could then be forced into the channels of this new reality.

Schlegel

In magic the Romantics attempted to intensify the world and whatever life could bring to such a pitch of extraordinariness that reality would necessarily fail to come up to expectations. Magic arose out of the boundlessness of Mood. Playing with possibilities engendered the "Romantic confusion" which so canceled the isolation of the Schleiermacherian individual that for a moment it seemed as if reality might invade the scene after all by sheer chance, by a surprise attack. But this would have to be pure extraordinariness, a miracle, not at all the "raw, crude chance" which struck Rahel when Finckenstein happened to be the one who wanted her to love him. Expectation of the extraordinary never lets reality have its say, so to speak. In expecting a miracle that does not arrive, the imagination conjures up "the most interesting situations" in order to distract itself—situations that are not impossible, that could occur, such as the death of the sweetheart in *Lucinde*. But since magic after all does not have any power over reality, since magic cannot make the sweetheart die, it can only conjure up moods which *would* affect the lover if his sweetheart *should* die.

This conjuring up of future moods which convert all reality into the neutralized "it has already happened," has a peculiar effect upon reality. In the fantasied mood direct affliction is anticipated. All possibilities, even the extremest, are translated into a future past in order to offset the present dread of them. This constant toying with possibilities becomes—in reference to the individual and his environment—a source of great confusion. Confusion overwhelms the possibilities, plays them off against one another, lets none dominate, none attain reality. But even the confusion remains without effect upon the person who is always balancing things out, instantly paralyzing any daydream by a new one. As a result of this balancing act, the narrow crack through which reality might have entered is closed up again. Mutual annihilation of opposites, the "harmony" of disorder, was the paradox in which Romantic contradictoriness as such existed. Any unequivocal language necessarily introduced actual chaos into the confused world of possibilities, just as any nonambiguity in life was necessarily a threat to the Romantic's existence. The rude force of unequivocalness not only destroyed the order of the confusions, but also shattered the magic of imagination. This magic alone could hold together a "self-formed world" and conjure it up again and again in the mind; once the magic went to pieces, the person was exposed to the reality of this world whose banality his imagination, which had already anticipated everything, could no longer endure. Either reality smashed the magic, bringing sudden sobriety; or else it attacked from behind in the shape of "unpleasant chance." But in any case, reality always came too late. From dread of the unequivocal, simplistic triviality of the Real, the Romantic always retreated back to the contradictions within himself.

That lasting ambiguities existed at all was the paradox of the Romantic life. Just as the paradox existed only in the moment, only in the last intensification of introspection, and could never survive the longer spans of life, so the Romantic's paradoxical existence was possible only as an ephemeral phase. The continuity of life imposes upon it a simplifying consistency and gives its fragmentary character a destructive reality. Then continuity produces not "new circumstances and new forces" (Herder), but the boredom of empty time.

Friedrich Schlegel had not been able to endure the process of aging, the continuance of life. He had been incapable of coping with time; his magic could only stand up to the deceptive reality of the moment. Schlegel possessed the same kind of personal magnetism which made Rahel famous during that period. She too, once she had become rigid, was able to play the part demanded by the moment. She could work her magic upon all who came to her; she was able to handle the miscellaneous personalities of her salon; she was in her element when she was able to play so upon her circle that each person said exactly what was most brilliant at the particular moment. Never again was she as effective as she was during this period; never again did she wield such power over people; never again did she impress people as so entirely herself in all her uniqueness.

Magic has power over people, but no power over time. It cannot command time to stand still. It can no more prevent aging than it can prevent the triumph of the "absurd regularity" to which everyone ultimately succumbs if he has not the dubious good fortune to die young.

In "romantic confusion" there lay a chance to permit reality to break in. Schlegel threw that chance away because he himself could endure his confusion only in the imagination, in the enchantment of mood; he never really created confusion within himself; for he desired balance and ultimate harmony.

Wilhelm von Humboldt

Of all the Romantics, only Humboldt took confusion seriously and realized early what a person had when he had nothing but himself: "a tinkling cymbal." The "emptiness" which was his "sickness" was something he could fill neither by imagination nor by productivity. As late as 1821 Rahel said of him that he was "always something only as long as he was nothing; as soon as he became something, he immediately was nothing." [3] Rather, he began establishing romantic confusion right in his own life, instead of merely imagining it and picturing what he would feel in what situations; he actually played the imaginary game of Romanticism, disguising himself, pretending to emotions, always hoping that he would really become what he believed he could only appear to be.

"The principle that one ought to have been in many situations of all sorts is so strongly with me that every situation in which I have not yet been is welcome for that reason alone." Feeling nothing but his own emptiness and so apparently condemned to ineffectuality, he managed to make a woman fall in love with him: "By this sham I really became what I merely wanted to seem." He contrived, overwhelmed by the reality of the situation, to become "excited" until he actually spoke in a "half-stammering voice" and "kissed her hand with warmth." In engaging in such experiments he showed no more consideration for the other person than for himself. He gave the reality of the experiment a chance to take hold of him. The proof that he had been taken hold of would come, he knew, only later on, if, with the door shut behind him, he was not again seized by the "heart's emptiness" which had driven him into this situation. These experiments, in which he was not himself, these situations in which he always pretended to

[3] Conversation noted by Varnhagen as of December 16, 1821.

be something else—whatever was required at the moment in order to amass experiences—allowed no fixations to become established. His "heart's emptiness" remained a situation in the world, did not become a quality of his own personality. He knew that reality was productive only if it had a future; but he knew also that in the most absurd regularity there still was contained a remnant of such reality. And therefore he could persist and wait.

There is a good probability that Caroline von Dachröden, who later became his wife, also first met him merely in the course of one of his experiments. The probability is supported by the curious disparity between his letters to his fiancée, in which he constantly represented himself as the inferior, the one in need of aid, and his diary in which he has her speak to him in the very words which in actuality *he* used in speaking to *her*: "I am not worthy of you, I can do nothing but love, but that I can do . . . ," etc. In any case, this encounter pulled him up sharply and stopped his experimentation; he had exposed himself to life until at last it really struck him. Destiny struck him in the form of happiness, and in happiness he learned to think: this is what life is like. He founded his marriage upon happiness. The happiness which enabled Humboldt to go on living, to wait out the eventualities of a long life, was more than a single piece of good luck. Chance, which came to him in the form of happiness, became in his mind a divine power—"there is nothing more divine than fortune and misfortune." His first happiness was at the same time a good sign for his whole life, an assurance that he would not be forgotten by destiny, that although man is at the mercy of powers outside himself, he can stand on a good, human footing with these powers, can come to an understanding with them. Given such an entente, every single grief would be parried at once, would be transformed "by means of its formative depths into a fruitful work of the soul." Suffering could no longer destroy the continuity of life because one awaited it in "submission" and "willingly yielded" to it—all of which had nothing to do with the sentimental intoxication with grief of Julius in *Lucinde*, who expressly imagines the death of his sweetheart. In Humboldt's case grief is merely accepted, when it really occurs, as part of human destiny. Man ought to confront the divine powers with gratitude for happiness and with willing submission to unhappiness. Consequently, what counted was not "to live happily, but to fulfill one's fate and to exhaust all human possibilities in one's own fashion."

In happiness the world had become a closed "cosmos" into which chance could no longer penetrate. The divine power acted only once in man's life, but after that once everything that followed bore the imprint of its operation. Once he had entered this cosmos of happiness, nothing, no action, no thought could be lost, everything was transfigured by it. Humboldt defined this happiness as "a feeling of universality in which the good is independent and tied down to no particular personality, and whose emanations enrich humanity even though they never pass over into the world or into action." For Humboldt, who liberated himself from himself by experiment, and thereby became free to live, there was nothing greater than life. Life did not have to accomplish anything, not even the cultivation of the personality. Humboldt could use the life span given him to learn to feel at home in "humanity." "I should like, when I must go, to leave behind as little as possible that I did not place in contact with myself." Life was the way "to measure all humanity purely by itself"; every inch of the way had a meaning for the whole, every action had an effect "and even if no one were ever present to observe it, it would nevertheless make its impression . . . upon dead nature itself." Humboldt had given himself up to life and had met with glorious success—that was his distinction. For by his "natural endowment" he was "destined neither for great deeds in life nor important works of the mind." He was nothing, a "tinkling cymbal," but he had known how to take everything that was given to him; his "proper sphere was life itself"—and he was lucky enough to find happiness.

4

FLIGHT ABROAD
THE BEAUTIFUL WORLD
(1800–1801)

IF happiness was really the guarantee of the continuance of life, then unhappiness as the central experience of life was really "disgrace." "It's all over with me in the world; I know it and cannot feel it; I wear a red heart like others, and have a dark, inconsolable, ugly destiny." Rahel was ashamed of inconsolability, of ugliness. It was useless to think that after all it was not her fault. Faced with unhappiness, you don't have a chance to speak up; to whom can you say constantly: it's not my fault? Everyone will believe you; no one desires his own unhappiness. "Real unhappiness" which "can be recognized by the fact" that you are "ashamed of it," is so overpowering that it shuts out all excuses. Once you have submitted to chance, have renounced your autonomy, once you decide that you "don't want to belong to those who do not risk their very selves," you must count on being unhappy, just as you might have been happy; you must count on being disgraced, just as you might have been blessed.

It is unhappiness and disgrace when everything you have seems to exist only in order to point up what you do *not* have, when "in spite of the tremendous gifts and presents" you always "lack the glory and the point of things." It is unhappiness and disgrace when you are not forgotten but neglected, as though you were not worthy to live to the end the life which you had not given yourself; as though you were not even worthy of keeping what you had received.

Everything you do after unhappiness has come is always tinged with ignobility because the unhappiness seems to forbid continuance. Only someone who dies of unhappiness remains noble; only then is it no disgrace. "I have experienced something *frightful* just because it did not kill me." To have experienced unhappiness once was to be marked, distinct; and being distinct was something else in addition to a distinction. Someone whom destiny forgot still had hope; but Rahel had to flee "for nothing." Having no hope.

She fled abroad from Berlin because she could no longer endure the disgrace. Because she was condemned to go on living, to enjoy every new day with the natural "innocence of all creatures." But it was no longer innocence when one knew "thoroughgoing unhappiness," "when anguished by grief, humiliation, in *despair,* one would gladly give up life in order not to be capable of pain; when one has thought everything, *all* of nature, cruel." Natural as gladness was, it had become inappropriate, a pleasure she could no longer allow herself, to which she merely succumbed. What was natural had become artificial. In despair she had already given up her own existence, and now it was returning again with each passing day, in spite of herself, like something imposed upon her by nature, cruel nature. Unhappiness brought disgrace. "One is no longer a pure creature of nature, no longer a sister of the silent things."

"I know, the business goes on." What business? Her life was over; how could something that was over go on? She went to Paris because "all whom I loved here have mistreated me." Who had mistreated her? Had not they all respected, admired her, showered her with flattering appreciation? Had she not achieved more than anyone else, although she was not rich, not beautiful, without a position in the world, not even married? Had she not by magic, by the fascination of personality, drawn to her everyone who was at all well known in the society of the day?

Apparently Rahel had not wanted them to fall prey to her magic; rather, she had hoped that someone would ask how things stood with her. The possibility of fascination was inherent in her situation, and, after all, how were all these others to know that she had wanted them to break through this fascination in order to get at her herself—that is to say, at what had happened to her? Each of them had enjoyed the "spectacle" which she offered to all; none had wanted to accept the truth which she had always been ready to scream out at the slightest provocation.

Her desire had been to tell the truth at all costs; instead she had made herself impenetrable. She had wanted to be completely passive, but she had grown steadily more "austere." Confronted with this impenetrability, people had finally drawn back, just as they had previously been drawn in by her fascination. "*Everyone* is retreating from me; only I do not *want* to retreat." She had really hoped that her austerity, her impenetrability, her hardness, would render her visible, that her resistance would make her tangible. But alas, all this had only made her obtrusive, tactless and obtrusive, as Wilhelm von Humboldt candidly said; she had lost her "inner grace." The world was full of opinions, and truth did not become visible simply because someone cried it aloud into the world of opinions. Who was going to distinguish between opinion and truth? "The truth and I—both not visible, both lack luster." In the world of opinions the truth itself was only an opinion; it was lackluster.

That was why the world had mistreated her. Now people, too, were giving her a wide berth, her whom fate had rejected. "They don't know it; I won't say it; that's why I'm going. Do not imagine I am hoping to be received decently there. God forbid! The farce will only start all over again." Absurd regularity which in spite of all despair had become the order of the day, youth's infamous lust for life was "longing for new arrows." In rigidity she should have been able to fixate her life at last; the mistreatment by her friends, the repeated rejections—though often expressed only in trivialities —had shattered her impenetrability. Even the truth, into which she had some insight, thanks to what she had experienced, remained lackluster and was no protection against other people. What good were impenetrability, austerity, standing above the battle, when "one *must* work for a world which one does not know and which irresistibly demands for itself everything, everything one loves."

Unhappiness had shown her at one blow: this is what life

is like. Such a general experience provides—if it does not altogether crush out one's life—a degree of foresight for the future. Everything would be repeated, for no one had understood. In consequence, everything that she had experienced slowly became illusory as it sank deeper into the past; with each passing day it became less true, less real. The result was that "she *is* true and *must be* untrue; and that she is *untrue* and must be *true*." She had to go on because the world was not content with what had happened once, because its mark upon her was not yet patent enough. She *"had to* love again." "Only it was *impermissible* for me to remain with *this* troupe." From another place in the world she would be thrown into the stream again, only apparently untrue, in truth obeying the consistent principle, the objective pattern of her life which she had called "the business"; only apparently true, in truth yielding, despite all memories, to new realities, open and ready to accept every new chance. For: "There are born soldiers and born gardeners; I must go into the battle and, as a common soldier, silently meet the cannon balls. Whom I obey, I do not know; but I am being pushed, not commanded." As a common soldier, as one who had no name, no standing, no prestige; and in whom whatever happened could be read most distinctly because he had nothing in himself to set against the events that inflicted themselves upon him. Pushed, without respect for desire or will; not even commanded; for if a command is given, a name is spoken; it is assumed that the person commanded is someone who can disobey. Only someone who is nothing and no one, the product of circumstances, the plaything of destiny, is merely pushed.

Pushed, then, Rahel went to Paris in the July of 1800. She left behind in Berlin a large number of people who had become dear to her; in Paris the only person she knew was her friend Caroline von Humboldt. She was waiting for something new and had realized that in life not even unhappiness had the last word. Now she intended every unhappiness merely to "serve as a maid" to her. This was convalescence.

Once more the past few years rose up again in all their bitterness—when her sister Rose married and Rahel had to wish her sister the happiness she herself did not have. Far off in Paris Rahel felt the contempt which her family had for her and her unhappiness; for they viewed her misfortune as pure extravagance or the silly hard luck of a girl who was not pretty. Her letters to her sister are more bitter—and more vulgar—than anything else of hers. For a moment it was as if she could see herself as her family could not help seeing her, in the full vulgarity of the "common things, which one must possess for all that they are common." She had lost part of her innocence when she learned, learned out of her own experience, that the "common things" could play their part even in the tale of love. "Innocence" existed only as long as "one does not know true unhappiness"; it was inherent in unhappiness that it dragged one down into the common lot which in happiness one believed oneself superior to. "Those who remain innocent for a long time are privileged souls, royal spirits; they find the common hard to grasp, and always forget it again." She, too, would forget it again, but now she saw her unhappiness upon the sister's commonplace level: the sister had married and she herself had not. "So you are happy. I wish you may have all this that I lack; how dreadful!" Her abdication of magnanimity—even as a gesture—was a painful but certain token that she was beginning to live again, that in despair she had learned to love life. "As long as one does not love life, everything remains at least tolerable."

Bitterness was only the ugly consequence of melancholy, that gloom which permitted "no dilution," which was not one of those sadnesses "that pass again, that, like a glow breaking through clouds, obscure or illuminate a region in pleasantly melancholic fashion." When the melancholic emerges from his sadness, in which the world and life and he himself, his life and his death, have been so vividly present to his mind, although without fixed outlines; when he emerges and forgets that this sadness of his was the final, the ultimate sadness (one which could arise unexpectedly from any pretext whatsoever); when he emerges and fixes his attention only on the pretext and realizes that that at any rate is past and done with; when he begins to draw comparisons between himself and others, he is already beginning to love life again. Later he will defame his melancholy by calling it ordinary unhappiness. Thinking only of the pretext, he forgets the truth which melancholy had revealed; forgets the general nature of sadness which needs no pretext because it can rise up unpredictably out of anyone's inner self, because it is deeply rooted in the fact that we have not given life to ourselves and have not chosen life freely.

Loving life is easy when you are abroad. Where no one knows you and you hold your life in your hands all alone, you are more master of yourself than at any other time. In the opacity of foreign places all specific references to yourself are blurred. It is easy to conquer unhappiness when the general knowledge that you are unhappy is not there to disgrace you, when your unhappiness is not reflected by innumerable mirrors, focused upon you so that it strikes you again and again. It is easy, as long as you are young, to surrender to the pure force of life, which always advises submergence and forgetfulness. It is easy to forget yourself when the reason for all your unhappiness, your "infamous birth," is not recognized, not observed, not counted.

"Foreignness is good"; to submerge, to be no one, to have no name, nothing that serves as a reminder; and thus to experiment, to try out, to see what things can still give pleasure; to avoid blows, to be without pretensions, to lose yourself in all the beautiful things of this world. It is possible to fall in love with so many things: with beautiful vases, beautiful weather, beautiful people. All beauty has power, all things of the world have a character and can be beautiful. "Lovely weather and climate is the most beautiful thing on earth. This is a true god." Out of a lovely summer day even happiness can emerge, a wholly unexpected happiness for someone who always expected it to come only from human beings. From "people no happiness comes," Rahel concluded. But falling in love without pretensions held no perils: "He is a Roman, twenty-two, head of a brigade, wounds on his neck and leg, and handsome as a god," she wrote from Paris to Brinckmann in February 1801. His belonging to the "race of gods" was quite sufficient, and the fact that beside him she did not feel fine at all, but simply "ugly." For, thank God, he was by no means "extraordinarily *spirituel* and *sensible*," already had an *"engagement,"* and Rahel could cheerfully "feast on his beauty," although in one sense that was annoying, *"facheux."*

From abroad, relaxed, without pretensions, it was easier to maintain natural ties. Her brothers and their children became objects of pleasure and concern for her. In the children she most immediately found an innocent counterpart to her own joy in life, a legitimation of her own, hard-won vitality, which was constantly in need of defense. She attached herself to the children as later she attached herself to every scrap of the natural world which remained unaffected by society and personal history; to everything that could not enter into her own life and become part of her own history. "The company of children also has the advantage of having almost nothing human about it; it gives pleasure like a garden—more—leaves one peaceful." A foreign land, beauty, weather, music and children made life worth living and loving.

Abroad, having perspective on wishes, hopes, unhappiness and renunciations, Rahel slowly and happily learned the joy of "denying one's own existence," the receptivity to enjoy new things without always and obstinately referring them to herself, the freedom to love a person as he was, to have a male friend without making demands upon him. This friend, eight years her junior, was a businessman whom David Veit had recommended to her. He had come from Hamburg, his name was Wilhelm Bokelmann, and he remained in Paris for two months.

"Until now I loved people only with my own powers; but you I love with *yours*." Her spasmodic efforts to understand people had hitherto always been guided by the obsessional desire to measure herself against them, to find herself reflected in them. Here she reached the point of pure acknowledgment: "You deserve so much love." She submerged herself in this friendship with the much younger man as she had submerged herself in the foreign city, renounced the exercise of her own forces as well as the tormenting concern with herself. In this conduct there was already a trace of insight that the world she did not know (any more than she knew the world into which she had been born), upon which she could make no claims, could be conquered and comprehended if she did not foolishly insist on examining everything solely in order to see whether it guaranteed or denied her own existence; insight that there are differences among men, and that not every encounter is equally a matter of chance. For Bokelmann "calls forth as much love as hitherto I could only give with an effort and by the noblest, finest kind of lying."

Still, this had come too early. In this way she would later love Alexander von der Marwitz; in the present case it remained without consequences, for it had come too unexpectedly; "I had no intention of attaining this goal." It remained merely a gift outside of life, whose course it for a short time pleasantly interrupted. Because this happiness had nothing to do with her unhappiness, she could not demand anything, either of herself or of the man; she could not insist on something's coming of it. "I demand nothing of you. . . . And I demand nothing of myself either. Not even that I should love you. Not that I always love you, not faithfulness, nothing!" And therefore she accepted this friendship as she accepted the weather, with the same gratitude and the same intensity of pleasure; in fact she loved him "as a child loves, a happiness . . . that may be had by anyone . . . who meets him. I have met him, and who can deprive me of that!" Much as she trusted herself to Bokelmann, she did not permit him to hurt her in any way.

They parted quickly. Bokelmann left Paris. "So you will receive a world into yourself, without me, and so will I, without you." She released him, let him go as one might let go of a happiness to which one had no claim; she had received him, the "loveliest booty in my life," gratis. It had "flattered" her that for once something had simply fallen to her lot. She could hold him no more than she could hold a lovely summer's day; she had no claim upon him, as one has no claim upon everything that is received without being wished for,

for which wishes and needs have not paved the way—in other words, for all the things that make life bearable, but do not change it.

Bokelmann, who found her worthy of loving, had helped her to find the world worthy of being loved; he had taught her to take pleasure, taught her that it was possible for her to get at the world by being completely passive, simply by letting the reality of existing things enfold her. Now that he was gone she was once more thrown back upon herself; the world now resisted her enjoying it. "Dead and mute and malignant and fearful is the whole world, the whole sunlit world." And once again pain and not pleasure was "the only thing that remains of life."

She could not hold him; she had no claim upon him. But apart from him, utterly renouncing all claims, she could implore him to remain the way he was. She did not want him; she wanted to know that he existed. For her it was "enough . . . to have possessed such a quiet friend if only for a moment." But she urged him not to deny this moment; she desperately wanted him to remain her friend, not to become an alien like all the others, not to fit himself into an alien society which would have nothing to do with her; she wanted him, though far from her, to remain with her. "I don't want to see you again—but do not change, always understand me, so that I may say everything to you"; she begged him "always to have the courage to injure yourself by questions and doubts," to "destroy the most charming, most comfortable structure, which would otherwise do you for life." He was not to let himself be "lulled by any nice, protective morality . . . or even prompted to admiration." She urged him not to become habituated to anything, neither to the world nor to his friends nor to the things "you know for a long time, or that are old"; not even to himself, to his "manner of expressing himself." If he obeyed these injunctions, he would remain her friend.

That was the most important thing. For her indefiniteness, her natural lack of ties, appeared to her, when she saw them in him, as freedom, incorruptibility, absence of prejudice.

Thereby she received a legitimation for herself; her freedom was only the positive aspect of her natural lack of ties to the world around her; his freedom was something he had achieved by his own merits and was therefore more imperiled than hers; only such freedom could assure her that she was not a freak.

"Do not change," she pleaded. "Have no prejudices; remain free in every sense of the word!" This was not a matter of anything definite, for all definiteness was a fetter hindering the "living play of life," life which one ought not "to sigh through almost unconsciously, as a duty," because then one was only being bound to a mechanism which simply went on turning of itself. He could remain her friend only if he remained outside of the world, uncorrupted by it, as he had been when she met him. She, who was already born outside of the world, could stand together against the world with those who remained outside it from a sense of freedom; with such people she could discover the reasons for rejecting a bad world and desiring a better one. But it was difficult to believe in the trustworthiness of such friends when she herself had no alternative and did not know what it was like inside the soul of someone who did have an alternative.

"If you change, I must leave you." She herself no longer cared to try doctoring up her rejectedness for the sake of the world or of a particular person. She would not keep faith with him, not with him as Herr Bokelmann of Hamburg or as a friend who had once done a great deal for her. As soon as he took his place in the world, allowed himself to be fitted into it, into everything from which she was excluded and excluded herself, he would be lost to her. She would not try to cover that fact up by any sort of profession of faithfulness. The man in particular, Bokelmann of Hamburg, mattered little to her. "No mortal will ever again hold me back unworthily." She was that independent of him.

She had to woo friends. After all, the pridefulness that imagined it could get along perfectly well all alone, outside society, was nothing but defiance. Bokelmann had awakened her pride; now she needed him in order to sustain it. "Unfortunately I again felt that I am dependent upon you, that my courage and my defiance toward everything I have lost, comes from you." Not for a moment did she really want him for herself: "You can love whomever you want." But his friendship was necessary to her as a surety that she need not go on through the world so defiantly alone. That dependent she was upon him.

Thus, in Paris, she had become both independent and dependent. "There is a despair in which one asks nothing; and there is also a mood of love—as I should like to call it—in which one also asks nothing." The despair was over, and the mood of love was also over; life had snatched from her what she had desired and had long ago driven her into the despair of desirelessness; but life always went on; she could no longer desire what she had once desired. Despair was over; what remained was not pain alone; there remained the renunciation of possession, there remained the insight that "life is not arranged for permanence." That was "proved not alone by death, but by everything imperfect, and most of all by our painful, drifting vacillations." Naturally she wanted to possess, naturally she wanted to hold on, to the bad as well as the good, but "if nothing changes, at any rate our mood changes." You could "scold" life for not being arranged for permanence, for not allowing man to linger, for compelling him to hope and to renounce, to desire and to surrender; but as long as you lived, life was right. "So desire and be satisfied; life is not more than that."

Renunciation of everything you would like to cling to, sorrow and joy both, the hope of possession and possession itself, was more than merely abnegation of happiness, more than the resignation which had made Rahel say at the very beginning: "I am so very glad not to be unhappy that a blind man would surely be able to see that I cannot be happy at all." The twenty-year-old's resignation had been without basis in experience, had been blind to the things life could bring, had been arrived at only in the isolation of introspection. In her present renunciation there emerged a last reconciliation to the life that had been given to her, as it was; renunciation was only the obverse of contentment. Ultimately she did not owe too much to happiness; the world, the "beautiful world," had helped her "to dismantle the structure of . . . noble grief and ignoble holding firm."

"For it is beautiful"; the world could be enjoyed. It did not only distribute blows; it was also a refuge that was always open, that always remained the same. The happiness of sheer enjoyment was something Rahel could reach only by renunciation; for a time enjoyment substituted for the reality which she had wanted to hold on to and which she had been forced to see slipping away from her. Good fortune which merely gave what a person desired and what was attainable suddenly seemed to her unworthy. "The worthiest happiness on earth is going on living in spite of many a deprivation." Happiness could give only finite, mortal things which concealed the fact that life was not made for permanence. "What might be divine, nobody can possess." Pleasure gave something that was not divine, but real, something a person could live and die with. It was "the final and only reality" which was permitted to those who had already experienced the finiteness of life, to whom life gave precisely what they had not desired.

Pleasure provided Rahel with a reality which she did not have to wait for. She did not have to wait for it to encounter her; she needed only to "open her eyes," and she could let herself be carried away by the "beautiful world," could let it enfold her. "Fortune does not strew rose petals before one, but if she allows one to open one's eyes, one must hasten to recognize what a great deal that is, and must drink in all the loveliness of it. If it is truly lovely, one does not want to possess it; one wants to see it blooming. In the end all our tears and bitterest sufferings are merely over possession: we can never possess anything but the capacity to enjoy."

Rahel returned from Paris to Berlin with a plea that she not be awaited; with the hope that she would meanwhile have been forgotten, so that she would not be coming home, but to a new foreign land in which she could unconcernedly go on pursuing her Parisian happiness. "Speak to no one about me . . . let it be said . . . I am not coming back at all." She had forgotten what she had known when she de-

parted, that the "business" would go on, that everything
would be repeated. To her "soul peace, to her heart equanimity, to her mind its proper elasticity" had returned. But the
future was no longer transparent to her; in pleasure a part of
reality had become accessible to her, and that sufficed. She
had learned renunciation. Why should anything else happen
to her? "Let him come and tell me that a second time."

5

MAGIC, BEAUTY, FOLLY
(1802–1804)

Soon someone would indeed come and tell her everything for a second time. But for the present she remained at peace. Berlin had become dull, the people cold, and they had stood still; she cared about no one. Personally she herself seemed to become more and more elusive. The last person to whom she remained attached was Bokelmann—"the last human being between my previous and present life." However, she could become the friend of all who sought her out. Not in order to help them—"there is no consolation"—but in order to be witness of their suffering; not so much for the sake of the people themselves, but "out of preference for and acquaintance with this old boy, suffering." She had not cast off her old indiscriminateness, in spite of the ennui people inspired in her, in spite of the disgust they aroused in her. But whereas her old indiscriminateness had been the expression of her alienation, of her indefiniteness, it now sprang from the feeling that people did not matter but only what happened to them, their suffering, their living and dying. To know about this living and dying of theirs was enough for her; for herself she wanted nothing more, neither suffering nor joy. Such was her composure.

"In my heart people press and die as on a battlefield; none knows about the others; each must die for himself." Rahel was no longer in the battle, had forgotten that she had once believed she was born to be a soldier; she would no longer co-operate, would not have anything told twice. She carried about with her the outrageous pretense of being herself the "battlefield"; that being herself nothing but the scene of action, she in reality provided the essential connection between disparate events: "Since I do not want peace, and since people are plentiful as the sand on the beach, I bear it like the earth: no one knows whether it hurts the earth; perhaps the earth is linked with all other beings." What she wanted now was to be no longer concerned with herself, no longer to ask after her own happiness or unhappiness, but to be something as unquestionable as the earth, whose reality everyone testified to by walking upon it. If she knew everything, she would be the link between all those individual facts which, by themselves, life denies and wipes out again. She did not herself want to become entangled again; she wanted to be the immutable soil which absorbs everything into itself; she wanted to preserve all the tribulations that people suffered and could not retain because the next day snatched it from them.

In becoming this, she became devout. Because she placed herself outside of all this worldliness, because she wanted to contain everything in this world, she needed some link to "other beings," a link to God, who was thus to be the ultimate guarantee of her existence, whose "child" she was and upon whose "mantle" she lay. She believed neither in the god of her ancestors nor the god of Christianity, believed least of all in the "new-fashioned" religiosity which was characterized by a bigotry she hated—as did every thinker of the Enlightenment. She needed neither "founders" nor "proofs"; in respect to religion she was just as traditionless, just as blind to tradition, as she was in everything else. Driven into a corner, she would defend her faith with any deistic, Enlightenment arguments that came to hand; for that purpose she took whatever suited her from Christianity, merely to make herself intelligible, not from any need to belong to a particular sect which preserved a particular revelation of God as a historic fact. Her religion was altogether a private affair; she wished to convert no one to it, explained it only in response to direct questions and said little about it in her diaries—which in any case never told more than she would have told in letters.

Just as she wished to stand outside reality, to merely take pleasure in the real, to provide the soil for the history and the destinies of many people without having any ground of her own to stand on, so she in turn needed God as the ground on which there took place whatever constituted her own destiny. Just as she could no longer prove her reality because enjoyment did not reveal her own reality but always the reality most foreign to her (so that, automatically as it were, she had to attribute the highest degree of reality to whatever was most foreign to her), so she needed the essence of the Unknown—God—for "proofs of our existence." Because she was a person who wanted to be "like the earth" which bore everything, she needed the "mantle of God" to lie upon. She could scarcely afford to deny God, for if she did she would sink into a bottomless abyss. Of course everyone who confided in her, who made her the soil and the preserver of his history, guaranteed her existence in some sense; but on the other hand, everyone who left her, shut himself off from her, or betrayed her, annihilated her again.

At the end of the year 1801 Rahel met Friedrich Gentz. In the few months during which they lived in the same city—by 1802 Gentz left for England and afterwards moved to Vienna for good—the curious ups and downs of a relationship that was to last to old age and death were permanently defined: a love never realized; a desertion never consistently carried out; his forgetting her, which she never took quite seriously because she knew the power she had over him; and her indignation at his betrayals, which he never took seriously because he knew the power he had over her.

Gentz, like Schlegel and Humboldt, was in search of reality. He surrendered himself to pleasure, to the beautiful world, naïvely, directly without reservations, and let it consume him in pleasures; he surrendered also to his own ego as if it were something over which he had no jurisdiction, "took pleasure in himself" (Gentz), found himself just as delightful as any other portion of the world. At the time he made Rahel's acquaintance he had already radically reversed himself on his original enthusiasm for the French Revolution, had unqualifiedly chosen the existing order; later he threw up everything for the sake of reality: principle, prestige, and a good name with posterity. In the world he recognized only real power. Since Austria represented power in Europe, Gentz became Metternich's most trusted adviser. He fought everything that threatened to undermine this power, the power of autocratic rule. At the end of his life—after the July Revolution in France—he knew that he had fought for a doomed cause, that "in the end the spirit of the age will prove mightier" (Gentz). But even if he had already known this at the beginning of his political career, in those days when he began "to think like Burke, but continued to live like Mirabeau" (Haym), it would still have been out of the question for him to take up the cause of something that lay in the future, something unofficial and therefore intangible.

Gentz could not endure invisibility. He was tremendously vain, not because he deceived himself or paid "flattering visits to himself," but rather because he wanted to see himself "happy without any fuss"; because he could not endure even the briefest moment of being at a disadvantage, being put into the shade, being held aloof from the real world. Even in old age, for all that he was immensely blasé, he could always be cozened by flattery.

But Gentz was not only vain; he needed more than merely an "asylum in the world." He had succeeded in doing what remained impossible for either Friedrich Schlegel or, at bottom, Humboldt: intervening actively in the world of reality and adjusting constantly to circumstances. He succeeded in doing something and representing something in the world which he never for a moment wanted to change. The very fact that the world was susceptible to change seemed to him a threat to his good terms with it. Because what exists is real, he wanted at any cost to preserve it, and thus became the bitterest foe of freedom of the press, the most brilliant advocate of absolutism; he wanted to make nothing of the part the people had played in the Wars of Liberation against Napoleon; he was determined to retain the policy of arbitrary administration known as *Kabinettspolitik* and to withhold from the people the constitution that had been promised them.

Gentz wanted to conserve everything that existed, but he

was no conservative, and none of the advocates of conservatism ever took him as their mentor. He defended reaction as a man of the Enlightenment; his style and his arguments produced so "liberal" an effect that it fell to the liberal Varnhagen to discover him as a great writer. But Gentz was by no means a liberal, and no progressive would ever have broken bread with him. He was the last Romantic; long after all his friends had become respectable, pious and philistine, he still refused to recognize for himself the applicability of the very conventions whose political expression he defended. But Gentz was also no Romantic; for he had after all succeeded in representing something in the world, in establishing a contact with reality without *sacrificium intellectus* and without conversion. He was equivocal because he wanted nothing but reality, neither good nor evil, but reality without reservations. He never understood the liberal attacks upon him, the liberal arguments that an Enlightened, unprejudiced person could exist only if he also supported Enlightened, hence liberal, policies. He also never understood the conservative attacks upon him, the arguments that conservatism was a creed which also had to be borne out in a man's personal life. And he practiced the same naïve double game in the theoretical field (and therefore served no one's ends). On the one hand he opposed to the arrogance of Reason "man's frailty"; on the other hand he insisted on the relativity of the principle of legitimacy; it was not "absolute," he said, but "born of time," "caught up in time," and must be "modified by time." He was interested as little in the one principle as the other; at most he was concerned with the "great old world" whose decline he had been forced to watch and could not endure—any more than he could endure the thought of the transitoriness of his own life and the thought of death.

The fact that Gentz succeeded in playing a part in the world separated him from his generation, the generation of Schlegels and Humboldts. But in his aims he had much in common with them. He was proud of nothing so much as his being on the inside, boasted of no decorations as much as he did of being "in the know." "I know *everything*; no one on earth knows as much about contemporary history as I do." In the same way Humboldt, when the time came for him to go, wanted to leave behind as little as possible that he had not come into contact with. In the same way Schlegel in old age wanted to follow the course of world history by "participating in thought." They were all of them alike in believing that to participate in the world through knowledge was the greatest thing they could do. The satisfaction Gentz took in knowing everything allowed him, in the end, to accept with equanimity the downfall of everything he had striven for in politics. Out of such disinterestedness in all particularity—and not out of any particular conviction or principles—came the sentence with which he concluded his "political confession of faith": *Victrix causa diis placuit, sed victa Catoni.*

When Rahel met Gentz, she already knew pleasure and the beautiful world. To yield without reserve to reality did not lie within her power; the world would not accept her, after all; she was not free to renounce her freedom in favor of something else. Should any of the Berlin Jews have been prone to illusions on that score, they were sharply recalled to reality during these years. A harmless forerunner of a far more critical development, a wave of anti-Semitism spread through the Prussian provinces right at the beginning of the nineteenth century. It was propagated and represented by Grattenauer's pamphlet *Against the Jews.* This first modern hate-sheet, in the midst of a process of assimilation which was still going forward, wreaked injury upon the Jews immediately—according to the very well-informed Gentz—especially in Berlin. Grattenauer was concerned neither with religious questions nor with tolerance. His complaint against the Jews was not for failing to assimilate; he attacked them *in toto.* He emphasized that he was speaking "not of this or that Jew . . . nor of any Jewish individual, but of Jews in general, of Jews everywhere and nowhere." He recognized no distinction between cultivated and even baptized Jews and other Jews. The Jews who no longer displayed any outward differences, who "to prove their culture . . . publicly eat pork on *shabbes* . . . and on the promenades learn Kiesewetter's *Logic* by heart," were to him more typical than caftaned Jews. This type of thinking, expressed though it was in a disgusting, rabble-rousing manner, made a great impression upon Gentz, even though he respected and loved Rahel dearly. And not only upon Gentz. Scarcely changed, only a little more polished, the whole of Grattenauer reappeared seven years later in the patriotic speeches of the *Christlich-Deutsche Tischgesellschaft;* the arguments advanced by Brentano and Arnim go straight back to him.

To take a lofty attitude on this matter was, therefore, scarcely possible for a man who wanted to assimilate to society under all circumstances. But just as the Jews made it a matter of policy to attempt to penetrate society solely as individuals, so every anti-Semite had his personal "exceptional Jew." Gentz loved Rahel and in Vienna went to Jewish houses even while he was reading Grattenauer's pamphlet. In later years the Arnims were frequent guests of the Varnhagens, without in the least revising their opinions. The same was true even of Brentano. The Berlin Jews considered themselves exceptions. And just as every anti-Semite knew his personal exceptional Jews in Berlin, so every Berlin Jew knew at least two eastern Jews in comparison with whom he felt himself to be an exception.

What remained, even in the most favorable situation, was the necessity "of having always to show who one is; that is why it is so repulsive to be a Jewess!" The necessary legitimation kept her from devoting herself directly to the world and to present circumstances; it killed any desire in her to conserve a world in which such repulsive behavior was necessary. The difference between Rahel and Gentz would always be that she could not reconcile herself to the existing order. Even abandoning any desire to change the world, she still could not possess enough of reality to yield herself wholly to it; she could not be "in the know"; all she could possess of the world was the sun which shone equally upon all, the beautiful things which existed for all; so that when she became involved in society she had to be revolutionary or, as Gentz called it, "anarchic."

That disposition also allied her with Gentz, since Gentz was, after all, no conservative. In order to be understood personally, he was dependent upon a kind of liberality which he could find only in individuals, in the invisible, unofficial people who had no power. No one had understood him so well as Rahel. She knew that he was no hypocrite; she understood his hunger for reality and loved the naïveté with which he surrendered to everything real; she perceived that naïveté was his kind of sincerity, and that his genuine innocence removed some of the stigma that always clings to choosing the existing order, decreased the unsavoriness of that choice by laying all cards on the table, by exposing the thing for just what it was. Thus Rahel loved her friend precisely "when he said or did something thoroughly childish. . . . That is why I repeated his words when he said with a delighted smile and looking me straight in the eye: he was so happy to be the foremost person in Prague, so that all the highest authorities, the great ladies and gentlemen, had to send to *him*. Every well-brought-up, corrupt rascal is clever enough to conceal this; but who has the simplicity of soul, the charming childlike disposition, to *say* it?"

Gentz betrayed her a thousand times over. He wrote to Brinckmann: "Never has a Jewess—without a single exception —known true love," and then on almost the same date wrote to Rahel that no one knew how to love so well as she, that in fact she was "the finest being in this world." He betrayed her not only for the sake of his public life; his attitude toward her from the start had been equivocal, an inherent duality. For his private life he was dependent upon her understanding; but he hated being understood because it divided him from the reality to which he had dedicated himself. At bottom he had only the alternative of officially loving her or officially denying her. If he wanted to live in the world without reserve, then "association with such a mightily unleashing, such a thoroughly disorganizing genius as that of [Rahel]" Levi's must necessarily be "ruinous" and the "secret passion which this great, bold, divinely diabolic creature" had for him must constitute a threat to him.

It was by no means easy for Gentz to decide not to take up this passion. For it contained, after all, another chance for reality, a different kind of chance to know more than anybody else, a chance to have everything anyhow, in the world's despite. He would have been able to oppose to reality a second reality so strange, so unique, so complete within itself, that the true world could scarcely have surpassed it. "Do you know, my love, why our relationship is so grand and so perfect? . . . You are an *infinitely productive*, I am an *infinitely receptive* being; you are a great *man*; I am the first of all the women who have ever lived. I know this: that had I been physically a woman, I should have brought the globe to my feet. . . . Note this curious fact: from within myself I do not draw the most miserable spark—my receptivity is wholly boundless. . . . Your eternally active, fruitful spirit (I don't mean mind, but soul, everything) encountered this unlimited receptivity, and so we give birth to ideas, feelings and loves, and languages, all of them wholly incredible. What we two together know, no mortal soul can even guess. I reproach myself bitterly now for not having, that time, insisted upon enjoying what you called 'that trifle.' Something so new, so extraordinary, as a physical relationship between people whose inner selves are reversed in each other, cannot possibly have existed yet. And I must have that, too. Promise me that the next time we meet again, this will be done; if you promise me that solemnly and in writing, then I promise you that I will never marry again."

Rahel did not give him what she called "that trifle." Nor did he make her do so, although possibly it was something he sincerely wanted. Not for a moment did he want her and her only; what he wanted was a situation, a connection, a "relationship whose like there have perhaps not been many in the world." Precisely because he did not want her alone, neither for love nor for pleasure, at any rate, but at most for understanding—for precisely that reason he would have had to give up everything for her. This experiment would have cost him his naïveté, his clear conscience, his position in the world—in short, everything. It was intelligent of him not to insist and to remain "stupidly dazzled by the physical charms of an insignificant creature" (Gentz).

At this same time Rahel made the acquaintance of the handsome secretary of the Spanish Legation, Don Raphael d'Urquijo, and fell head over heels in love with him. Had Gentz and his naïve gospel of pleasure influenced her when she fell in love with Urquijo? Had she really persuaded herself that she would be able to let herself be consumed unreservedly? After all Urquijo was merely handsome—handsome as the Roman in Paris who had unfortunately had an *engagement*.

Ever since she had met Gentz, reality had been tempting her again. Since she had seen that pleasure need not be merely a lovely parenthesis in life, pleasure had begun to exert a strong attraction upon her. Suddenly she no longer wanted to be merely a theater for the actions of others; she wanted to have her share also, to take part. She no longer desired something extraordinary, a great love, or marriage to a nobleman, but the natural, everyday experience that was accessible to almost everyone. She wanted to try to take this handsome Spaniard as Gentz had taken his beautiful actress.

Gentz enjoyed the things of the world not because they were beautiful, but because they were real. He was captivated not by beauty, but by reality. For Rahel, however, since she was excluded from the world, there remained only the small segment that was beautiful.

By its very nature the beautiful is isolated from everything else. From beauty no road leads to reality. To be sure, the beauty of a poem can provide the inspiration for endless meditation, but this meditation is tied to the magic of the moment, has neither past nor future. A *beautiful* evening is not the evening of a day, and is not a symbol for anything. Perhaps it is evening itself, evening without day or night. But always day and night come to spoil the beauty of the evening, and only language, with its capacity for giving names to beauty, preserves the evening in an eternal present. Always the real evening shatters the magic of the word "evening"; always the continuity of life would annihilate the beauty of twilight.

The specific and definite always set limits to the wide horizon of the indefinite and unspecific. Always the one is separated from the other as by prison walls; always life prevails over the magical enchantment—and always beauty remains unaffected in its isolation, unconquered by this victory. For beauty insists upon its visibility and audibility, even when it accomplishes nothing and is nothing but a monument to itself. Beauty retains its magic, even though reality resists enchantment, even though temporality, the succession of the days, is not susceptible to any magic. Beauty has power through magic, although the greater power is still time's, since even the enchanted soul must die. The power of time always affects the person who has already lived and who will still live. The power of beauty affects the naked human being, as though he had never lived. Beauty in its isolation seems to abolish all ties and to thrust the human person into the same nakedness in which it was encountered.

Man can place himself at the mercy of beauty, just as he can be at the mercy of nature. Independent of everything that life gave or denied, there always remains the boundless delight over the first day of spring, over the ever-returning warm fragrance of summer. Just as beauty remains invincible in spite of the victory of life in which it is submerged, so the power of the seasons is invincible; there is always the certainty of their eternal recurrence. Rahel succumbed to the most natural passion, to the "violent magic"; she succumbed to the "beautiful object"—and hoped in this way to fend human beings off, to keep them out of her life. Indeed, she hoped, within magic, to be able definitively to throw off her life, just as beauty or the joy in earth and trees could make one forget life. She believed that in this very nakedness to which she was exposing herself she would find the elements of permanence, those aspects of herself which were independent of circumstances. She hoped to find herself as she had been in the beginning. She gave herself to love as though she were nothing but a creature of nature, and hoped since she had been "pushed out of the world by birth, by ill luck not admitted to it," to be able to circumvent ill luck and birth through love. Beauty could not entangle her in reality, and perhaps it could release her from the inhumanity of being like "the earth linked with all other beings." Perhaps the happiness to be had by losing herself in the beauty in a man was a happiness without all pretensions, the most human kind of happiness, akin to the happiness of sun, warmth and earth, the happiness of all animal life.

Urquijo was a foreigner to whom Rahel was no Jewess; there was no need for her to justify herself to him; he would not even understand justification. So she hoped that he would provide her with the longed-for refuge. Perhaps he of all people, knowing nothing about her, having no prejudices— that is, not the prejudices she was familiar with—would be a human shelter to her. To her just as she was before life dealt with her and made a shlemihl of her; to her who had never been shown any consideration; to her gifts, which life had regarded as of no consequence. Perhaps this man would recognize or rediscover her true nature—if she put herself at his mercy without reservation, regardless of everything, heeding nothing but the original joy which every human being takes in behaving naturally. That was it: he must take her as she was originally, as God made her: *Telle que je suis, Dieu l'a voulu; et je vous aime.* This love was to have no connection with the rest of her life, no connection with her past. Rather: *Je suis née pour vous aimer.* She now saw love as a "gift of Heaven," the mightiest of magics; with it the earth, when it was beautiful, could allure, could enthrall. "My heart belongs to you for all of life! . . . Eternally, eternally, beautiful object, you enchant and possess it."

The enchantment released Rahel from herself. What bliss to be free of herself: "Do you know that my heart is altogether sore from the bliss of being so wrenched loose?" She had made up her mind to enjoy the world; for this, aloofness was required. She was going to bring the same aloofness to the pursuit of this pleasure. But she had forgotten that everything would have to be repeated. Being who she was, she was simply unable to maintain the aloofness and had carried the pleasure to the point of utter enchantment.

"God has placed in my soul what nature and circumstances have denied my face. I knew that, but hitherto I did not know that God would grant me the inexpressible happiness, the greatest and complete happiness, of being able to reveal this soul." She wanted, then, to reveal her soul instead of her ugly destiny. But then, who was she if she forgot her life? What else had she to reveal but that she was not beautiful and a shlemihl? What was she being so conceited about? After all, her soul had already been abused and crippled in her youth. A crippled soul was not a pleasant sight. Had she not yet understood that it was precisely the soul for which life showed no consideration, that the fact of life and death was more important than the convolutions of the inner self?

Urquijo promptly thwarted her. He did not at all want to know her soul. A soul of his own was sufficient for him; why should he burden himself with another? Nor did he like her boundless, intemperate love. Aside from everything else, it was not seemly for a woman to love a man so much more than he loved her. "Is it true; are you really still glad that I love you? Oh, do not grow tired of my speaking of that again and again. I would gladly force myself not to show my love, so that it will not become a burden to you; but if you love me, show me, I beg you; I need it." No, it was quite clear that he had no intention of becoming a refuge for her.

Moreover, he never felt at ease with her. The less he understood her letters, which implored him for a kind of love unknown to him, and which he was certainly not willing to give, the more jealous he became. He made life a hell for her. And she made her old mistake: she admitted him to the circle of her friends, who could only mock at him. For she alone was sensitive to the magic. Among her friends he justly felt insecure, as Finckenstein had, and therefore jealous. With his Spanish prejudices he undoubtedly thought she was having an affair with every man who called on her. Once again everything was smashed by mischance: the fact that Urquijo was the kind of man he was. Since she nevertheless held on to him, did not drop him as an unfortunate specimen of the "handsome man" type, she surrendered once more to chance, which apparently could strike her from every direction because she fitted in and could fit in nowhere. "Oh! Why did he have to be the one to wield magic over me!"

When Urquijo grew jealous, Rahel realized that he was not only a "beautiful object," but a human being. At this point she thought she was loved; only at this point did the love affair really begin. Urquijo became the token of chance for her, just as had Finckenstein when she "yielded to chance where she should have been able to calculate everything." Once again love was "more important than the object" to her. "One surrenders to love, good or bad, as though it were a sea, and either luck, strength, or skill at swimming takes you across or lets you be swallowed up. That is why Goethe says: 'Does he who trusts to love consider his life?'" In the course of the affair Urquijo more and more became Finckenstein's double: like the former he did not want her love, repulsed her, rejected her. *Ma plus sainte volonté est repoussé, foulée! . . . et le premier besoin de mon coeur m'est refusé.* And he, too, was as "innocent as the axe that hacks off a great man's head." Within the relationship, however, he was far more to blame—he was not so decent or well-bred as Finckenstein; he was a liar who swindled his way through the world; he was accustomed to being despised by people; he was a "craven rascal" who years after their break always remembered her as soon as he needed money.

Rahel did not clearly see this difference. The drama so thoroughly wiped out distinctions between the persons that they seemed merely to be playing their parts and stepping off the stage. The event imposed a role upon the individual so forcefully that he had no opportunity to display his differences. Humboldt was not alone in charging Rahel with indiscriminateness because of this complete overlooking of individual differences. Gentz wrote, when he learned of the affair with Urquijo, utterly incomprehensible to him: "I am afraid that Humboldt will be madly triumphant again. What food for his hatred of *la petite!*" Rahel's choice seemed to be a demonstration of everything that was unendurable about her. She did not defend herself; she merely described her love to Gentz, not the object of it. "Your love," he replied to her, "I thought charming, magical, divine . . . but between this love and the object of it lay, for me, an immeasurable gulf. . . . I always judged him favorably and with good will. There appeared to me to be no particular depths in his nature; he always slid contentedly and with utter self-satisfaction down the commonplace track of life. . . . But in everything I saw and heard there was not a single point which could ever have made me guess he would be capable of kindling a passion in you. In a word: profound astonishment closed my mouth. . . . Urquijo seemed to me an extremely ordinary person. Now, of course, I myself am not so sub-ordinary as to imagine one must love only the extraordinary; but I thought that if inward depth could not explain the affair, there must emanate some superabundant outward breath of physical attraction from the beloved object—such as there undeniably breathes from Christel, whom you have . . . never quite forgiven me for!" Gentz certainly might have forgiven Rahel, since he could no more understand that Urquijo of all persons should exercise such "violent magic" upon her than she could understand why he had fallen for the actress Christel Eigensatz, who had been his mistress in Berlin. One thing was certain, however: Gentz would not misjudge the limits of such an affair; he would not allow himself to be "dragged around by suffering" on account of it; he would certainly not, on account of it, let himself be "torn apart to the point of transparency." He would know every single moment what the whole business was worth. It had been very foolish of Rahel to attempt to imitate him. The extravagance of her passion was for Gentz the "strange, paradoxical, inexplicable phenomenon." "Selling out life and the heart" to an unworthy object struck him as tasteless, offended his justified demand for dignity and poise. He saw in Rahel a provoking lack of grace.

Rahel had long known that she had "no grace and not even the grace to see the cause of that." The cause was her lack of position in the world, her excludedness, whose reason she did not properly understand. The cause was that if she wanted to live at all she had to expose herself to chance, a principle she sensed very strongly, but which others did not understand. The cause was also that she was disoriented and had no alternatives, that everything assailed her immoderately because she had nothing with which to defend herself. "I must let everything pour down upon me like rain without an umbrella." To be sure, no one understood the rain better, no one showed so clearly what rain was like, than the person who happened to have no umbrella and therefore became soaking wet. But how did such knowledge help her? How was it possible for her to remain moderate and maintain her poise when everything that other people protected themselves against she had to take directly and without protection?

The lack of grace was not the result of Rahel's letting Urquijo entrance her. "Why should one not be beside oneself? There are in life good parentheses which belong neither to us nor to others; I call them good because they give us a freedom which neither we ourselves nor others would allow us to have when in sound mind." The whole thing became ugly and repulsive only when she attached herself to the "beautiful object," when the magic became a love affair, when in the sphere of magic she once again encountered loving and being loved and quite forgot whom she was dealing with. "Urquijo, too, could have kept me faithful, if he had wanted to," she wrote in her diary after that last meeting with Finckenstein. The whole thing became ugly and repulsive only when she insisted upon draining the twice-told experience to the dregs again, when even at the cost of her human dignity she would not renounce even the worst experience; because everything, even in the worst, even mendacity, provided a revelation of what love and chance could do.

"It was a protracted murder." It lasted for two years. Urquijo's jealousy gave the impression of having sprung from a great passion. Yet he paid no more regard to her as a person than she did to him. *Je t'aime mais je ne t'estime pas*, he wrote to her again and again, as though he had taken the very words from her mouth—except that on her lips those words would have been most apt. Urquijo's saying he could not respect her was merely absurd. He had very definite ideas about women in general, their duties, their subordination to men. Rahel must have seemed a kind of witch to him, a "monster." What he knew of her life—what he had heard from her—only made him the more certain of himself; he assumed that in all probability she had to be treated this way, since Finckenstein had done the same. Much sooner than she, he saw the parallel; his insight flowed from a natural male solidarity against *monstres* of all sorts. *Que veux-tu, Finck t'a déjà traitée comme cela, cela ne doit pas être nouveau pour toi.* She did not want to accept any longer what was given to her; she did not want to let go any more what was being taken away. She was full of rebellion and full of fear: *Mais je te demande en grâce, trompes-moi un peu! Il me le faut. Nommes-moi "vous" dans ton âme, mais que je ne le trouve plus dans tes billets.* She no longer wanted the truth; above all, she no longer wanted to be an exception. She preferred lies; she was ready to give up everyone she was fond of, to give up anything, rather than be cast off by him, disenchanted and rejected. Long since she had realized what he was and what he was not. If she had not known, the letters from Gentz and the judgments of her friends would have made it abundantly clear. Nor had she any claim to his love; she alone was responsible for "the greatest turpitude of my life." *Tu n'as rien fait; il t'est arrivé une chose,* she wrote in express exoneration of him. "All the blame is mine; I bear it gladly," so she said at the beginning. But she could not take the responsibility upon herself because in the end she was incapable of desiring despair; because she had surrendered herself to magic; because she had subjugated herself entirely; because her former life and everything she had learned had dropped away from her, as though there had never been anything in her life but Urquijo. She had really succumbed completely to him, as if she were the same person she had been before she met Finckenstein.

But that was not the case. She was older than she had been then. Even if everything that happened to one was forgotten, time itself settled into a person, changing him utterly. Time itself forbade insistence on a vague originality. Rahel had grown older; whatever she might experience now was "experienced for ever," because there simply remained no time for other experiences. In the affair with Finckenstein it had taken despair to make her grasp the finality of experiences; now she knew beforehand that they were final, and consequently she was afraid, which she had not been then. She no longer provoked a break; rather, she tried to postpone it as long as possible. A full two years before their separation she was already writing: *Je veux me soumettre à tout; mais je ne veux pas anticiper la mort. Ne me faites pas mourir avant le temps.*

"I lied. The loveliest lie, the lie of a truly great passion." Why should not such a lie be permitted, when loving and being loved were at stake, when there was no other possible way to love and be loved? Was there not enough truth inherent in passion and its story for it to survive a poor, wretched lie that a poor, wretched human being invented for its sake? What did dignity and taste amount to? Had not Gentz also renounced his dignity when he surrendered to reality at all costs? And had not Rahel lied before when she loved Finckenstein "with effort and by the noblest, loveliest sort of lying?"

"But the value and the very possibility of my Being were at stake." This time she dared not lie. She had never let herself be consumed by Finckenstein; there it had really only been a question of loving and being loved. Here she was trying to get rid of her self. If she had any right to give herself away at all, certainly it must be done without lies, and certainly it must not be to an unworthy object; if she were going to do that, she should rather have given Gentz "the trifle" and sent "Urquijo to the devil" (Gentz). Since she refrained, obviously she had not entirely given up being the repository of events, a sign and an example. She did not voluntarily bear witness, but neither could she voluntarily give up doing so. This time she lied to escape all that: "I lied in order to obtain a reprieve for my life. I lied; I did not declare the demands of my heart, my proper deserts; I let myself be suffocated; I did not want to let myself be stabbed; wretched cowardice; I wanted, unhappy

creature, to protect the life of the heart; I simulated, I dissimu-
lated, I twisted and twisted and twisted." Rahel lied to obtain
a reprieve, as though life would not go on anyway without her
doing anything about it. She wanted to let herself be consumed, but she kept in reserve certain "demands of the heart"
and "proper deserts" which she merely concealed. That was
her lie. It was not possible to get rid of her self.

"When at last, basely treated, I laid my own heart upon
the shield, and as if with the sword demanded that the '*oui*'
be written on the envelope, it was really over. My soul knew
it beforehand. As I wrote to him I surrendered to despair,
which I did not yet know; no one knows it, it and death." Finally she knew that she must provoke the "no"; that he was no
longer a "beautiful object," not after having treated her basely;
that his actions had gone far beyond anything she had originally wanted of him; that his behavior had more weight than
her craving to be free of herself; that despair was as much part
of this affair as death was part of life. No lie availed against
death either; to death also one could not say: No, I don't want
it. Despair and death: "Whoever does not fear these two
merely does not know the meaning of not knowing. Yet at
times one must choose them both." If you could not choose
death, you were foolishly depriving yourself of the freedom to
die when you would; you became then a mere animal creature
whom death seized in the end. If you could not choose despair,
you despaired nevertheless. Lies and lack of awareness accomplished nothing but the nameless humiliation of not doing
consciously something that in any case would be done to you.
"I believe that if the Governor of this earth had wanted only a
single example of such love, in all its twistings and possibilities, in its supreme strength, genuineness and purity, coupled
with the highest consciousness of itself and therefore with the
ultimate potentialities of its torments, wherein the circum-
ference of the whole soul served, as if supplied with facets,
to reflect back every grief—then I would have sufficed as his
example."

"The darkest things and everything we have ever read become true in our case like the most hackneyed saws." Rahel

now suddenly saw herself not as an example of anything special or extraordinary, not destined for anything remarkable, but as an example of "the hackneyed," both the darker and the brighter aspects of it, of the things every human being encountered and was affected by—but everyone experienced these things in such isolation that he was easily tempted to think of them as something special and guard them like a secret. She was the example of love in its most banal form, of chance of the chanciest kind. She was a living example of everything that "hackneyed saws" had to say about life in general. Her love for Urquijo was the "shipwreck," the being "storm-tossed" that everyone knew, everyone felt now and again; but not everyone had to drain the cup to the bitter dregs, to pursue the matter to the ultimate consequences inherent in it. The true meaning of shipwreck, after all, came only to the person who achieved ultimate despair. That she had become an example was the sum of the meaning she herself saw in this affair which so frequently seemed altogether ridiculous: "What fault have I committed that one man should toss me into the hands of another until the goddess herself calms me by turning me to stone."

"I am as unique as the greatest phenomenon on this earth." It was not, she felt, that she was by nature exceptional, but that it had pleased life to make an example of her. For that reason "the greatest artist, philosopher or poet is not above me. We are made of the same element. In the same rank, and belong together. . . . But my assigned task was *life*. . . . And I remained in the seed until my century, and have been wholly covered with earth from outside—that is why I say it myself." After Finckenstein left her she had wanted to be a sign and symbol in the world, the "mouthpiece of eternal justice." But the world had not taken cognizance of this desire; life had stirred her up out of her petrifaction and forced her to go on living. "Wholly covered with earth from outside," she had found no language in which to tell the world of her experience. And because the world therefore had not confirmed it, from day to day it had lost reality. And then everything had begun from the beginning again. But now "the circle was complete"; to be sure she would "leap from hell to hell for eternity" if there were no natural end point, no limit of vitality —and age; "if the Primal Spirit would not make my nature fly apart." Now, however, things would not so easily be repeated again; now she must only seek for "an image that would define existence"—existence not being enough in itself, for there was no slate upon which life would write itself. Consciousness was a part of being an example, and so was communication, for one who "has a destiny" was only someone who "knows what kind of destiny he has" and could report it.

"And I think I am one of those products which humanity has to bring forth and then no longer needs and no longer can" —because only a single example of a thing is needed; provided it is without confusion and equivocation. She would have had to renounce this uniqueness if she had "correctly thought over" her life and had given Gentz "the trifle." In exchange she would have had to become, together with him, something quite unique, namely something like the perfect human being dimly conceived by Romanticism in its idea of the androgyne: the essence of humanity in a single specimen. Had they made any such attempt, both would have lost all solid ground underfoot. In an abstruse, curious manner they would have cut themselves off from all ordinary human destiny. Neither of them had wished that. Neither had ever been able to forget this possibility; neither had ever been able to forgive the other for their not having been happy together. Gentz's attempts to forget Rahel were never successful. He was the "only one who has forgotten me—as I predicted to him a thousand times that he would—and who *cannot* forget me because I realized, in fact created, one of his moral ideals." She remained the price he had paid when he committed himself to reality. He could not forgive her for not having kept him from doing so. Eight years after their separation, in 1810, he wrote: "It was really a frightful mistake that we did not attain to love to one another, I mean to real, complete love! If at that time I had been able to see, instead of being stupidly dazzled by the physical charms of an insignificant creature, how extremely fond you were of me, I would have insisted stubbornly, even if only out of curiosity, frivolity, etc., on what you called the trifle—an affair would have broken out between us whose like the world has perhaps not seen many of. . . . And yet it was principally *your* fault; you stood higher, saw more clearly and farther than I; you should have freed me from Christel and sent Urquijo to the devil. In consideration of my soul, which had remained innocent in a corrupt husk, you should have set aside traditional reserve and even done violence to me, in order to make me tremendously happy. . . . It is strange that even the true man . . . must in the end say . . . that he wantonly thrust away the best. And at bottom . . . is it not always the basest of all human vices, namely vanity, the senseless striving for appearance, which . . . cheats us of the whole genuine reality of existence?" It is difficult to say which was the genuine reality. With Gentz it is impossible to decide whether he grasped reality only out of vanity, or whether vanity only served to lead him to reality, to show him that man was nothing when he remained invisible, when he excluded himself from history, which could only progress along its way through him.

In any case, whenever he met Rahel again in later years, "something constrained, uncanny, like a guilty conscience," took possession of him in her presence. She knew only that he "must love" her and that she had "never given him up, although we can no longer communicate in letters." And he came to her again, to her alone, shortly before her and his deaths, when he had already resignedly accepted the fact that the *Zeitgeist* was more powerful than he; when history had at last left him by the wayside; when he was no longer living for what was official and visible, but only for his last great passion for the young dancer Fanny Elssler. Disillusioned, griefstricken and lovesick, cast out by the great world, disgusted and bored by everything, the old man came back to her. And she was at once ready to forget all his "perfidies"—for *"his* perfidies—and he committed many of them against me—are different from those of others; he glided, soared in Fortune's toboggan, down a track that he alone followed; and no one can rightly compare himself with him. . . . But now, in sum, there remains to me only pure living love. Let this be his epitaph: he always stirred me to love; he was *always* receptive to what struck him as true. He seized upon untruth with a passion for truth. Many people must be praised item by item; and they do not arouse love in our hearts; others, a few, can be reproached for much, but they always open our hearts, move them to love. Gentz did that for me: and he will never die in me."

6

ANSWERS
THE GREAT GOOD FORTUNE
(1805–1807)

"Since then. . . . No joy reaches to my heart; like a ghost he stands below and presses it shut with a giant's force; and only pain can find entrance; this ghost, this distorted image—I love it! Tell me, when will this madness, this gruesome pain end? What will make it end?"

In losing Urquijo, Rahel lost the beautiful world. Even the elementary and always alluring simplicity of natural existence —to have the man she desired—was forbidden her. The divine powers which brought consolation where human comfort was lacking, and which had once enabled her to go on living, now failed her. She was failed by "weather, climate, children, music, the true realities." Nothing could reach her any longer, not so long as she remained under the magic. Yet this magic, now powerless to build pleasure domes or castles in the air, was like a *danse macabre* in which she was swept along. Suffering had once been the guarantee of her existence, an undoubted reality. She had been able to cling to it in the past, to use it to shelter herself a little from the power of time which brought "new consolation and new circumstances" (Herder). But now she no longer needed to struggle against the "absurd regularity," against the natural joy in a new day. She had given away her senses, had concentrated everything she was upon an object, and now, having grown unaccustomed to all rule of reason, she pursued it and was blind and deaf and dumb to the "beautiful world." All she had left was "gruesome pain."

First she had hung on to Urquijo much too long out of fear of disenchantment. Now she could no longer disenchant herself; even her despair lay under a spell. Although separated from him, she was not free. Because she went on living with him without his being physically present, everything became ghostly. Again and again she read his letters, and hers to him, which she had made him return. For the longest time she had ceased to understand why her caprice had fixed upon this particular man, this Spaniard; yet her fixation became all the more inexorable; no reasoning could assail it, no understanding dissolve it. Once having "sold out" herself, she could not buy herself back by recognizing that she had made a mistake.

"This man, this creature, wielded the greatest magic over me, still wields it; I sold myself out to him, gave him—this is no cliché; accursed that I am, I have experienced it—gave him my whole heart. And once your heart is given, only love and worthiness can give it back; otherwise it is gone from you. Then do curses, magic, really exist? . . . But it is as though he still had something of mine which I must have again, and as if his love could still delight and cure me. . . . In short, so long as I cannot love someone more intensely, the part of my self necessary for happiness remains in his power, the source of clearest, most intimate being lies stricken under the weight of magic and a curse." In her life she would not be able to love anyone more intensely; the parting from Urquijo had converted the magic into a curse. Part of the curse was that for the first time she could not bring herself to accept what had happened; could not bring herself to, in spite of her knowledge that bitterness was useless because time allowed freedom only for affirmation of the past; freedom for negation existed only in self-destruction, in death.

"Outrageously, I remained alive nonetheless, and that is my crime, my sin, my injustice, my disgrace, and God's hard, great curse which should have struck me down. I resign myself to the most eternal suffering, and ought to be silent. You see only distraction, life, movement, helping others, you see vanity saving me; but when I am alone I put together millions of hells, as children do with building blocks or sand."

Playing with the building blocks of her own history, Rahel inexorably tore apart events, the world and things, shattered their connections, crazily shifted them now here, now there, in order to provide some distraction for a soul crazed with grief. Despair and playful frivolity approached so closely that only in their strange and cruel compounding was the ghostly quality of human existence in general illuminated—a ghostliness conjured up by the careful sculptor's hand of one to whom everything had become meaningless. It is not madness but only the shadow of madness that appears before the eyes of a person who even in despair cannot cease to insist obstinately and persistently upon the meaning of events.

Because being isolated and under an evil spell was not the same as being mad, there arose, out of the frivolous play which was destroying all connections between things, something new and surprising, something that led by wearisome detours back to continuity and reason: namely, a peculiar clarity of vision in perceiving the contours of the individual building blocks. If you playfully force yourself to forget for a moment that the glass in front of you is there for drinking, you will stop knowing whether you are dreaming or awake, but you will also see the contours of the glass more sharply. It will seem menacing; the very fact that glassy things exist in the world will appear frightening. Thus Rahel, in the menacing, painful, ghostly eeriness of her situation perceived the pieces of her own life more distinctly; she saw her life from outside as a mere game, like something she had never lived. The dual phantasm of frivolously playful aloofness and despairing isolation enabled her to see the contour of her life so clearly and unequivocally that she could relate it in all its bareness. Her life became a narrative to her.

At the time the affair with Finckenstein came to an end, she had wanted to speak the truth directly. Immoderate in her estimate of her sufferings because she was ignorant and without experience, she had thought herself "beyond," superior to the historically developed world in which she lived and to which she turned. An outsider and therefore without modesty, truly (in Schiller's phrase) a *Mädchen aus der Fremde*, she had upset and enchanted society with her "answers" and had discovered that a truth at the wrong place and the wrong time remained merely one opinion among others, that truth bore no identifying label, that it was by nature unpretentious. Speaking out, pouring out her soul, had certainly been permitted, had been interesting, exercised fascination, as confessions always did. But such utterances were promptly forgotten because they really mattered to no one. Proud of her discovery, she had at the time been altogether indifferent to whether anyone was interested in her truth. Helplessly, she had repeated in ever-new variations: "And the kind of suffering I know is a life also"—had repeated this without realizing that life was not tellable so long as it was focused solely on suffering, on the confirmation of reality.

No one paid any attention to the things that mattered to her; she had remained alone with all her conclusions and had gradually forgotten them. For to the world and in the world the only things of permanence were those that could be communicated. All things uncommunicated and incommunicable that have never been told to anyone and have never made an impression on anybody; that have never entered the consciousness of the times and have sunk without importance into the chaos of oblivion—are condemned to repetition; they have found no permanent resting place in reality.

Rahel had learned that and half understood it when, right after the break with Finckenstein, she fled abroad from the lack of understanding and sympathy at home, fled to Paris knowing that everything would be repeated and that she was being allowed only a breathing spell in which to recover. But anticipation of experiences, the knowledge that prematurely and precociously converted the future into the past, also stands outside history; it forestalls nothing and vanishes as soon as one surrenders to life again, capitulates to life. Then, as one is being helplessly carried along, every event and every new acquaintance take on a tormenting note of *déjà vu, déjà entendu.*

It took reiteration to make Rahel learn to dread forgetting. Pure continuance of life, with accompanying loss of her own history, could only mean "leaping from hell to hell forever." Pride, pretensions, arrogance out of contempt for those who were prepared to listen must not stop her from communicating.

In any case she must try to escape oblivion and to fit herself into history, to save her own little portion of history, no matter how, to tell it to no matter whom.

Out of building blocks which Rahel had collected in her despairing, experimental frivolity, she built up a kind of tellable story. With this story, not with herself, she turned to the outer world once again, trying the find comrades in misery. If she were to succeed, she would have to renounce superiority and pretensions. She knew now that one became an example only of triviality; she had learned that destiny not only operated upon one, but one vigorously took part in it. What happened to her was not only a matter of being helplessly exposed to an event, of enduring sacrilege to the purity of self, the nobility of personality. Rather, she herself erred just as much as anybody; she herself was as mean and, in the end, no less vulgar. What, then, was the situation with Urquijo? Certainly it *had* been a "turpitude," but only at the beginning. Later: "I saw myself mistreated, where I thought to be treating the other with love. . . . Hitherto, nothing had seemed so contemptible to me as a person's not knowing how he stood with another. . . . I thought myself not liable to this kind of error . . . always secretly hated people who made such mistakes. Even in love . . . I retained a balanced judgment; for I never hoped. But suddenly I saw that I, too, could be mistaken about it. . . . I see now that I may have been erring all my life, that I cannot be sure about the future and the past. This shattered me." This insight, which at first seemed more shattering than unhappiness or disgrace, because it involved self-blame, turned out to be her salvation. Because she herself had acted no differently from other people, she was forced into solidarity with the rest of the human race, who also do little else but err. Her very regrets enabled her to feel that she may have erred all her life, and like everyone else she could no longer be sure about past or future.

Unhappiness, suffering, disgrace, had been foreseeable, and foresight, even though it might develop only later into understanding, afforded a perspective on events, provided security, produced an attitude of dignity toward destiny. But hatred directed against oneself, loss of pride and security, were "alien" and "intolerable." They forced her into solidarity with the others. Only "conversion of the heart" forced upon her this additional understanding, this identification with the unequivocally ugly, this acceptance that she could be merely an example and without any distinction.

Rahel told her life story to a certain Rebecca Friedländer. This was a person "insufferable, unnatural, *pauvre* by nature in her pretensions." The daughter of a Berlin Jewish family named Salomon, the sister of Marianne and Julie Saaling, sprung from the same milieu as Rahel, she had separated from her husband, undergone baptism, and written bad novels under the name of Regina Frohberg.[1] She became Rahel's friend during the years 1805 to 1810; one hundred and fifty-eight letters of Rahel written to her during those years, of which only a fraction were published by Varnhagen, testify to the intimacy between the two women. Rebecca Friedländer was in a situation similar to what Rahel's had once been. She was in love with a Count Egloffstein, who partially returned her love, but had not the slightest intention of marrying this baptized Jewess. Rebecca, too, suffered from her love; she, too, fought for him; and for her, too, the fight was in vain. The only difference was that she used the affair for a *roman à clef*, "a picture of a German salon." The novel compromised both herself and her entire circle of acquaintances, since no one at the time had any difficulty dubbing in the real names. Rahel commented, "She is a greater fool than I thought" and cut off relations with her.

"I am interested in every person who I think is unhappy! That is my greatest misfortune—for that is how they all catch me. Pluck me and let me scurry off—and like a stripped fowl,

---

[1] Varnhagen published extracts from Rahel's letters to her in the *Buch des Andenkens*, frequently disguising them as diary entries or employing the code *Frau v. F.* Ludmilla Assing, in the correspondence she published between Rahel and Varnhagen, always calls her Regina Frohberg, although this name never occurs in the original letters of Rahel; Rahel usually referred to her as "the Friedländer."

my feathers and faith grow again—but unfortunately without the slightest convictions!"[2] Rahel, who always was and gave precisely what circumstance, persons and fate demanded of her at the moment, was late to learn that unhappiness could occur in the most stupid forms. At this time the fact that someone could be unhappy accredited him as a decent human being.

In telling about herself she kept nothing back, betrayed herself and everyone else. Not insofar as she related anything particularly secret to Rebecca Friedländer—there is scarcely anything in the letters that she did not occasionally write to others—but insofar as she told everything to one person; until Rebecca's stupidity became too apparent to her, she put herself at the mercy of this one woman, declared entire solidarity with her.

Ultimately, Rahel was right. Their solidarity was real and considerable, their fates much the same. She was obligated to tell all because she could understand and tell, which Rebecca could not do—*she* could only write novels. She was obligated to be the "loving witness" because she had learned how useless suffering was without someone who could be witness to it. "Let this be comfort to you in the horror: that a creature lives who knows your existence as a living witness and—I venture to say—sees the depths of it." Every grief that Rebecca told her of, she already knew, and proved to her that there were greater and worse ones, "higher suffering, which I myself have experienced."[3] She taught her friend that life goes on: "Hope for forces which you do not yet have. That is what is most impossible, and nevertheless, possible."[4] She pointed out that grief could serve as a confirmation that life had not passed one by. "Experiencing sorrows also means living." And that one must nevertheless not love grief, not confuse it with what had really happened: "Do not love your grief." That no feeling was permanent, and therefore could not be clung to, but that nevertheless feeling could supply the basis for an

[2] Unprinted letter dated January 8, 1808.
[3] Unprinted letter, December 1, 1807.
[4] Unprinted letter, end of December, 1805.

existence because it banished pure nothingness. That then, however, human beings not only endured every "glorious frivolity," but sought it out in order to be able to endure suffering; that one must remain "active and amusable," for only such an attitude, "joined to great endured suffering, gives to one's whole being the weight that makes it go." She did not scruple to impress upon Rebecca the most trite ideas—that youth is an advantage because youth has time and can wait, and because "the world is more prolific of events than are our minds"; that people do not die of grief and unhappiness, but generally hope quite solidly for the next day. "Since you must go on living, really live!!"; that hope of death is only one of suffering's deceptions, for "youth is violent and profound, but it does not yet know life"—for example, it does not know how beautiful and tempting is everything that irrefutably remains after the cruelest loss: "Pleasures crowd in upon us even in the worst state. The sun shines! We suffer, we lament!" And she tried to rouse in Rebecca that salutary curiosity which represents the first shy effort to settle with life and to love it: "Is it not worthwhile, if only out of curiosity, to live one's life through and to eavesdrop on sorrow and joy?" Out of curiosity emerges the way to insight, the ability to understand—"even if our understanding is only in retrospect"—and finally that ultimate consent which rebounds, as it were, from the negation of suicide and amounts to a voluntary submission to life, whatever it may hold, out of gratitude for the sun's always shining and for our being able to understand: "At the end of things it is good again—like everything, when we understand it."

It was evident that what life could teach, what conclusions could be derived from the despairing game with incoherent fragments of memory, were pitiful trivialities. As soon as one cast the beam of reason into the dark phantasmagoria of incoherence, with intent to communicate, the wonderful complex meaning which had seemed to lie in the chaos disappeared utterly, and all that was left was the weariest of old saws. From such impoverishment, too, only solidarity with certain others afforded salvation, with people to whom for special reasons banality was not native, but whose "infamous birth" marked them out for precisely the bitterest and most banal of experiences.

"Let me have suffered for you."[5] Rahel pleaded with her friend. That was the point of her lessons, admonitions, communications. It did not suffice to be an example; it was necessary to have been an example for the sake of someone else. There must be at least one person who could learn from Rahel's examples: "In the extremity of distress I asked this of God, and vowed to assuage my soul if he granted it to me; he and I have kept our word." She was not merely looking for someone who had already suffered a like fate; rather it seemed to her senseless that others should repeat the misfortunes which she had already tasted to the dregs, pursued to their ultimate conclusion. She wanted to fit herself into the world and into its history in which there was no need for repetition. And since she herself—if only because of her age—was now relatively immune to repetition, she wanted to shield anyone who might be able to repeat her experiences, to take that person's place; the past, she felt, had given her the right to do so. "I want to buy your youth's freedom; mine had to be lost . . . and so much is permitted to me—but I permit myself nothing more than to dole out the droplet of joy which some good soul may yet find in me!" Her life was undoubtedly lost, so why should she not permit herself anything? She could never again be happy: "The court painter from heaven has whitewashed my old suffering: and it takes away from me life, breath and prospects."[6] Why should she not let herself go? Was not clinging to oneself also a form of overestimation of the self? And what should she cling to, if it were not to be her old suffering?

It is possible to let yourself be deceived by your own hopelessness and so let life drift. But it is also possible to insist upon what events have shown, upon the "truth that it was true within me and remains so." You can insist that what has once been remained, remained in the world. You can refuse to let yourself be distracted and see yourself as the unique

[5] Unprinted letter of August 26, 1807.
[6] Ibid.

preserver of what has been. That was a difficult and a rough course, for it did not permit you to choose what you wanted to preserve, what you wanted to transmit. Once you set out on that course, it inexorably compelled you to "love everything that *has ever been.*" It tethered one permanently to things past. It would then not be possible to take a single step forward which would not be darkened by the shadow of what had been. If you forgot nothing, it was as if your road was walled in by familiar things; and even the future, the unknown, would have a phantom familiarity to the person who already knew everything and was no longer inclined to be stunned by the sudden shock of things never yet seen. Moreover, every encounter with new people would be familiar, for you would have only known and familiar things to communicate to everybody.

Rahel had nothing more to learn, but she was compelled to repeat in words what she had learned. She could not communicate everything to a single person and then creep away from the society of human beings again. Might not this one person die, and then would not all her communications be lost? Could she keep a check on this one person to whom she had poured out her heart to make sure that her words were treasured and not betrayed? After all, she was not living in any fixed tradition; she had no position in the world of men which guaranteed her permanence. Therefore she had to tread the road to history, which was open to her only on the basis of her life story, again and again. Her only guarantee of permanence lay in herself; only if she succeeded in remaining as she was, in preserving what she had learned, only if she felt the old sorrows with each retelling, did she have any guarantee that she could continue to transmit anything. "I would have come . . . if I had not been physically . . . low; as a result of a single conversation . . . about love, about my love; which brought my condition so close to me, and me to it, that I felt pangs in the heart—physical ones; and envisioned abysses of which I will not speak here, and which for all I talked of them I did not begin to *outline.* This talk made me recognize my whole . . . illness: and proves and demonstrates to me that I would not survive anything similar again for a week without the grave, yawning grave; and gave me also a few answers, and the truth that it was true within me and remains so."

Neither Rahel's meager answers nor the existence of fellow sufferers had sufficed to assure her a kind of historical existence. Her attempt to communicate would have remained hopeless and altogether without direction if she had not found for herself a "mediator" to whom she could attach herself, whose words she could repeat. "Listen to Goethe," she advised her friend. "With tears I write the name of this mediator, in memory of my extreme distress. . . . Read [him] as one reads the Bible in misfortune." For "through all my life this poet infallibly accompanied me." All young people require such companionship and such guides to introduce them to life, to develop their personalities, to help them to discover the few great, simple things that matter. When Rahel was young and the first volume of *Wilhelm Meister* was published, she and her friends discussed at length whom she most resembled: Aurelie, unhappily in love with Lothario, or Philine, who irrepressibly found the appropriate phrase and the appropriate joke for every situation, who embodied that frivolity without which life could no more be borne than the novel itself if it had contained only Mignon and the harpist. Rahel had given up such speculations long ago. Only the young model themselves on characters out of books, because in life they are still seeking themselves. The person who has become emancipated from himself flees to the artist out of terror that everything he has learned may pass away; he flees to the model, to the representation in which there glows again and again what otherwise he can only dimly surmise.

That Rahel attached herself to the poet at all was due to her healthy determination, which no suffering could entirely shatter, to understand everything ultimately. "Vigorously and soundly, he put together for me what I broke to pieces, unhappiness and happiness, and what I obviously was unable to keep together." Goethe taught her the connection between happiness and unhappiness: that they did not simply fall from heaven upon the poor creature below, but rather that happiness and unhappiness existed only in a life which already possessed a certain coherence. In *Wilhelm Meister* happiness and unhappiness are formative elements; as a matter of fact, the unhappiness with Mariane in the First Book is what starts Meister out on his "education." Nothing could be more instructive and more comforting to Rahel than a life in which every event had a meaning, in which only comprehensible happenings took place, so that there remained scarcely any loophole through which the purely destructive elements, which compel a person to give up, can penetrate; a life in which even chance appeared in the guise of a "cultivated man" (Schlegel). How determined Rahel's search for clarity, insight and comprehensibility was is most clearly shown by her passionate protest against Goethe's *Wahlverwandtschaften.* "The subject matter . . . is repulsive to me. The cadaverousness of the end extends backward to the beginning, where one already begins to feel somewhat depressed in spirit. But I find Ottilie particularly repulsive—she with her one-sided headache, her dark relationship to nature, her lack of talent."

Rahel's life for the present had no history and was completely at the mercy of the destructive elements. She needed and utilized the example of another life and learned from it; learned that love, fear, hope, happiness and unhappiness, were not merely blind terrors, but that at a specific point, proceeding from a specific past and toward a specific future, they meant something which human beings could grasp. She owed it to Goethe that she possessed something tellable beyond the mere "answers"; otherwise, what she had to tell would have fragmented into the weariest of saws. Without Goethe she would have seen her life only from outside, in its phantom outlines. She would never have been able to establish a connection between it and the world to which she had to narrate it. "His riches gave me company; he has eternally been my sole and surest friend"; for in his works he was the sole person whom she had to love in such a way "that the measure is marked off not in me, but in him." He overwhelmed her with his greatness and forced her to bow to objective reality, not to seek originality aimlessly and immoderately. Because she understood Goethe, and understood herself only through him, he almost served her as a substitute for tradition. She professed him as a religion, kept "company" with him, let him introduce her to German history. He was "eternally my guarantor that I do not merely live fearfully among fleeting ghosts, my superior master, my most compassionate friend; of him I knew what hells he had looked into." He was the assurance that she was not a curiosity, that her unhappiness indicated something more than her being under an evil spell, that her solitude was not peopled only by phantoms. He shattered in her the inhuman clarity of outline and showed her the transitions and connections between her as a human being and all things human. She could refer to Aurelia and Mignon when she told about herself and her isolation. He had accompanied her from earliest youth to age: "In short, I grew up with him, and after a thousand separations I always found him again; he never failed me."

It was the great good fortune of Rahel's life that she found one person whom she trusted. It was her great opportunity to confide in history, in language. She realized that her individual experiences could be generalized without being falsified; in fact, that within these generalities her individuality was preserved, was destined for permanence. "My friend has expressed it for me this time, too," she said when she read the Prelude to *Faust*. Her knowledge, her sufferings, her joys, would die with her, but these verses would not die. And they would carry her with them into the future. And so it is: again and again that rhythm will carry us away, carry us along to the place where those who come after us, no matter what they are like, will learn what we know.

"Everything that Goethe shows is an essence." Poetry, that is, converts the individual matters of which it speaks into generalities because it not only employs language as a means for communicating a specific content, but converts language back into its original substance. The function of language is preservation; what it embodies is meant to remain, to remain longer than is possible for ephemeral human beings. Thus from the start the representation, being destined for permanence, is stripped of its singularity, becomes an essence.

The generalizing power of poetry is achieved only if it arises out of an ultimate and absolute precision in the use of words, if it takes every word seriously. Thus, for Rahel, "all of Goethe's words seem different as he uses them from the same words used by other people, words like hope, fidelity, fear, etc." Only in the wholly liberated purity of the poetic, in which all words are, as it were, spoken for the first time, can language become her friend, one to whom she is willing to entrust herself and her unprecedented life. Goethe provided her with the language she could speak. For as she read the poet's words, "just so my life seems to me. It always seems to me that in the true sense, in the sense torn from the bleeding, living heart, other people do nothing." Again and again his words freed her from the mute spell of mere happening. And her ability to speak provided her with an asylum in the world, taught her how to treat people, taught her to trust what she heard. She had Goethe to thank for her being able to speak.

She thanked him most of all for *Wilhelm Meister*. "The whole book is for me simply a growth, grown up around the kernel which appears in the book itself as a text and which reads: 'Oh, how strange that man is denied not only so much that is impossible, but also so much that is possible!' . . . And then this other thing: that every patch of earth, every river, everything, is taken from man. With a stroke of magic Goethe has preserved in this book the whole prosiness of our infamous little lives, and in addition twitted us nicely enough about it. He catches us and describes us at the moment we were clinging to these lives of ours; he bids the burgher who feels his wretchedness, and yet does not want to kill himself like Werther, to turn to the theater, to art, and to deceit also; just by the by, he shows the nobility as it is, good or bad, however it comes—the nobility whom the others vaguely picture as an arena—I cannot think of the right word at the moment—which they would like to attain. Then there remains the matter of love, and on that score the most concentrated commentary is the one I quoted; on that score the stories in the book move toward baseness and toward tragedy; people do not meet one another; prejudice parts them once they do meet—the harpist, Aurelia, and so on; and since man here on earth understands nothing because there is wanting in him that other half to which this mad game may belong, Meister and Goethe burst forth with the observation that the best we can possibly do on earth—what we think is the best—may also well be fettered to pilasters which rest upon other worlds which we do not know; meanwhile, however, men move about—and this is what he shows us in his book as if it were a mirror."

Wilhelm Meister was, for Rahel, not *the* German *Bildungsroman*. From it she did not learn the "art of existing" (Friedrich Schlegel), nor did she grasp that each of the characters paid "for his position by desiring to contribute to the forming of Wilhelm's mind and to promote his total education" (Schlegel). The development of the novel as a whole did not concern her very much, and she never paid attention to the contrast between Meister's life and her own—her own being not at all, of course, the story of her education. She scarcely gave thought to Meister's life itself: the opening up of a purer and richer world as the novel progresses, yet the characters of his old world never leaving him entirely, as though they seemed no longer of any importance; the connections between events and persons shown by forewarnings, secrets or attractions. She overlooked the way nothing ever sinks into ultimate darkness; that Meister's life is never entirely clouded over; that Mignon and the harpist alone remain, all through his apprentice years, in the same place, lending weight to the whole by their unchanging melancholy, thus proving that it is impossible to wrench entirely free from the past. And finally the mystery surrounding the harpist and Mignon is unraveled when dark horror and unknown pure longing threaten to shatter a brighter world. But Mignon's death leaves behind a "bottomless abyss of grief" which is not overcome by anything that follows.

In the whole novel, Rahel always saw either too little or too much. Either she saw only the relationships of the characters, Meister's parting from Mariane, Aurelia's love for Lothario; or she believed that the darkness hanging over every single book of the novel never brightened "since man here on earth understands nothing because there is wanting in him that other half to which this mad game may belong."

Nevertheless, she too thought the novel "the greatest spectacle of humanity" (Schlegel). Within its scheme the world was like a stage on which each person counted for what he could represent, on which each took the part that corresponded to his nature, and had to speak his lines accordingly. No one concealed anything deliberately except in order to say it at the right place and the right moment. Even the mystery surrounding Mignon and the harpist was not self-concealment but rather darkness itself, the darkness and the "wild grief" of one who does not know his past and therefore cannot communicate it. All other characters represent themselves; even Aurelia "is actress through and through, by character as well, even though she may represent and play nothing but herself"; "she makes a display of everything, including her femininity and her love" (Schlegel). Boundless frankness to the point of making a display of oneself was the only way to become "visible" for the burgher who was bidden to turn to "theater, art and deceit," who otherwise represented nothing. Thus, even in the "Confessions of a Beautiful Soul" there was the element of display, even though the "beautiful soul" had retired completely from the world: "Fundamentally, she too lives theatrically, but with the difference that she unites all the roles and that her inner self forms the stage upon which she is . . . actor and spectator simultaneously" (Schlegel).

Rahel acquired to the point of mastery the art of representing her own life: the point was not to tell the truth, but to display herself; not always to say the same thing to everyone, but to each what was appropriate for him. She learned that only as a specific person could one say something specific in such a way that it would be listened to, and she learned that "unhappiness without a title" was double unhappiness. The ambiguity which everyone else inherited by birth and along with his language, in which conventions were guaranteed—

the ambiguity, namely, of being not only a self, but also having a specific social quality, and of being not only a single person, but a person naturally intertwined with many others in the intricacies of social life; of existing simultaneously as mother and as child, as sister and as sweetheart, as citizen and as friend—this she had to learn. She had to learn the ambiguity which is at the same time politeness, the knack of not embarrassing anyone by what one is or what one knows. Originally there was "a lack of grace in me, so that I cannot assert myself."

Perhaps she had also learned from Mignon that the person must die who has lost all relationships and insists solely upon what is "for human beings unattainable," upon the "richness of alien worlds." That richness attracts everyone as the goal of pure longing and as an unfathomable abyss, because everyone, after all, "carries it around with himself"; yet in its mute purity it blasts all human relationships. Perhaps she had learned from the harpist that true and bottomless melancholy, the sadness of the person who has experienced too much for it to be worth his while to tell the story, strikes others merely as horrifying, for all that it may express his personal truth; that much as his madness may mean something, be a sign of something, he remains for other people merely a madman.

She had learned that the pure subjectivity which makes a point of "bearing a world within itself" is doomed because this inner world is never able to replace what is merely given to human beings. She had learned to despise the kind of pride which leads one to retire into oneself and which plumes itself on its ability to renounce; for pride is either empty and mendacious, or else it is outright hubris attempting to fortify itself by a kind of fanaticism; it is an effort "to sit in a cell with one's inner world" and to produce the "outer" world by thinking to oneself, by "inner" processes. "But he would be mad who could imagine something unsupported by reality, and not know that it is imagination."

She had learned that love could guarantee the whole of a human life only occasionally, that such love came only as an unpredictable stroke of fortune. And even then it could do so only if it transformed itself and ceased to be the "richness of alien worlds." She saw how Goethe in *Wilhelm Meister* "made all those die for whom love had been the whole of life, Sperata, Mariane, Mignon, Aurelie, the harpist." And it was a consolation to her to know that not only for her did every love end with the approach of death.

She had learned that anyone who went on living did not have the right to despise life, or merely to exploit it in order to shelter and protect the life of his soul. One had the right to say, "Life is not much," only at moments when one held it "in one's hand like a pea" and threw it away "with full consciousness." Life was much, was important enough so that it would be foolish not to fight for it; one had to rise in its defense, cling to it at any price. It would be the height of hubris to ignore an external world which was threatening to snatch away or destroy the life one lived only once. Such a ridiculously proud gesture of subjectivity with all its defenselessness before the external world had nothing to do with that ultimate consent which affirmed life as it was out of gratitude for the gift of life. To throw life away—"this is something anyone can do for a great price, or else precisely because there is no price. But to let oneself be robbed of it, deprived of it from minute to minute by an institution—a virtually sanctified one!—of human beings? And is Reason to bow its head and consent to it all, and appear in good burgher's clothes at the feasts which are prepared out of my life's essence?"

If she wanted to live, she had to learn to make her presence felt, to display herself; she had to unlearn her previous acceptance of the bareness and the sketchiness of her external existence as something final; she had to renounce originality and become one person among others. She had to prepare to occupy a higher social position. For as she was, of "infamous birth," people did not want to accept her. To go about with a Jewish name when she considered such a name a disgrace meant renunciation of "external existence," meant being eternally peculiar, meant having to prove herself by the possession of an exceptional inner life, meant never being able to pass unnoticed. At least she must try to normalize herself. Since she considered being a Jew a disgrace, remaining a Jew was nothing but defiance, and pride in her inner world, as if she were pointing out that her inner worth was so great that even being a Jew could not detract from it. Such defiant claims upon superior qualities of soul were, in all circumstances, always at the mercy of the spiteful indifference of the outer world. Indeed, "the more multifarious this inner world is, the greater the demands the outer one makes upon it, and every incongruity only disturbs it in more ways, more deeply, and offends against richer harmonies."

In order "to become another person outwardly" Rahel would have to cover the nakedness of Jewishness with, as it were, a dress—"as it is I do not forget this shame for a *single* second. I drink it in water, I drink it in wine, I drink it with the air; in every breath, that is. . . . The Jew must be extirpated from us, that is the sacred truth, and it must be done even if life were uprooted in the process." Full of illusions about the possibilities of the outer world, she imagined that disguises, camouflage, changes of name could exert a tremendous transforming power. Therefore she decided to follow the example of her brother Ludwig and call herself Rahel Robert. (All her brothers had assumed the same surname when they underwent baptism.) That was in the year 1810, four years before she, too, decided upon baptism and, following the custom of the times, changed her first name to Friederike. Not Rahel Levin but Friederike Robert—like a magic formula the new name was intended to help her become one human being among others.

7

ASSIMILATION
(1807–1808)

For Rahel it was too late to become one human being among others; the world had changed meanwhile, and people had deserted her. "At my 'tea table' . . . I sit with nothing but dictionaries; I serve tea no oftener than every week or ten days, when Schack, who has *not* deserted me, asks for some. That is how much everything has changed! Never have I been so alone. Absolutely. Never so completely and utterly bored." She wrote this early in 1808. The salon which had brought together people of all classes, in which a person could participate without having any social status at all, which had offered a haven for those who fitted in nowhere socially, had fallen victim to the disaster of 1806. The age of Frederick the Second, in which Jews could live, which gave "room for every plant in his sun-welcoming land," was over. Only now, in a time of breakdown, did Rahel realize that her life also was subject to general political conditions. "Until now I have lived under the auspices, in the strictest sense under the wings, of Frederick the Second. Every pleasure from outside, every good, every advantage, every acquaintance, I now see, can be ascribed to his influence: this has been shattered over my head: I feel it especially hard!" Her personal history might possibly link her privately with certain people, but she could find no way to escape from it and make herself part of the general public destiny. The unfortunate war had penetrated her consciousness no more than had the French Revolution or Napoleon. Events struck home only when she became aware that they were destroying her small personal world, the one world in which she had managed, in spite of everything, to live. "I have investigated it; what oppresses me is the world, which is in ferment and no longer, in my eyes, in flower; to it I have referred myself in my thoughts—that I now see. And its case and mine conjoin. And I lie here actually fallen, stunned."

The salon in which private things were given objectivity by being communicated, and in which public matters counted only insofar as they had private significance—this salon ceased to exist when the public world, the power of general misfortune, became so overwhelming that it could no longer be translated into private terms. Now personal matters were separated from the things that affected everyone; all that really remained to be communicated was pure gossip. The possibility of living without any social status, as "an imaginary Romantic person, one to whom one can give true *goût*," was now blocked off. Never again did Rahel succeed in becoming the actual center of a representative circle revolving solely around her own personality. Never was she able to forget the period which was now gone forever. "Where are our days, when we were all together!" she lamented as late as 1818. "They went under in the year '06. Went under like a ship: containing the loveliest goods of life, the loveliest pleasures."

It was not that the salons disappeared from the capital of Prussia. Rather, they now formed around persons of name and rank. The most noted were those of Privy State Councilor Stägemann, Countess Voss and Prince Radziwill, whom we met ten years before in Rahel's attic chamber. To these salons came Adam Müller, Heinrich von Kleist, Clemens Brentano, Archim von Arnim—the younger generation of Romanticists who had been born between 1780 and 1790. They were ten to twenty years younger than Rahel's circle, and from 1809 on determined the intellectual tone of Berlin society. It was significant that officialdom now came to the fore, right alongside of the hereditary landed nobility and the higher-ranking officers of the army. Hitherto, the bureaucratic class in Berlin had been unable to compete socially with the Jewish salons. These groups bore all the earmarks of patriotic secret societies; they were, moreover, in deliberate contrast to the indiscriminateness of the Jewish salons, highly exclusive. The members of this new type of thoroughly politicized social group were not content with mere salons; they sought a form which would keep the circle more closely knit. The first attempt in this direction was the *Zeltersche Liedertafel*, in which, however, everyone was "too serious for singing" (Humboldt). Out of the *Liedertafel* there sprang the *Christlich-Deutsche Tischgesellschaft*, founded by Arnim, a curious epicene creation in which Romantic and Prussian elements united in a brief marriage. The *Tischgesellschaft* had written bylaws and was a regular club. Numerically, the nobles were superior, but the Romanticists set the tone. The bylaws banned admittance of women, Frenchmen, philistines and Jews. For each of the meetings there was a fixed program: a serious patriotic story was read aloud; there followed a second reading in which the same story was told in a grotesque and farcical variation. The ironic attitude toward principles and the deliberate play on the same material is a plain mark of the Romantic element.

The nobles had been the first to admit the Jews to a degree of social equality, and it was among the nobles that systematic anti-Semitism first broke out. Social prejudices were taken up once more and intensified to the point of crass, brutal exclusion. It took the Prussian Jews a long while to realize the significance of the quiet disaster that had descended upon them. They, like their historians, were living at that time in a delirium of hope for political reforms, which finally came, bringing emancipation and civil liberation. Meanwhile, however, the nobility, and still more the "political Romanticists" who were in its employ and under its influence, rendered furious by Stein and Hardenberg's reforms, turned their entire fury against the Jews whose edict of emancipation was at this time being prepared.

"Jews, Frenchmen and philistines" were generally considered to be the representatives of the Enlightenment. Philistines, Brentano declared, despised "old festivals and sagas of the people, and whatever has grown gray with age in a few isolated places where such things are safe from modern insolence." "They call nature whatever falls within their circle of vision, or rather their square of vision, for they understand only square things. . . . A fine neighborhood, they say—all paved roads! They prefer Voltaire to Shakespeare, Wieland to Goethe, Rammler to Klopstock, Voss most of all." To France, the classic land of the Enlightenment and the political enemy of these patriotic Germans, the Jews owed the realization of equality of rights. That the arguments for civil equality had first been formulated as a program by Prussian officials (Mirabeau virtually copied Dohm), and that the social assimilation of the Jews had been begun by the representatives of the Prussian Enlightenment in "cultivated Berlin" (the representatives of the French Enlightenment were, with the one exception of Diderot, more or less hostile to the Jews) was little known or in any case not taken into consideration. What counted now was that these patriotic groups came together because they were intellectually against the Enlightenment, politically against France, and socially against the salons. The exclusion of women must be understood as a direct protest against the Jewish salons of the day; the same protest underlay the choice of the time for meetings, at lunch in contrast to afternoon or evening tea. This temporary union of Romanticism and Prussianism came to a natural end in the Wars of Liberation, for the Prussian nobles, and for the Romanticists in romantic conversions.

Rahel sought to escape from this new situation, which was isolating her, by flight. Later on she was to win great praise for patriotism, but it was by no means her first reaction to the downfall of her country. "There is peace and order here, and we feel the concern and the kindly treatment of our conqueror. I say this with truth, and this gives me confort." She did not become patriotic until she realized that otherwise she would be wholly isolated from people. As long as she did not know the reason, and saw only her solitude, she tried to strike up friendships with the French. Henri Campan, whom she met first when he was one of the French administrative officials of the Berlin occupation force, remained her friend. He was not the only one. At first she seemed to be unaware of the nationalist indignation, the rising chauvinism, which had gripped all her friends; she was suddenly so isolated that apparently she did not at first think of the possibility of such a reaction.

She diligently learned French, which to her represented the "European" language; she saw in Napoleon the representative of the Enlightenment, and in his wars and effortless victories the beginnings of a united Europe which would be broad enough to become for her, perhaps, a native land. She planned a trip to France, which she now thought of as synonymous with peace and breadth of vision. Her native land had never been Prussia in any case, but rather the protection and enlightened views of Frederick the Second.

These private concerns and personal adjustments had far more weight with her than the general climate of opinion all around her, which had long since become wholly patriotic. Many years later she was still capable of referring to her friends who had been killed in the war, Prince Louis Ferdinand and Alexander von der Marwitz, as victims of a "self-instilled delusion." Nevertheless, she soon began to be careful, and for many years she expressed such heretical opinions only in letters to her brothers, from whom she could count upon agreement.

This enthusiasm for Napoleon should not be misinterpreted as Jewish reaction. Rahel, like all those who wanted to escape from Judaism at any cost, did not hail Napoleon as liberator of the Jews or as the late heir of the French Revolution. Her initial departure from the opinions of her milieu could not be explained by saying that she had more urgent interests closer to her heart, or that she felt solidarity with the oppressed Jews—who were liberated in all the provinces conquered by the French. Demands for emancipation were raised only by those very few who were unwilling to pay the price of baptism for their "European entry ticket" (Heine), those who wanted to remain Jews even though it meant renouncing all political aspirations. These latter, who were active in cultural and reform associations, were in spite of appearances actually fighting for the preservation of Judaism. Rahel's contemporaries quite clearly understood one fact which was later proved true over several generations: that it would be incomparably more difficult to escape from a reformed Judaism than from orthodox Judaism; that associations for the assimilation of the Jews could lead ultimately to nothing but the preservation of Judaism in a form more suited to the times; not to the disappearance of the Jews into non-Jewish society but to the establishment of a Jewish group within the womb of society. Rahel was consistently opposed to all reformist trends, for she felt them as a menace to herself: "People like us cannot be Jews. I only hope that Jacobsohn [Israel Jacobsohn, leader of the Westphalian Jews] with all his money does not succeed in bringing about a Jewish reform here. I am afraid the vain fool will. . . ."

For her Napoleon was not (as he was for Israel Jacobsohn) the liberator of the Jews. He was simply the victor. "Napoleon has won, and I join the victor." Having lived so long under the protection of a great man, she now wanted only to turn to the "next great man." That was Napoleon. Under great men all subjects are equal, and one was not forced to choose any side. To be capable of choice it was not enough to love the country; your own past had to be identical with that of the country. "My history begins earlier than my life, and that is the case with everyone who understands his life." That statement of hers was proving its truth at that very moment, though certainly in an unexpected way.

But it was no longer possible to go on living in Germany without making a choice. Her isolation made that plain to her —and this isolation was now accentuated by a necessary separation from her family. "To leave one's family, to go away from the living beings to whom one has become so accustomed, without going somewhere else, is as unrespectable and crazy as it is sad. I do not have to run any errands or do any thinking for anyone except myself! Never, never, never, before have I been in such a situation." For she had fled back to the family at the time of Prussia's collapse; political disaster had momentarily wiped out the differences she had had with her family. Relationship alone had become a social bond. Now her plan to flee to Paris—to join Campan and her other new friends— failed; she had to remain in Berlin "alone in the strictest sense of the word, and without any hope, without a plan, with the profoundest insight, with the most wracked soul, without courage to take up any occupation." Hence she would have to try to find her way back into society, to assimilate, to become like the others. Once again she succeeded in arriving at a simple, obvious thing, a course imposed by circumstances, only by long and complicated detour through generalities. For all that her later patriotism may have seemed opportunistic, for all that it assumed parvenu forms, the fact remains that she reached it strictly by insight, reason, general convictions. It took the endeavors of no less a person than Fichte for her really to assimilate: "Fichte's hour, my sole comfort, my hope, my riches."

Rahel assimilated by way of Fichte's *Addresses to the German Nation*. Fichte himself expressly referred to these addresses as the continuation of his lectures in Berlin on the *Fundamental Principles of the Present Age*, in which three years before he had developed his philosophy of history. It may be safely assumed that Rahel was familiar with them. These lectures had no topical theme; in fact all topical references were strictly avoided since "no one is farther than the philosopher from the delusion that by his activities the age will perceptibly advance." Rather "time proceeds along its fixed course, which is determined by Eternity, and no single force can hasten or force anything within it" (*Fundamental Principles*). The course of history is *a priori* predetermined; it remains for the philosopher only to trace its laws. If he knows the fundamental laws, which are perceptible to him "without any instruction from history," he need not limit himself to delineating the past and judging the present, but he will also know—being a kind of *a priori* prophet—its future course. "The philosopher, who deals with history as a philosopher, pursues every *a priori* continuing thread of the world plan; that plan is clear to him without any history; and he does not use history to prove anything by it, for his dicta have been proved beforehand, independently of all history. Rather, his use of history is only for the purposes of elucidation; he demonstrates in history, in life as it is lived, that which is also comprehensible without benefit of history" (*Fundamental Principles*).

Man, then, can be so privy to the innermost nature of history that not even the future is concealed from him. Nevertheless, he is outwardly so fixed to his place in the "stream of time," bound so fast by the "*a priori* continuing threads of the world plan" that in practice there is no future at all in which he can meaningfully intervene. Fichte's resolution of this duality of the power and the impotence of man in history was, ultimately, highly unsatisfactory, but for the unsophisticated hearer he appeared to resolve it forthrightly enough. The *Addresses* called for some action to escape the catastrophe. They did not appeal, overtly or covertly, for rebellion against France, however. Rather, they made their point by envisioning far more spacious realms of the future. By means of a mighty educational plan, the next generation was to be trained for a wholly changed world. To be sure, Fichte nowhere expressly denied his original conception of *a priori* successive ages; nevertheless, in the *Addresses* the basic distinction is unequivocally plain: man has the power to translate his thinking into reality, to reshape the world according to plan, freely to create something historically new. As if he were determined to parody his own earlier theses, Fichte now argued in the *Addresses* that for the philosopher "history, and with it the human race, does not evolve according to the mysterious and strange law of a circular dance, but rather the true and proper human being makes it himself, not only by repeating what already has been, but acting creatively within time to shape something altogether new." In order to give men power to change the real world and yet not deprive man of his "fundamental impulse" toward the "aprioristic," Fichte distinguishes between the "already given and existing world, which, of course, can only be taken passively, as it happens to be," and the "world which is to come, an aprioristic world, one which will be in the future and will eternally remain future." Between the immutably given world and the world which needs no change because it is absolutely lawful and eternally in the future, there lies the human sphere whose worth or lack of worth depends on the "clear perception" of the *a priori*, eternally future world. The new age which Fichte called for was (according to the subdivision in the *Fundamental Principles*) the "epoch of rational science: the age in which truth will be recognized as supreme, and will be loved supremely." The schematic outline of five world epochs was tacitly taken over in the *Addresses* from the *Fundamental Principles*, only the epochs were reduced to three. Fichte eliminated the first epoch, the "rule of reason by instinct," which had occupied a special position in the earlier lectures, because it took place before all of history, and without freedom; for, he argued, the business of man and of his freedom was "not *being* rational but *becoming* rational" (*Addresses*). For the same reason he dropped the fifth epoch, "when mankind with a sure and infallible hand will form itself into an accurate image of Reason." Thus he avoided the "strange law of a circular dance," that "wizardry" through which the listener, to use a phrase of Schleiermacher's, "finds himself horribly transported among ghosts."

"Whoever believes in a fixed, permanent, and dead Being, believes in it only because he is dead in himself," Rahel learned from Fichte. Had she not, in bitterness, transformed the world to which she could not find admittance into such a "fixed, permanent, and dead Being"? Had she not, on that account alone, created for herself in the salon another, pleasant and living world in order to escape this "permanent dead Being," in order not to be under bondage as a "link in a chain," but instead to be "gripped directly by the truth"? The catastrophe of 1806 not only destroyed the ethereal, idyllic and illusory society of the salon, but above all showed the fragility of that other fixed, permanent world in which it had been possible for one to live only as a "link in a chain." Perhaps, therefore, the breakdown of the old world would provide Rahel with a chance to enter a new one, in spite of the fact that the narrow fringe of private life which the old world had left inviolate was carried along and destroyed in the general disaster. The old world had been shattered, and Fichte was a "comfort and hope" to Rahel because he desired to exclude all tradition from the reconstruction of a new world. According to him, the coming generation ought to be separated from the still living older generation, protected during its education from the corrupt influence of the latter. Fichte called for the destruction of the natural relationship which underlies the historical continuum, namely, the succession of the generations. The pillars of the new world were to be the whole nation rather than a class privileged by birth and by history. Not "dark feeling" but "clear understanding" (Fichte) was to be made the true basis and starting point of a new social order.

Perhaps in this new world everyone would be welcome. After all, anyone could acquire clear understanding; anyone could participate in the future if its basis was to be "the governed, the citizens" (Fichte). Belonging, in fact, was promised precisely to the person who had "annihilated" himself as a "sensuous individual" (Fichte), in his sensuous specificity, with a particular origin and a particular situation in the world. The historical community of the future would be determined not by individuals, but by "us as a commonality in which the individual person is absorbed by the concept of the whole, is absolutely forgotten in a unity of thought" (*Addresses*).

To belong to the new community, then, Rahel needed only to annihilate herself and her origin, her "sensuous" existence—which for many reasons she had been trying to do for a long time. As she had written to her brother, "the Jew must be extirpated from us; that is the sacred truth, and it must be done even if life were uprooted in the process." If she annihilated herself in her sensuous individuality, she would only be affirming life, which in any case had never shown the slightest consideration for her concrete, sensuous specificity. It would be pure gain for her to receive gratis a history whose past could be grasped *a priori*, whose future could be shaped by pure thought. The separation of the coming generation from the existing civil order, which Fichte had called for—was this not equivalent to establishing precisely the kind of isolation in which Rahel had always lived? Under these circumstances, her "disgrace," not having any status, would then become a privilege.

"What else *can* human beings place above the human mind, since after all it is through the mind alone that we understand everything." That the outsider can understand history and the world without benefit of tradition, and without the natural self-assurance of social status, is more than merely a triumph for him. It is the only possible way he can bind himself to the world. Rahel learned from Fichte the willingness to understand; she learned from him to avoid the pariah's arrogant conceit in exceptionally profound experiences and emotions. To have learned these lessons was so important for her that it did not matter if, ultimately, she took over from him nothing but an empty pattern which could be used to comprehend everything or nothing. Her new patriotism, which so often had embarrassing overtones, was nothing but a premature conclusion which she derived from Fichte under the oppressive force of circumstances. She had to establish herself somehow in the new societal situation. Or at least try to do so, for she did not succeed until the wars of 1813. Patriotic anti-Semitism, to which Fichte too was not averse, poisoned all relationships between Jews and non-Jews. Social and class prejudices formed along new lines while the nobles, on the basis of their very political and economic defeats, were trumpeting their old social pretensions with the greatest success—and receiving support, on the whole, from the patriotic intelligentsia. Rahel's newfound patriotism faded swiftly since, as it turned out, it did not help to break through her isolation. She had missed the chance to re-establish social ties because, in general, the Jews were unable to enter society until the new war began.

She spent the years of the war, 1813–14, mostly in Prague, and there she recalled her patriotic emotions again. The war which had driven her to a foreign land erased social differences to some extent. In Prague she found, for the first time in her life, a definite occupation—she cared for wounded soldiers, provided quarters for them, raised funds. There her patriotism had a meaning, even though her accounts of her own fervor do sound childish. There, for the first time, she really belonged, was really a German woman, and enjoyed a certain prestige for doing what she was permitted to do.

8

DAY AND NIGHT

SINCE Rahel in spite of all her efforts could form no social ties, since her inclinations toward assimilation remained entirely suspended in an unpeopled vacuum, she was unable to become one human being among others. What should she do about her inability to forget Urquijo? No need to forget what had happened to her, neither the magic nor the rejection; but she had to be able to forget *him*. She must be able to remain calm when she saw him, must rely upon her disillusionment, upon the unmasking of him that came with her perception that she could detect "envy in his nose," and "between eye and mouth, running down the cheeks, the uncertainty of his opinions." She must be able not to succumb to his voice, but rather to hear in his speech "the vagueness and lack of cultivation." She must be certain that her senses behaved rationally. Instead, her senses were disloyal to her; they conjured up his image when he was not present because it was and remained true that in him she had "found the image for her senses," and that for that reason she "cast her heart to him forever." Her senses and heart had grown disloyal, betrayed her and her understanding which in spite of everything governed her days and determined their rhythm. If she did not want to lose her dominance over her daily life, she must deceive that daily life, deceive the others, deceive herself, so that in the end nobody, neither herself nor any of her friends would know "what the state of my soul is like; whatever I say is a lie, without my fault." She could no longer trust her opinions because she had lost herself. But whether lies or truth, whatever she said determined her daily life, forced it into a specific pattern of unanimity and unambiguity in its living continuance. The other element, which she concealed by a vague silence, did not have to concern anyone, because it was "unspeakable"; it was no one's business even though she knew that it was the "essential" thing. The shame which was ashamed to name the ultimate misfortune must not be breached; it was the sole protection her life had. Others, and Rahel herself, had no business being concerned with anything but the events of the day. Only "happiness or death," so she declared, could "open my mouth." Happiness because it rendered unhappiness historical, reduced unhappiness to the triviality of an era over and done with. Death because then continuance no longer mattered and shame consequently lost all meaning.

Unhappiness does not entirely disappear, even though it is concealed; daily life and the will to lie have no power over its mute lament. Unhappiness, banished from the day, flees into the night where it rages unchecked, even though it cannot affect the day. Then the night ceases to offer its necessary protection from the unbearable glare and fullness of the day, no longer brings the neutral comfort of unvarying darkness nor the featureless peace of what is put into the past, of what is over and done with; then the night, ordinarily so vast that it makes mock of the strivings of the day, narrows, contracts into a tightly sealed container of despair. It is terrible when the night, coerced by the force of a specific unhappiness, engenders a specific parallel; when the past becomes a specific past event which once filled the day and took refuge in the night only when it was expelled from the day, and which now peoples the darkness of the night with phantoms of the day. It is terrible when something that was once of the day assumes the featurelessness and eternal repetitiousness of the night. Terrible when peace is transformed into consuming, hopeless yearning.

We might possibly still escape the mute and consuming lament of night if the specific parallel did not also press forward into sleep, manifest itself in dreams which assail the waker in the shape of memories, and which he cannot blanket by the activities of the day, because they repeat themselves. Ultimately, then, night and sleep become identical with certain dreams whose meaning penetrates into the day, and which the day recognizes from days past. The duality of day and night, the salutary division of life into the specific and the general, becomes ambiguity when night turns into a specific night, when dreams insist, with monotonous repetitiousness, upon certain contents, darkening the day with excessively distinct shadow images, troubling its occupations, and again and again reverting to things past without the clarity of memory.

Rahel dreamed the following dream for ten years; it came for the first time during her engagement with Finckenstein. As long as everything went well with Urquijo, she was free of it; after the break it returned, characteristically altered, but with the same dream landscape. She wrote down this dream, as well as the following dreams, only after she had ceased dreaming. The dream was:

"I always found myself in a splendid, inhabited palace, with a magnificent garden beginning right outside of the windows, a fair-sized terrace in front of the building, and then linden and chestnut trees of equal height on an almost irregular plaza which led to walks, ponds, tree-lined paths, and the usual appurtenances of such gardens. The rooms in the building were always illuminated, open, and filled with the movements of a large number of servants; I always saw a long vista of them opened before me, in the last of which was the actual assemblage of the most distinguished persons; however, I could not imagine a single one of these people, although I knew them all, belonged to them, and was supposed to join them. But this, in spite of the fact that the doors were open and I could see their backs—lined up at a large gaming table—like a bench—I was never able to do. I was prevented by an incapacity, a paralysis, which seemed to be in the atmosphere of the rooms and in the illumination. I never conceived this obstacle as a whole, and merely thought each time that I was hindered by different chance circumstances, and each time I also thought that I would reach my society. But every time, whenever I was still six or eight rooms away from it, there appeared, in the room in which I was, an animal that I could not name, because its like did not exist in the world; of the size of a sheep, though rather thinner than sheep usually are, pure and white as untouched snow; half sheep, half goat, with a sort of angora pelt; pinkish snout like the purest, most delightful marble—the color of dawn—the paws likewise.

"This animal was my acquaintance. I did not know why, but it loved me *tremendously,* and knew how to tell me and show me that it did; I had to treat it like a human being. It pressed my hands with its paws, and every time it did that it touched me to the heart; and it looked at me with more love than I ever remember seeing in any human being's eye. Most commonly, it took me by the hand, and since I kept wanting to reach the company, we walked together through the rooms, without ever getting there; the animal tried to keep me from going, but tenderly, and as though it had an important reason; but because I always wanted to get there, it always went along, compelled by its love. Quite frequently in the queerest manner, namely with its paws down to the second joint sinking through the floorboards, through which I too could see down to another story, and yet these floorboards were solid; sometimes I also went that way with the animal, now on the ground floor, now one flight up, but generally down below. The servants paid no attention to us, although they saw us.

"I called this loving darling my pet; and whenever I was there I asked for it, for it wielded a great power over me and I do not recall having felt during my whole waking life so powerful a stirring of the senses as the mere touching of hands which this animal gave me. But it was not this alone which defined my attachment; it was also an overflowing of the heart in sympathy; and that I alone knew that the animal could love and speak and had a human soul. But especially I was held by something secret, which consisted partly in that no one saw my animal or noticed it except myself, that it turned to no one else, that it seemed to be concealing a profound, highly significant secret, and that I did not in the slightest know where it stayed or went when I was not there to see it. But none of these things alienated or disturbed me even to the point of questioning myself; and on the whole I was captivated by the animal's love—and its apparent suffering from that love—and by the fact that my mere presence would make it so supernally happy, which it was always eager to show me. Only sometimes, when I was leading it by the hand in that way, and pressed its hand again with deep tenderness, and we looked into each other's eyes, I was suddenly startled by the thought: How can you give such caresses to an animal; after all, it is an animal! But nothing changed; these scenes were repeated again and again, with small variations: namely, in new dreams all the time, in the same place.

"The time came, however, when I had not had this dream for a long while; and when I again dreamed it, there it all was again: the castle, the rooms, the servants, the garden, the company; I again wanted to join them; only this time there was somewhat more movement, and a kind of excitement in the rooms, though without any particular disturbance or disorder; I also did not see my animal—which, it seemed to me, I had already missed for a long time without being especially concerned or troubled, although I had spoken about the matter with the servants of the house. Because the restive movement disturbed me even more than the usual force which had prevented me from entering the last room, I stepped *de plein pied* through large French doors on to the terrace which soon merged into the plaza with trees, without any boundary between; there, between the old trees, bright lanterns on tall posts were lit; I regarded in a leisurely way the illuminated windows of the palace and the brilliantly lit-up foliage of the trees; the servants trotted back and forth more busily and frequently than usual; they paid no attention to me, nor I to them. Suddenly I see, close by the trunk of a large tree, half on top of its stout root, my animal, curled up with head hidden, sleeping on its belly: it was quite black with bristly hair. My animal! My animal is back, I shout to the servants who pause, with utensils in their hands and napkins over their shoulders. They pause in their activities, but do not come any closer. It is asleep, I say; and poke it with my toes in order to shake it up a bit: at that moment, however, it rolls over, falls apart, and lies flat, a mere skin; the rough side on the ground, dry and clean. 'It is a skin; so it was dead!' I exclaim.

The dream vanishes; and never again have I dreamed of the black or the white animal."

To this dream she herself added the interpretation: "At this time I knew Finckenstein, who was extremely straw-blond; afterwards Urquijo who was brown . . . almost black; if I were to interpret the dream, which at the time I did not do: he was bristly toward me, and I found no heart in him." [1]

The torment of such dreams does not lie in the clarity of their interpretation. What, after all, can a dream make clear but something that the day clarifies anyhow? That Rahel always found herself in a world more distinguished than the one in which she belonged, but which always turned its back to her or permitted her only to peer through cracks. That her lovers had only kept her farther removed from the great world, prevented her from entering it. That in the eyes of society her lovers, whom she had always tried to introduce into her society, were mere "animals," but for that very reason of tremendous importance to her—namely, gifted with human voice and as animals therefore representing the natural in contrast to the social, and hence what was essentially human. Finally, her own interpretation says the decisive word. What was tormenting was only the insistency of the dream, its repetition, its refusal to let her alone; intolerable the precise representationalism of the dream, its fundamentally unsymbolic landscape, and its shattering of the symbolic character of the animal, replacing symbolism with a ghostly realism. Intolerable, finally, the explicitness and clarity of a world which was not provided for in the day, which, moreover, not only symbolized the day, but also—by virtue of the powerful repetition and precision of the dreamworld—strove to replace the day and destroy it utterly. She did not dream continuance of the day, so that the next day would bring her the certainty of a logical consequence or of an answer—as when she dreamed that everybody had found the ideal, and then she recognized that this ideal was a living person who could not restrain his laughter, and announced this fact to him, whereupon he put

[1] The interpretation of the dream published in *Buch des Andenkens*, II, 52 in the posthumous papers of the Varnhagen Collection.

his arms around her, danced with her and everyone else stepped back.[2] Nor did she dream only the shadows of the day, the things that clouded it or were concealed by it. Such dreams, too, banish the peace of the night because they extend the day endlessly; but they can do no harm to the day.

She wrote down two such dreams, far more innocuous in spite of the incomparably more frightful overt content, because they were only dream-continuations of the day. One of them dealt with Finckenstein, the other with Urquijo. This is the first:

"In this dream I found myself upon the outermost bulwark of a very considerable fortress which extended in a broad, flat, sandy plain far out beyond the town. It was bright noon, and the weather on this day was characterized by those too bright shafts of the sun which produce a kind of despair because there is nothing refreshing about them; they pierce their way through no bracing air, nor fall upon any objects that might cast reassuring green shadows. This weather affected me all the more because the whole region consisted of parched, grass-less, sandstony earth which deteriorated into actual sand; bumpy and uneven, like the look of places where gravel is dug. This overbright sunshine, which made everything else overbright, irritated my eyes and ears excessively, and worried me in a peculiar manner. There was nothing to be seen on the accursed plain; and the impression was as if the sun were hastening through, angry because it could not entirely pass by this insignificant place! So I stood with my breast close to the edge of this old rampart—for it was in poor condition, like so much round about—pressed by a whole mob behind me. These people were all dressed like Athenians. F. stood beside me, bareheaded, dressed like the rest, but in pink taffeta, without looking in the slightest degree ridiculous. I was to be thrown down from this rampart, which was the last of the entire fortress; deep down, among stones, chalky sand pits, rubble and broken-off fragments of the fortress. The mob was demanding it, and shouting to F., who was their king, to give his consent.

2 This is the second of the five dreams in her diary of July 1812, *Buch des Andenkens*, II, 49; Varnhagen did not publish it.

He stood there cruelly sullen, and looked down into the depths; the people shouted louder and more violently, insisting that he consent; pressed closer and closer to me; with their eyes on F. gripped my clothes; I tried to look into his eyes, and kept shouting: 'You won't say yes, will you?' He stood unmoving, ashamed before the people for not yet having consented. The people were shouting too, and he—'Yes!' he said. They seized me, threw me over the wall; I fell from stone to stone, and as I was about to fall into the ultimate pit, I awoke.

"And I knew in the depths of my soul what F.'s attitude toward me was. Moreover, the dream gave me the complete impression of the story's having been true; I was silent, but I had not been mistaken."

This dream, which apparently was not repeated, could be carried over into the day without harm; it merely explained something that belonged to the day, something that was in any case reality: that Finckenstein simply sacrificed her—who was already driven by fate to the brink of the abyss in any case—to the people, to public opinion, to his family. Not that Finckenstein had pressed her to the verge in the first place; it merely lay within his power to push her over. She knew all that anyway, without benefit of dream symbolism. Therefore the dream was not repeated; it had no independent force of its own.

In the other dream of the same sort, which dealt with Urquijo, she simply dreamed that she killed him in rage. But when he actually began dying, she tried to make him well again by kisses. It was no use. She suffered such anxiety that she felt on the point of death herself, so that she awoke. "So *that* is the way you think of him? I said to myself that night. You must forgive him everything. You have forgiven him everything." Then she fell asleep again and went on dreaming that he actually did die. Once more she was seized by anxiety: "It was certain (as life or something of the sort) that as soon as he died, I would die with him. And I constantly thought: so this is his and my end; this is the way we are dying; this is our death; so you have killed him after all, for you are dying with him!"

This dream, too, belonged to the day. What the day ultimately preserved of the dream was not a consequence or an insight, but the tormenting question: why had she not actually killed him? She would have paid with her life. "Believe me, that is the way I am. But what, in actual life, keeps me from acting this way, I do not know precisely, I do not know how to name it."

This night (and that is why she wrote of it) made her realize that she had banished from the day everything that really concerned her, everything that she basically desired; she saw that she was paying during the nights for having remained alive. Because she had never done any of the things she might have wanted to do, such a dream pursued her for years after she had parted from Urquijo and made everything gained during the days appear illusory. The repetition which she believed she had already expelled from her life, when it became "historical" for her, went on playing its old game at night, grotesquely transformed into the insistency of the identical, or mockingly inviting the attempt to retrieve the irretrievable. What use was the day's constant urging of gratitude for life's being understandable, if the night insisted upon life's incomprehensibility and persistently provided, in a succession of unvarying and specific images, a whole nexus of incomprehensibilities and impenetrabilities? What use was the day when a "whole enchanted heart's existence" made the night seem more important than the day? What use was all insight when the "other land" of night forever presented opaque riddles and again and again conjured up delusory visions of "freedom, truth, unity, native soil?"

What use was it to be brave and taciturn, to deny the ultimate burden and the profoundest unhappiness, to be proud, too proud to let even oneself share the secret, if the night nevertheless revealed everything; if the night refused to keep silence, refused to fulfill its function of providing merely a dark, lulling background for the wearied soul; if the night absorbed into its darkness what was concealed by day, what was merely a shadowing and obscuring by day; if it deceptively transformed these shadows into life's ground and native soil.

Rahel dreamed:

"I lay on a wide bed, covered with a gray blanket. On the same bed opposite me, without touching me, feet also under the blanket, somewhat to my right, lay Bettina Brentano, and in Bettina's direction, to her right but to my left, the Mother of God. Whose face, however, I could not see at all distinctly; in fact, over everything visible there seemed to lie an extremely fine, very thin gray cloud, which, however, did not hinder seeing—only everything was seen as a kind of mist. At the same time it seemed to me as if the Mother of God had the face of Schleiermacher's wife. We were on the edge of the world. Close on the right, beside the bed, a large strip of earth fairly far down under us could be seen, something like a very big highway; on it microscopic human beings ran back and forth, performing the world's work; I only glanced at this cursorily, as if it were something very well known. We were the maids of the earth and no longer living; or rather we had departed from life—though without surprise for me or sadness or thoughts of death—and I had an obscure knowledge that we were to go to a certain place; but our business on this bed, our occupation namely, was to ask each other what we had suffered—a kind of confessional! 'Do you know mortification?' we asked each other, for instance. And if we had ever felt this particular form of suffering in our lives, we said: 'Yes that I know,' with a loud cry of grief, and the particular form of suffering we were speaking of was rent from the heart, the pain multiplied a hundredfold: but then we were rid of it forever and felt wholly sound and light. The Mother of God was quiet all the while, only said Yes! to each question, and also wept. Bettina asked: 'Do you know the suffering of love?' Whimpering and almost howling, I exclaimed, while the tears streamed and I held a handkerchief over my face, a long, long Yes! 'Do you know mortification?' Yes! again yes. 'Do you know enduring wrong, injustice?' Yes! 'Do you know murdered youth?' Yes! I whimper again in a long-drawn-out tone, dissolving in tears. We were finished, our hearts pure, but mine was still filled with the heavy burden of earth; I sit up, look excitedly at the other women, and want my burden taken from me; in words spoken thickly, but with extreme distinctness, because I want to receive the answer Yes to this question too, I ask: 'Do you two know—disgrace?' Both shrink away from me as if in horror, though with still something of pity in their gesture; they glance rapidly at one another and try, in spite of the confined space, to move away from me. In a state bordering on madness I scream: 'I have not *done* anything. It's nothing I have *done*. I have not *done* anything. I am innocent!' The women believe me; I see that by the rigid way they lie still, no longer unwillingly, but they no longer understand me. 'Woe,' I cry out, weeping as if my heart were threatening to melt away, 'they do not understand me either. Never, then! *This* burden I must keep; I knew *that*. Forever! *Merciful* God! Woe!' Utterly beside myself, I hastened my awakening.

"And even awake the burden remains with me, for I really bear it, and if only there could possibly be persons who would wholly understand it, I too would be relieved."

Never again and nowhere else had Rahel expressed so brutally, so utterly without adornment, the thing that hopelessly separated her from others, as she did in this dream, which she related to Alexander von der Marwitz.[3]

Only the night, only the despair which had taken refuge in the night revealed in its depths what the day had tried to circumvent, to improve, or to distract her attention from. In the definitiveness and the supreme generality of the dream it was impossible to divide day from night, to unravel the tangle of truth and lie, to tell native soil from alien ground, to distinguish confession from concealment. Night and dream confirmed and reproduced what day glossed over or hid. The dream stopped at nothing, exposed the naked phenomena and did not mind their incomprehensibility. With ease it conquered the will which was reluctant to accept what it could not understand or could not change. It dragged all hidden things into the light.

[3] An abbreviated account written down immediately after Rahel's oral narration is to be found among Alexander von der Marwitz's papers. A copy in Varnhagen's hand was in the Varnhagen Collection.

But night's confirmations were deceptive, for they deceptively pretended that the burden of the day was the basis of the whole life. The day tended by nature to conceal, but still in the end it would accept the truth of the night—"for I really bear it"; indeed, the day could be induced to speak out—"if only there could possibly be persons who would wholly understand it, I too would be relieved." The more the day had hidden, the more defenseless it was against the deceptions of the night which in spite of being deceptive still revealed truths.

Thus the continuity of the day was constantly challenged by the night and the night's mute, stupid lingering over what was long since past or successfully concealed. Thus it came about that everything subsequently took on the color of ambiguity, of a barely conscious, by no means desired ambiguity. Recurrent dreams, nights which had specific testimony to give, would certainly not conjure up a life continuity of their own. But when a dream landscape has become known and familiar, it is easy to let oneself be drawn into it, as though there existed alongside the clear reality of the day a second land in which one would establish oneself comfortably. Once consciousness is clouded, once it is no longer so certain that only one single world accompanies and surrounds us from birth to death, ambiguity enters of its own accord, like twilight in the interval between day and night. The disgrace which no man and no God can remove, is by day an obsessional idea. Moving on, assimilation, learning history, are at night a comically hopeless game. When such a gulf yawns, only ambiguity points a permanent way out, by taking neither extreme seriously and engendering, in the twilight in which both extremes are mixed, resignation and new strength.

9

THE BEGGAR BY THE WAYSIDE
(1808–1809)

In the spring of 1808 Rahel met August Varnhagen in Berlin and a few months later became his mistress. It was typical of the suddenly altered mores of the day that only two persons knew of this, whereas her affair with Urquijo had been the talk of the city; it was likewise typical, however, that when she admitted it, she added: "I would be ashamed to deny it; I cannot deny it to decent people."[1] In Rahel's acquaintance, apparently, the number of "decent people" had dropped to two.

Varnhagen, born in 1785 and thus fourteen years younger than Rahel, was one of the students whom Napoleon had driven from the University of Halle. There, in his eagerness to acquire culture, he had from the first neglected his official study of medicine. Equipped with some knowledge of philosophy and some of literature, he had already fallen in with literati before he met Rahel, and together with Chamisso had published a literary almanac which had such bad reviews that it soon folded. There followed the publication of a satirical novel written together with his friend Neumann. From these works of his youth it is evident that Varnhagen would in any case have made a good journalist, if the type had existed in his day.

Born in the Rhineland, his mother a Protestant Alsatian, Varnhagen had been raised as a freethinker by his father, who was a Catholic altogether out of touch with the church. In Düsseldorf, his birthplace, his father had a thriving medical practice which he subsequently abandoned in order to move

[1] From her letter to Varnhagen of September 24, 1808. Omitted in the original edition. See *Rahel Varnhagen. Ein Frauenleben*, edited by A. Welder-Steinberg, 1917, pp. 35–36.

to Strasbourg, then in Revolutionary France. For him and for his son, whom he took with him, this move marked the beginning of decades of a wandering life; he lived almost constantly separated from his wife and daughter. He left Strasbourg again because he was a freethinker only in religion; politically legitimist, he was repelled by the radicalism of the Revolutionists and outraged by the beheading of the king. Since he feared that unrest would spread to Alsace, he returned to Düsseldorf, whence he was promptly deported as having been an adherent of the French Revolution. After numerous moves he finally landed in Hamburg in 1794 and sent for wife and children. A few years after settling down in Hamburg, he died, leaving behind an almost impoverished family. August Varnhagen had at this time just turned sixteen.

A friend of the father's befriended the boy and sent him to the Pépinière in Berlin to study medicine. These studies, the first and last regular learning he pursued, lasted only for a few years and were never concluded. At a very early age he began drifting rather aimlessly from subject to subject, his studying constantly interrupted by literary productions. He wrote poems because Adalbert von Chamisso was his friend; he became enthusiastic about medicine because he met young Johann Ferdinand Koreff, who was soon to become one of the most famous physicians of the age, and who introduced him to nature philosophy. His intellectual vagabondage acquired a kind of system after he went to Halle, where Friedrich Schleiermacher, the classical philologist Friedrich August Wolf, the nature philosopher Henrik Steffens and the general atmosphere of student life provided some content for his craving for culture. Here for the first time he was really content with his life. He even thought of completing his medical studies, in order to have a means of livelihood. The war of 1806–07 destroyed the university life at Halle, however; both professors and students were banished from the city. Schleiermacher and Wolf went to Berlin. There was as yet no university there; the professors merely gave courses which Varnhagen, too, attended. Under such circumstances a definite studious milieu did not take shape, and Varnhagen soon gave up the plan to resume his studies and turned again to his old literary and social life. In this way he met Rahel, whose salon, however, no longer existed. He came to her at the time of her greatest isolation. "At my tea table I sit with nothing but dictionaries; I serve tea no oftener than every week or ten days. . . . Never have I been so alone. Absolutely. Never so completely and utterly bored. . . . In the winter, and in the summer too for a while, I knew a few Frenchmen. . . . They are all gone. My German friends—how long it is since I have seen them; as if they were dead, scattered!"

Varnhagen's poems were bad, his novel not only amateurish but outrightly tasteless, his philosophical observations altogether without originality or depth, his culture far too scattered, far too dependent upon the divergent opinions of others under whose spell he would fall for a while, for him to be considered a cultivated person. Since no one liked him for very long, he was vain. But he had no real craving to be liked; he merely prolonged artificially the attachments he could not retain because for all his pliability he was possessed of a certain stubborn clinging to principles, and because he had no ability to sense the climate of his surroundings; he saw all relationships sharply, in terms of well-defined alternatives. Nevertheless he had one great advantage: he was highly teachable; he strove to understand because he was rational.

He described himself splendidly: "My soul came into the world in extreme poverty; whereas others in this earthly society have been given a stake to start with, or at any rate can be given it at any time, I have had to draw timidly back from the game. All is emptiness in me, real emptiness most of the time; I do not produce thoughts, nor figures; I can neither represent relationships as a system nor endow the elements with individual life in the form of wit; no springs bubble forth in me! . . . But in this total vacuity I am always open; a ray of sunlight, a movement, an aspect of beauty or even only of strength, will not escape me; I only wait for something to happen; I am a *beggar by the wayside*."

Rahel confided her life to the beggarly curiosity of this man, who listened to it with avid interest, never again forgot a single detail, made it his own. Varnhagen knew how to seize all the advantages of a "beggar by the wayside." Who knows better what is happening, what is passing by, than one who waits by the wayside and is himself never entangled? He called himself "incapable of a great passion"; and in fact he was wholly amorphous of himself, ready to become everything, to let anything be made of himself. He was without any impulses at all, overwhelmed by every minute, if only it brought him something; he was also prepared to remain somehow faithful to such moments, although rather out of habit and in order to achieve mastery over time until the next "love moment." There was nothing in the world to set limits to his vagueness. He was nothing and had nothing; early uprooted from his parental home, he was without family and without talent. Living a life of his own was impossible for him; moreover, he did not want to give up his place as a beggar, for that was his sole unquestionable advantage: to see more, to learn more than others. Yet what he seized, what he saw, was never a whole; he collected nothing but details, features, anecdotes. Rahel became the great opportunity of his life because she voluntarily placed something whole in his hands. Her life became *the* anecdote on which he fed all his life. That he ultimately degraded her life to an anecdote, that he praised her for her qualities, her kindliness, her cleverness; that he admired her passions, her wit, her capacity for love; that he lamented her unhappiness, her solitude; in short, that at bottom he saw her only as a tremendous curiosity—was the fundamental misunderstanding of his "priestly fidelity" (Varnhagen).

The beggar by the wayside was no one; he was *sans* name, *sans* history and *sans* face. He was *the* Unknown stranger. It is possible really to speak out only to the unknown stranger, since with such a one the risk of self-exposure does not exist. Since the unknown is not identifiable, the speaker himself gradually loses his identity, his name, his face, everything the other person is unaware of and does not need to know. What remains is only the story, the pure narrative. Every acquaintance, every "known" person whom one encounters here and there, with whom one is related by various ties, will ignore the story and concentrate upon the speaker, fascinated by the opportunity of getting to know thoroughly another human being. Instead of taking in the story he is being told, he will grasp at the qualities he believes the story reveals. And once a person is endowed with qualities he is no longer unique; qualities we share with everybody. It is better to be only an anecdote than to be a person with qualities.

One who stands by the wayside cannot forget anything, for there is nothing in his life which demands that he forget for its sake. One thing is certain: he will always remain by the wayside, for he would die if he did not receive sustenance from outside himself. On the other hand, it may happen that, in the course of his career of beggar, he is given so much by one person that he need no longer ask anything of others; such a gift guarantees him security. In gratitude he will gladly desist from his begging, will accommodate himself to the gift as if he were just as rich and full of life as others. Thus, the present of another's life, of experiences he never had, which could never make him either happy or unhappy, served Varnhagen as a complete surrogate for a life of his own.

Rahel gave him everything she had, all her diaries, all her letters, whatever copies of letters to Finckenstein she had, the letters she had demanded back from Urquijo. She also gave him the letters of others which she had kept. Only a few months after they met Varnhagen boasted to Jean Paul that he possessed three thousand letters of hers. These letters became the landscape of his life. They did not provide him with experiences, did not tell him what life was like, did not give him any basis for generalizations. But they created for him a specific psychological milieu. "And although I can never attain to the celestial vault, which like nobility takes men fully into its embrace only at birth or not at all, at your side I shall nevertheless wander about in high forests and upon mountains whose desolation holds none of the terrors of the desolate open plains round about" (Varnhagen). The beggar by the wayside can be consoled for his poverty if the gift is great enough to last a whole life. The man to whom destiny never came, who had known neither unhappiness nor happiness, who was always left in the lurch by human beings and had apparently been condemned to live in the "desolate open plains round about" was comforted by the breath of another's life, which blew by him and touched him "with secret caress." If he were permitted to live beside Rahel, to "see her see" and "hear her speak," life itself seemed to be bending toward him with kindly intent, life itself seemed "enough for me."

The beggar, finding himself denied that life which man can only live from birth to death, which only becomes comprehensible through experience, whose general nature can be perceived only in day to day continuity—denied this which ought to be everyone's privilege, and yet, able to look on "curious and comforted," because at last he possesses something whole rather than scattered particulars, possesses a whole life belonging to someone else—such a beggar will feel the need to personify that life. The whole is too large for him; it becomes the landscape replacing his own soul; it acquires a specific physiognomy, as though it had been shaped by a person with a special passion, a special love of truth. Life forfeits its symbolic meaning, becomes the heroic act of one person; it forfeits its temporal character, becomes a rounded whole in the center of which stands a single person. Rahel's life became for Varnhagen the emanation of her person.

The beggar by the wayside had nothing beside this life, nothing beside this person. He had to preserve both, guard them like a precious gem; he had to glorify both. He had to become avaricious for every utterance of the glorified giver, as the idol worshipper craves every miracle of his god. "Do bring the letters of Gentz and Louis with you to Vienna; I say this not out of covetousness; I crave only yours, would like to possess all of those, conscious of my priestly fidelity; the others I only want to read!" The letters of her friends, too, must pass by him like a breath and touch him, but they amounted to no more than anecdotes subsidiary to the main story. It was hers he wanted to possess, because they alone were "genuine" emanations. He was as fascinated by Rahel as the priest by his idols; he had to "cherish and accompany [her], devote all life to her, serve [her] as if [she] were a Greek classic" (Varnhagen).

Varnhagen had nothing to lose. In his urge to represent at least something, he stopped at no grotesquerie. No native dignity warned him against the preposterousness of making himself the prophet of a woman. No reticence restrained him from telling all. What did the privilege he had been given amount to, what the magnificent fact of his having been chosen, if he could not display everything? How else was anyone going to recognize him? He talked about her shamelessly to anyone who crossed his path. He displayed her, her utterances, her story, as if it were a justification of his no longer having to remain in the background, of his no longer needing to stand by the wayside. He not only played the priest who alone knew the way of salvation but the prophet who felt it necessary to proclaim: "I should like to live as your apostle; in this function I feel best, feel my destiny fulfilled in the most multifarious ways! And yet blindness will remain blind forever; even now, you know, there are more pagans than Christians; but let those who do not want to adore hold their tongues and petrify. I spoke about you at Steffens's house . . . as the third glory of the Jewish nation, the first and second chronologically being Christ and Spinoza, but you the first as far as content goes; they accused me of idolatry, but Steffens was nevertheless delighted with my fervor."

It is highly improbable that Steffens or anyone else was delighted with such fervor. Many of Rahel's letters to Varnhagen suggest the opposite; in them she begged him not to make himself ridiculous by talking about her. But having once put herself at the mercy of the unknown stranger, she could no longer prevent his desiring to make himself known by exploiting her. He was, after all, no longer the "beggar by the wayside"; he held something in his hand now; he wanted to represent something in the world, and he wanted to become "worthy of her." To this end he left her temporarily and went to Tuebingen in order to finish his medical course.

She could not and did not dare dissuade him from this,

although she knew that it was pointless for her; that it would not help her at all if he ceased to be an unknown; that he was mistaken if he thought he could become a person in his own right, independent of her. For all that he really possessed was someone else. That could serve no other end than to make him vain.

Varnhagen's departure changed everything all at once, forced her into the position of the pleader. He left, taking with him all his knowledge about her. She would have to hold on to him. After all, his desire to become something sprang from what he had learned about her. He was not going to remain an unknown; therefore she must hold on to him, for if he should attain his goal, should make himself "known," he would have her in the palm of his hand. All this meant was that she had to yearn for him, for we bind ourselves to others only by yearning.

In Tuebingen, alone, relying on himself alone, without society and without stimulus, Varnhagen almost forgot why he had come. He lived in a state of oppressive vacuity, of deadly boredom. Right at the beginning when he first met Rahel, he had been violently convinced that he loved her. Rahel had fended this emotion off with the sure knowledge that love could not help her. She had referred to Urquijo and said that she was no longer capable of love. Now, in the ambiguous situation of separation, she confused her yearning with love. Varnhagen, however, did not respond to love. She wanted to hold him by love and also believed that she owed it to him, since he had after all consecrated his life to her. But Varnhagen evaded her; he left her in uncertainty about his plans, toyed with a relationship to another woman, a young girl whom he knew from Hamburg and to whom he felt obligated. But when Rahel for her part treated this as a serious matter and asked what he intended to do about it, he wriggled out of the whole thing: "The bond which fetters me to her extends over the whole earth, and so I am free, completely free!" He wrote often and a great deal, without expressing himself directly, as if he were in a state of "lukewarm numbness." Again and again he pointed out the uncertainty of his livelihood, made covert references to the freedom which Rahel had promised to allow him, and which she demanded for herself. The whole business threatened to turn once more into an unhappy and ridiculous love affair.

At the same time Rahel could not even succeed in convincing herself that she loved him. What did the yearnings of the day and the day's clever schemes to hold on to him amount to as against the unvarying dreams of the nights, which would not release her from their spell? Was not her love just as equivocal as his evasion? Certainly she needed him in order to retain the reality of her past. But did not every night give the lie to this reality? Was she not being swept away from him into another country every single night? And even if the day tossed her toward him again, toward him and his "lukewarm numbness" and the tortures of uncertainty, there remained an aloofness, for the nights were unknown to him; there were realms which she had not confided to his beggarly covetousness.

This aloofness enabled her to tell him what she found unbearable in him. It was not that he drove her to issue an ultimatum as if it were a logical conclusion which she merely had to draw; rather, of her own accord she confronted him with the demand that he choose—simply because her nerve failed her, because she could no longer ask her "heart muscle" to put up with "ambiguities." She told him that his equivocation had nothing to do with freedom or lack of it: "I declared you free. . . . But in the midst of the first consummation of the first scene of an action one is not free; to stop in the midst of the consummation means not completing it and has nothing in common with being free or not being free. Anyone who wishes to dance the fandango and ceases in the midst of it from awkwardness or lack of strength, has not carried out an act of freedom." Once more she drew wholly back upon herself. "And I thought for a moment that I was not alone! I am that again, in a sense." She was not even risking very much in delivering this ultimatum, for Varnhagen had once more become the "beggar by the wayside." Whatever he had held had slipped away from him in his solitude and boredom. He had little left but a new pretext for his introspections.

Then something astonishing happened; Varnhagen reacted to her criticism with understanding. He was not offended, did not sulk, but admitted that she was right. "Nothing in your words offended me," he wrote. "I looked them courageously in the eye, although I felt myself shrinking smaller and smaller under their gaze; for I found myself at last cutting the figure I have always cut, and the truth has nothing terrible for me because it is in harmony with whatever is true within me."

There is nothing so reassuring as a person's listening to reason. Understanding is rationality which takes account of others and nevertheless retains its independence as an aspect of humanity. Rationality provides assurance that a person is not entirely at the mercy of external powers and of his own fallibility. It provides the comfort of knowing that one can always appeal to something, no matter what the nature of the other person, no matter how alien that nature is. For what blasts human relationships is never alienness or baseness or vanity but only the ignoring of this appeal, in which we want to have it recognized that we are human beings. If the appeal fails, if the other refuses to listen to reason, there remains nothing human, only the eternal differentness and incomprehensible otherness of physical substances. We can love alienness with the complex tenderness that lovely forms extort from us. We can turn away from the alien with that utter indifference or total disgust we reserve for abortive products of nature. But that cannot prevent the abortive appeal from reacting back upon ourselves, from transforming ourselves into a product of nature and debasing rationality to a mere quality.

Rationality, understanding, humanity, listening to reason— all these had hitherto played little part in Rahel's life. Truth directly communicated irrespective of the listener is not human; truth has no reasons. Varnhagen's rationality transformed Rahel's truths into understandings. Because he guided himself by them, permitted himself to be shaped by them, he made her human. Rahel's life became more human because it now had a pedagogical effect upon another human being, because for the first time the other person and his otherness did not constitute a doom for her, an immovable obstacle whose only relevance to her was that it showed her something different from what she was in herself. "The extreme differences in our temperaments and the ways of our minds are all too obvious." Although these differences were apparent at their very first meeting, they did not remain a crude and unassailable fact. Rather, thanks to Varnhagen's understanding and the human communication provided by language, they could be included in the development of a friendship. "Where we are separated by talents and nature, we are united by friendship, understanding, forbearance, justice, loyalty, honesty, true cultivation."

Varnhagen's understanding not only saved the relationship at a specific crisis; it became the general basis for many years of friendship and marriage. Rahel began to educate him. She loved him like a "son"—he was, after all, fourteen years younger than she. She also learned from him that a person was distinguished by more than the things that had happened to him, that a person's being was more than the sum of his happiness or unhappiness. That someone to whom nothing happened, who had to rely upon himself alone, need not remain merely the raw material of his own nature. That an outside event was not the only means of release from the isolation of ordinary existence; that rationality and the possibility of appealing to it could lend human dignity even to the most ignoble soul. That not only the person who was destined to be something, but the rational person also was from the first more than the chance arrangement of his gifts and qualities. Varnhagen was vain, but it was scarcely right to identify him with his vanity, since he was aware of it and subjected it to rational judgment. Varnhagen was empty, but Rahel had no right to confound him with his hollowness because as a rational person he was in a position to convert this hollowness into a capacity for acquiring cultivation; emptiness could also be viewed as potentiality. "*Dear* August! (I am flattering you now!) . . .

because no one I know on earth has so correct a judgment, so thorough a conception of the nature and range of his whole being as you. Yes, you are yourself what you judge best and most impartially and therefore you are also the person most capable of acquiring cultivation—perhaps I ought to say the most cultivated person. . . . We are also cultivated; we must cultivate ourselves as water must rush; such cultivation is happiness. . . . Yours is a noble act of your whole moral being; it is not only the morality imposed by your nature, but a morality that should be demanded of all rational creatures; from you and from your nature it emerges of its own accord."

In learning from him what rationality, what understanding meant, she took care of his unlimited teachability and strove to develop understanding itself into a specific talent which would provide the "beggar by the wayside" with a specific function in the world. "You know yourself with a greater understanding than, perhaps, any other human being of your kind, of the kind you describe yourself to be, has ever had. You are so honest, though with inborn tendencies not to be, that it is a miracle—not in the moral sense. This alone would have to originalize your talent in a manner such as perhaps has never been before, and create a talent such as has never existed."

Rahel educated Varnhagen for her own sake. Originally she had been able to put herself into Varnhagen's hands, so that he would be the preserver of her story, precisely because he was an unknown, a "beggar by the wayside." Now she tried to teach him to grasp the meaning of it. She gave him her life once more, not as an impersonal event which was the repository of truth, but as the comprehensible life story of a particular person: "Rejoice if you really do think well of me and consider my life and being something extraordinary. You have impressed humanity upon it." She realized that the unknown must become known, that among human beings her life could be preserved only in the form of a comprehensible, human life story. She grasped the tremendous opportunity inherent in the fact that someone who in himself was nothing in particular at the same time had the greatest degree of understanding, and she endowed that understanding with specificity, the specificity of her life. Thus she transformed the "beggar by the wayside" into her only reliable friend, into the person who would accompany her understandingly in the future as well as in the present. "You understand my nature as much as it was possible for one like yours to understand one like mine, grasped it with the most magnificent, most brilliant appreciation, with an insight which surpasses my comprehension, for it does not spring from a similarity of natures."

She had not been bound to the unknown to whom she had turned over her life story that he might preserve it. Any personal tie would have impaired the pure narrative of a person who did not want to be understood, only listened to and recorded. But now that she had taught Varnhagen to understand, now that she was employing his rationality in the struggle against his qualities, now that she listened to his love and depended upon him, now that he was her only friend, always at her disposal, she had to bind herself to him. He was no longer merely the spectator for whose "eye alone the frightful spectacle [of her life]" was there. When, with her encouragement and her tutorial aid, he began to understand the things that had only been thrown his way as a kind of loan, he became her friend, the strongest, the most unyielding tie in her life. "I feel as if my life substance had grown on to the place in your heart with which you love and understand me." He removed from her actual life, not only from her past life, all secrets, all obscurities, all concealments. Before him who was her permanent friend all ambiguities appeared interpretable and consistent, because he knew and understood the whole. Whether he understood her rightly or wrongly did not alter the significance of this. The fact that he gave his clear, knowing, enthusiastic approval to everything about her, conferred upon everything the same brilliant transparency. "You know everything. *That*, that, Varnhagen, is my joy and my love for you."

Yet the more Varnhagen understood, the more Rahel was compelled to keep back from him. A person can be understood only as a particular being with particular contours, a particular physiognomy. Everything that blurs the contour must be suppressed or the general understanding will be destroyed. And that Rahel did not want. It was not that she concealed anything definite from him, but she did not speak of the elusive misery of the nights, the confusing twilight of the days, and the painful effort it cost her to overcome her melancholia anew every single day. "Neither in the morning nor in the afternoon can I summon up the courage to get up out of bed, because I do not know what for. My heart lacks joy in life, stimulus— it won't do." She clung to Varnhagen as she did to the day, only to relapse ever and again into the ever-recurrent, insistent and importunate dreams of the night.

10

BANKRUPTCY OF A FRIENDSHIP
(1809–1811)

AMONG Varnhagen's numerous acquaintances, whom he introduced to Rahel, was a young, extremely talented student who was studying classical philology under Friedrich August Wolf. His name was Alexander von der Marwitz, and he was the younger brother of the Prussian junker who had fought Hardenberg's reforms most intensely and intelligently and whose concept of the nobility and its regeneration is set forth in one of the most interesting documents that class produced.

When Rahel met this young man in 1809 he was twenty-two years old. Alexander had little in common with his brother. He was not concerned with the interests of the junkers, desired no "reforms of the nobility." But he was also no renegade, no bourgeois; he too considered Hardenberg's various reforms and laws "a tissue of modern fancy stupidity, ignorance, mendacity and weakness." He took a passionate interest in everything historical, but the contemporary scene provided no place for him. He stood outside public life and yet was linked to it, involved in it by tradition; his position in society was too well established by his family history for him to be able to exist as a private person. He studied the Greeks out of a passionate love for "a *whole* life *completely* cultured in all directions." The classics were supposed to rescue him from the barbarism of history, to liberate him from the merely private nature of a life which could not find any public outlet, could not be effective outwardly in any direction. For no one accorded him recognition, although everyone paid tribute to this handsome, young and gifted nobleman. "Marwitz has an extraordinary talent for ruling, but no talent for acquiring authority, and I do not know how he is ever going to ascend

the throne, since destiny has not placed him there at the start"
(Varnhagen).

If he could train himself to acceptance, to renouncing all
ambition to attain the extraordinary, if he learned to respect
what lay closest at hand and to subdue the fine élan and the
truly impassioned quality of his existence, he might some day
also be content with "understanding everything human and
historical, and working understandingly at that" (Marwitz).
But at present he could not reconcile himself to this and he
felt at the mercy of the emptiness of time, which had no significance for him, no use for him—at the mercy of boredom.
"Les ennuis me consument, ma chère amie; I live too badly,
too solitarily, too mechanically, without any relationships,
without any prospects; and my inner strength can scarcely
stand against the colorless death that crowds in upon me from
all sides." The world to which he belonged, for which, by his
birth, he was responsible, was not a thing he could simply
abandon. His small, accidental existence at the beginning of
the nineteenth century could not wipe out the centuries of
forefathers who had participated in politics and history. Yet
everything to which he belonged aroused in him nothing but
boredom and disgust. He was repelled not alone by particular
institutions, not even by "disgust with the present" (Marwitz),
but by the whole world of humanity, all of which struck him
as "vulgar." He feared vulgarity, guarded himself against any
contact with it, therefore refrained from entering into relations
—and felt in the end that he was being rent asunder by his
"quivering passions." He was too young for misanthropy; he
had not yet had any unpleasant experiences with people—
experiences which might not have washed away his disgust
but which probably could have taught him some wisdom. And
so he always reacted with inappropriate intensity, with rage,
with a staking of his whole existence on each encounter; with
the result that he often seemed simply ludicrous. "I cannot
endure the touch of vulgarity; but (and this is the corrupt spot
in me) I also cannot fend it off where I ought, and I cannot
fend it off with prudence, but only with rage." Thus he once
stabbed "by accident" an innkeeper who was impudent to him;

this affair had cost him a good part of his career. What was worse, he knew that he could not endure the world; he knew he was cut off from it, that he could not live. Yet he also could not take his life; he felt inhibitions about destroying what he himself had not made. "I *can* go under, but to live an abomination to myself and a burden to others, or to end in an undignified, vulgarly horrible manner, I *cannot* do. During this period I have often thought of suicide, and it has always seemed to me infamous grossness to destroy the sacred vessel so bloodily, so deliberately."

Rahel listened to his lamentations as if they were her own. Into her replies she put everything she knew; she tried to mobilize all her experience in order to help him, in order for him to "get on more happily than I." For "you are the first man whom I would never want to see, to hear or to possess again, if only *you* could fare well, if only *your* nature, with its needs, could develop." She bucked him up: "You only *seem* to vacillate; the world that surges around you is sucked dry, colorless and marrowless." She advised him to accept the good commonplaces: "Live, love, study, be diligent, marry if the chance comes, make every triviality count and come alive; that is the tried and true course, and no one will hinder you from it." She was right, and he thanked her. He was, after all, ready to be resigned: "Henceforth I am done with all dreams and heroic grandeur and desire for importance in the world."

Would he really have come to something? Would he have learned to strike a peace pact with the world? Or would he not in the end have been destroyed by his disgust? It is impossible to say. When the Wars of Liberation began, he joined up, and so for a few months at least drowned out his boredom in the general enthusiasm. In 1814 he fell in a minor skirmish—still too young to have left anything behind but a few letters and an impression upon the memories of his contemporaries.

The friendship between Rahel and Marwitz was suggestive of an alliance against everyone else. Love was not involved, and yet there was an exclusiveness about this friendship; nothing else was allowed to enter it. Marwitz was the only person who ever succeeded, for a short while, in curing Rahel of her indiscriminateness. His disgust with people, his clear, malicious eye for their mediocrity, was so persuasive that she too began distinguishing people by their qualities. Her alliance with Marwitz imposed upon her an obligation to be exclusive. She had always been aware, for example, of the tastelessness of Henriette Herz, or Rebecca Friedländer's foolishness; she had understood Bokelmann's qualities and Gentz's great talent. But such knowledge had had little bearing on her relationships with them. Marwitz was the first person toward whom she felt the call of friendship solely on the basis of his qualities.

For the first time she recognized solidarity not based upon similar destinies, but only upon the plain perception of equality: "Marwitz was the last man whom I placed above myself; he paid for it with tears; and this angel found me stony, he who was nevertheless no more than I," she wrote years after his death. He found her "stony"—and ready to live his life with him. The quality of a person and his life seemed to her so closely allied that she knew no other way to express her solidarity, her friendship. To bear witness, as she had done so often before, in all her friendships, no longer sufficed her. "Keep back no word, no bad temper, no mood; honor me with everything; I want to endure your life as I do mine; to live doubly is lovely; as far as it is possible for a human being, I want to accept it gladly, to take it as it comes." She was as concerned for him as for herself; she was determined with an obstinate intensity that he must be happy. "With *my own* blood, with *my own* life, with the happiness that *unfathomable* divinities may yet send me, I want to supplement his." His happiness would constitute compensation, an adequate exchange for her unhappiness. "I comfort myself—as one may find comfort in the existence of a child, say—in the knowledge that a similar nature, with the finest abilities, with the most secret and delicate nuances, exists upon earth and is going to be happier than I am. . . . I know you, understand you and feel you so intensely that my happiness and your happiness flow in one stream!" It was not that his happiness could make her any happier; at best it could render her more content, more reconciled to the world. "Neither you nor I nor the gods without a miracle could renovate my destiny; I must play it out to the end. The flower on this plant is crushed; do not forget that. Its foliage creates an illusion." Only in general and in terms of personal disinterestedness could his happiness become hers—the sympathetic disinterestedness of a woman so much the elder who knew that the limits of this one life we have at our disposal had already been paced off; and in general because life is understandable only in general terms when one has at last realized: this is what life is like.

To the degree that she made his life her own, she was "diverted . . . from all contemplation and palpating of [her] own feelings . . . concentrating instead upon his being." To that degree her "heart," which was always entangled with itself, always reaching out to generalities only through itself, learned how to be objective, how to be "outside itself." Marwitz was the first and last person who meant more to her than the part he played in her life. He was the one friend whose "presence had become like the eye of the world to her," through whom she viewed the world for the first time independently of her own entanglements and her own state of exile from it. Even his disgust and his contempt helped her to grasp the rankings and differences in level in a society essentially foreign to her. For in spite of all his disgust, in spite of all his bored aloofness from society, Marwitz belonged to this world and its society, and even his disgust drew some of its justification from the world. He did not, like Rahel, have to "justify himself to thousands of years of stupidity"; he could see the stupidity for what it was and despise it. He taught Rahel this contempt of his, taught her the unworthiness of the higher circles she so longed to reach. "Be assured," she wrote, "that if today I should attain to rank or fortune or even to transient celebrity, I should treat everybody *en canaille*." Marwitz, who possessed rank, fortune and influence, taught her by the example of his despair that it was all worthless. He freed her from her dependency upon the world because he himself, with all his contempt, stood as the legitimate representative of that world.

By his legitimate contempt this nobleman and conservative

believer in history taught the Enlightened Jewess that reality was not merely whatever chanced to come a person's way, that the society to which she did not belong, and which disgusted him, recognized another kind of reality, a reality of heritage, of tradition, confirmed again and again by the succession of generations. He taught her that lines existed from the known to realms progressively more unknown, from the near to the far, from the present to the past; lines that dwindled to threads as they stretched farther back, that grew finer and finer, more and more invisible. Yet only through these ties, he taught her, could historical reality be grasped. But he taught her only the doctrines of a declining world; that became clear to her as she listened to his laments on the "disconnectedness and vacuity of the present, on the lack of continuity and cohesiveness. She became acquainted with something which, in the end, she could neither approve of nor utilize to her own benefit. For she and Marwitz would not have come together at all had it not been for the spiritual havoc the Enlightenment had wreaked upon this world. That alone was responsible for Rahel's very existence, so to speak, and for the fact that the junker and the Jewess could strike up so strange an alliance against the world.

Marwitz never wholly succeeded in drawing her over to his side, in making her feel his protest against the "disconnectedness and vacuity" of her surroundings, his contempt for "people without a proper comprehension of human relationships." He did not know—and she herself did not take this into account—that only in appearance was he dealing with her as an individual, that she was neither the first nor the last Jew who wanted to assimilate, to enter into the reality of an alien land. Perhaps it would have been possible to transform a single case, to take one person along into the alien world—a world, moreover, so cracked and brittle. After all, there had been many such single cases. But Rahel, for all her singularity, for all her isolation, put up a resistance, just as she had resisted with Finckenstein and Gentz: she resisted accepting a society and a view of the world whose foundations would inevitably always remain hostile to her—not to her personally, but to her as a Jew. For that society had never of its own accord granted her —as a Jew—the most elementary, most important and minimum concession: equal human rights.

The struggle of these two allies against one another was conducted covertly, by indirection, via the detour of Rahel's friendship with Varnhagen. In this context Varnhagen was not the "beggar by the wayside," but rather the liberal, middle-class intellectual of the Enlightenment, always keenly distrustful of class privileges, opposed to the nobility as a class and to the prerogatives of birth. Marwitz wrote that Varnhagen "seems to me, disregarding all exterior marks of culture, inwardly extremely vulgar, petty in his views and meager in the energy of his will, of the inner activity in which his life is rooted. And at the same time this vulgarity is so repulsive, so vexing. My first judgment of him, when I saw him in Halle three years ago, was just this; I hated the barrenness of his nature, which by adroitness and all kinds of little tricks had won a much higher place for itself than it merited. . . . I know very well that he has discernment, but it is never anything but discernment of miniatures, of a leaf, not of a landscape, of a smoothed hair, but not of a face, of a skillful and intelligent phrase, not of the inner depths of a divine nature. Nowhere does he see true greatness, and you know, dear Rahel, that is after all the only solid reality. But he is your friend—how is that? . . . Do you see him differently; am I wrong? Is he noble, for in the end everything depends on that, doesn't it? No, he is not."

Certainly Varnhagen was not noble; the question remained, however, whether for Rahel everything really did "depend on that." At any rate she did not write a word in defense of her friend; she left Marwitz undisturbed in his antipathy. In fact she often shared it to such an extent that Marwitz could confidently ask: "Must I help you break away from Varnhagen?" Yet the whole affair ended with Varnhagen's victory. After Marwitz's first disparagements, Rahel was hesitant, often ready to drop Varnhagen; later, when she had already decided for him, she still hesitated for a long time to admit it, and it was only toward the end that she came out with the fact which was crucial for her: "You see, Varnhagen is my friend, the one who loves me most, for whose whole pattern of life I am the essential condition; and it is not enough for me to know and feel him thoroughly, take and endure him. I must now, wave upon wave, go through the reefs with him." She had to cleave to him, remain with him, not only because he loved her most, but because his world—the world of a vain, meagerly gifted, adroit man—was still and all the world of the Enlightenment in which she was more at home than in the world of the Prussian junker, no matter how glittering and "noble" that was.

The decision against Marwitz was not taken immediately and cannot be attributed to Varnhagen's influence alone. On the contrary, never again was she to drop so utterly all reserves toward a person as she did toward Marwitz. She even told her friend about her nights, and not as a matter of chance, the way she informed everyone piecemeal about the things concerning her, but never told anyone everything. With him she set out deliberately, and with a clear knowledge of what she was doing, to lay bare to him the ultimate base of her existence. For that base, after all, had never been anything specific—it had been the day or the night or the entanglement of both; or even merely her having learned what disgrace meant, or what it was like to be a pariah, or to have a secret. She had only to declare that one or other of these things was the base and make it so, by dint of concealing the other features. But in recent years suppression of her dreams had withdrawn the night entirely from the control of the day and made the night into that ambiguous refuge which sheltered her from other human beings and therefore seemed like a home. *Je vous mets [le rêve] dans cette lettre. Mais je vous prie de me le rendre la première fois que vous viendrez à Berlin, car j'aimerais le conserver, puisqu'il ouvre et montre les abîmes de l'âme, où l'amour s'ouvre des routes inconnues à tout ce qu'on ne croit, ne dit et ne veut publier et qu'il n'est presque donné qu'à moi de descendre dans mes rêves dans les fonds les plus obscurs de mon coeur.* The nights had wrought such havoc on her life that her dreams appeared to her without any ambiguity as the true expression of her soul: "Believe me, thus I am"; she could in good conscience present the day with its compulsions, with the bustle that Marwitz despised and to which she always had only half adjusted, as a frivolous farce imposed by convention and intended only to dissimulate what others could not understand. She adapted herself to Marwitz's contempt for the world by playing off the nights and her dreams against society.

Hence, she was no longer turning the night into day and the day into night. By telling him about her nights she was showing him that she, too, held something solid which she could oppose to the world's demands and rejections; that she had a refuge which served her as a vantage point from which to make Marwitz's contempt her own. Here there came to her aid—as it did in other cases also—that exaggerated, high-wrought love of nature which is the escape of those who can be deprived of everything but at least not of the sun which shines upon all. She felt good only "walking alone, after much vexation, in mild weather, under a fleecy sky," only when she saw "a great deal of sky," with "the air rural" and still. "Like evil swathings it all fell away from me, all the alienation cast over me like a spell by the situation, and I too became still." Every social situation was oppressive to her, because she had nothing, was nothing, never was permitted to be natural. "And the most intolerable aspect of the situation is that I cannot and can never change it." Only the sky and the relaxation nature brought—blessings which were granted to every human being—were as unchangeable as her social situation. These became the two sides of the coin for her; both were equally impersonal situations, which she could in no way alter by her own powers.

"All this heaviness in me became light because my blood could flow right, my nerves vibrate right, and so momentarily I entered into a right relationship and reciprocation with the elements, colors, light and soil. I relished it listening, almost amazed, and then I cried to the heavens to let me keep this meager naturalness, and I cried against the heavens also." Society was as malicious and cruel as nature was healing and releasing—and both were alien. But she need not be troubled by nature's alien quality, since this was the same for everybody just as the sun shone equally upon all. If she walked through the city with open eyes, seeing nothing but houses, the sky, spaces, light and the earth, the people seemed to her mere ghosts and marionettes; her surroundings were nothing but stage-sets; the humanly inhabitable whole had a theatrically lifeless quality. "Yesterday on Unter den Linden I was swept by such a queer mood; the linden trees, the street and houses, the people, seemed all frighteningly strange, altogether shabby to me; not one of them had a face, a physiognomy; the silliest, most superficial, most wooden, most distracted expression; silly, vain women, not coquettish, not inviting affection or sex, or complete pleasure of any sort. The poverty of the city where I can calculate what everyone has, consumes, wants or can do; the frightful, vacuous unrelatedness, looking neither to the state nor to love, family or any kind of self-created religion. Their dizzying, vain, trivial, criminally repulsive chaos. I among them, still more unrelated, with full, empty heart, thwarted in attaining everything desirable, separated from the ultimate. In short, as if I stood before a temple of magic—for reality receded before my soul that was still not empty of life —a temple I can already see swaying; its collapse is certain and it will inevitably come down on me and everyone else."

She had learned some things from Marwitz after all, learned to see her own unrelatedness and alienation objectively, to fit them into the vacuity and emptiness of a city which was, so to speak, too poor and too empty of content to have the strength to absorb, to assimilate her. Her despair was no longer her own private affair; rather, it was merely the reflection of a doomed world. This was the light in which Marwitz saw his own despair, his own disgust—and he was right, for the world to which he belonged was indeed swaying and on the point of collapse. Rahel interpreted her own alienation accordingly, no longer believed it inflicted by an incomprehensibly abstract fate which could be understood only in generalized categories —life in itself, *the* world. She now saw it as the specific misfortune of having been born in the wrong place, assigned by history to a doomed world—like Marwitz. If the collapse crushed her along with everyone else, she would achieve belonging, even though only as part of the general ruin. And then, was not her alienation perhaps only the clairvoyance of the "unusual" person? Such despair and such contempt she could, at any rate, offer to Marwitz; these he could accept, could feel allied to her in sharing despair and contempt. As one great soul—or one "frightened soul"—was allied to another.

"I feel your walk on Unter den Linden," he replied. "Great, gruesome, true. Must I now remind you of the noble, moving words you wrote to me at the time of my great misery, on the helplessness of every frightened soul? Oh, it is horribly true. How many half consolations, and therefore utter vapidities, might I not say to you about the sublimity of your mind, the depth of your feelings, by virtue of which you annihilate your utterly insubstantial surroundings whenever you like, and enter into the splendors of true life." Marwitz, whose world was one of aristocracy and vulgarity, quality and sham, good and bad textures of the soul, was always seeking depth of feeling and sublimity of the mind. For him these were not traits of character, as they were for Varnhagen when he praised Rahel; rather, they constituted forms of existence, degrees of intensity and passion which form the very fiber of the personality. Rahel could only prove herself, only justify herself to him by displaying as a quality, as evidence of achievement, the sum of characteristics which she, in fact, believed to be nothing but the result of an evil destiny. The transformation that Marwitz tacitly demanded of her was a change from being nothing and no one to being a personality. Marwitz did not realize that a necessary attribute of a personality, of rank and quality, was a world in which certain things were recognized as constituting rank and quality; that a person must stand within a framework which keeps him from being at the mercy of chance and reality. But in taking Rahel as an equal partner, as, in fact, the sole person who deserved equality with himself, he also created (while their relationship lasted, at any rate) a world for her in which she counted for something as a person. Thus he was the first man, and basically remained the only one, who rightly regarded her as a whole, as a single human being. He was also the only one who had some semblance of right to see her as unique and extraordinary. He would never react wrongly to the personality he had unwittingly made of her, for as such he had, of course, understood her better than she could ever understand herself. "I can tell him everything just because he has never yet misunderstood me." He could never do or say the wrong thing, for in his world, which in spite of all his contempt for it was wellknit, she stood at a particular spot, had a place of her own as a person. For he did not become entangled in her life, or she in his. Thus nothing imperiled the picture he had of her. After her death, perhaps, he would actually have been able to transmit knowledge of her as something really "unique" to the world which had never been willing to accept her while she was alive, a world whose past she did not belong to, and from whose future she could be erased at any time. She hoped he would do this. "Oh, be my friend, and when I am dead rescue the image of my soul." In this appeal she was clearly turning away from Varnhagen. For a time she saw more hope in being one person among others, a great one perhaps in a realm that recognized greatness, than in being reduced to anecdote, recited and handed down to posterity by the ignoble, traditionless "beggar by the wayside."

There was much about her that met Marwitz, and the picture he had formed of her, halfway. Was not her life at an end? Could she not, like many others, display it as if it were nothing but the evolution of her soul? After all, when one was no longer distracted and involved in specific present concerns, in happiness and unhappiness, when everything was already decided and done with, was not the end the same as the beginning? Was not the beginning present once more, with all that had had to be forgotten in order to get on, all that had been drowned out by the fullness, variety and multiplicity of human life? And did not the beginning then prove to have been, all along, the essential, indestructible core?

That was all very well and good so long as she let him do the talking, so long as she contented herself with "depth of feelings" and "sublimity of mind," so long as she asked no more than generalized tributes and did not take it into her head to determine for herself why she was extraordinary. It took her a relatively long time to adjust sufficiently to Marwitz's way of thinking, classifying and judging to attempt to interpret for herself the things she so unreservedly told him. She told him only by way of her dreams what she was "essentially" and "really" like, without specifying the essential, the real, the "center." His very praise, his constant interpreting, stimulated her to attempt self-analysis as soon as she thought she grasped what sort of thing he looked for. "What would there be at all good about me if I could be unfair? It seems to me that the sole center, the axis of my inglorious, twisted nature, my unprepossessing, graceless and untalented nature, is that this center can be found, that I am fair to others as well as to myself. . . ."

No reply to this letter exists. A great part of the correspondence between Marwitz and Rahel, the one in Potsdam and the other in Berlin, was answered orally. The above letter ends: "Don't trouble to answer; come." It is necessary, therefore, to reconstruct the reply.

Fairness was not a quality with which Marwitz was directly familiar from the world he knew, nor was it for Rahel a character trait at all; rather, it was an attitude toward the world and a way of holding aloof from the world. From personal experience Marwitz was acquainted with the attitudes of resigned rejection of all action and all entanglement, of disgust at contact; building on this personal knowledge he might therefore arrive at an understanding of the inevitable guilt which all action involves. But fairness is something special: the fair person judges in every individual case; he is constantly intervening; his objective, aloof attitude is never anything but a sham. She might call herself fair, but Rahel was not at the same time willing to remain aloofly indifferent to the world. Rather, she was aggressive and at bottom believed it possible to change the unfair world. Certainly she held aloof but not, or not only, out of impotence and resignation. Certainly she thought herself different and special; but this specialness, she believed, was something one ought to be able to ask of everyone. In other words, everyone should be "fair to others as well as to himself." Marwitz escaped from the present, where there was no place for him, into the past; in so doing he put the seal upon his judgment that this world was necessarily doomed to decay. Rahel escaped from a present in which, she believed, there was not *yet* any place for her, and her refuge was not the past but a better future. That was why she pleaded: "When I am dead, rescue the image of my soul." The future, she hoped, would be fair to her. Marwitz expected nothing from the future; he found the image of his soul preserved and secure in the past, in tradition.

Fairness can also be a characteristic of age. It is possible to be fair when there is no longer any sense in wishing or hoping. Rahel, however, had always been fair, even while she was still young. In all her passions, in all her desires and hopes, there had always been implicit a knowledge that these could not be fulfilled and an ultimate indifference toward the fulfillment of any specific, single one of them. Therefore she was right in saying that fairness was the "axis of her nature." But she understood this and voiced this understanding only when she believed that her life was over.

"My heart is embers; . . . I considered this only yesterday: it no longer loves on its own account; its soul and spirit are barely alive; it is really dead. And in one respect Harscher [1] is right to be surprised that I continue to live. See how sad I am! I weep, too, and never say most of what I feel. And yet I look at even this quite differently, and can regard it as a sort of happiness. I am so infinitely free within myself, as though I had no obligations to this earth. Oh, I cannot say it in words. I still feel as I did when I was fourteen years old; then everything was for the others, for the grownups; that is the way I feel when I forget my horrible griefs, the fierce shame, and I really have no talent for dealing with these all the time, brooding upon them. It is still the way it used to be, because my nature was not made for unhappiness. My nature was overflowing and proud, wild with joy when the earth received me.

[1] A Swiss medical student, Varnhagen's friend.

But things went on, badly and well; that is to say, there has been a great deal, and nothing of much worth, but nothing especially making for unhappiness, although I feel it and savored it as few could." These words contained everything: knowledge that life had reached its end, and the deep joy of being through it at last; anguish at life's having been only a chain of mishaps, and pride at a destiny in which beginning and end coalesced, therefore proving its inevitability. This confession of ultimate sadness was written in a tone of exuberant hope, as though life were just beginning now that everything was over. "You will not believe how ironically I can rise above myself to the point of freest gaiety, without resentment or anger, and how ordinarily I turn my back on my destiny. New forces, new courage, new vision, a fresh, impersonal heart, a sound head, a really intelligent intellect—they help a great deal."

Evident in these lines also is her conviction that everything she suffered had only been inflicted upon her by people for whom she was really too good—yes, Marwitz was right—and who could not understand her because she was better and other than they. Was she not, just like Marwitz, alien in the world only because she was better than her surroundings? And had not her life been a ghost story only because she had never encountered anyone of equal rank who could have confirmed the fact that she, she too, was "real"? "And you, you help me too, you make what I love, what I love in myself, true and real to me; you assure me that I am no solitary dreamer."

Marwitz did not fall in with this solidarity. Not only because he was, after all, sixteen years her junior and his life was not yet over, but also because her boundless candor revealed to him that his contempt for the world was something different from her despairing sense of exclusion from it. Her fairness, which she could not make manifest because of her isolation and powerlessness in society, he tried to interpret as a sublime greatness of a soul. He replied: "Every just person . . . supposes himself the center of the universe, but how few greatly gifted persons have been granted, since the world began, the fullness of heart, the fairness of soul, the penetration of mind, to actually be that, as have you? Let Rahel's heart have sunk to embers; the human heart continues to beat in you, with a freer, loftier pulsation, turned away from all earthly things, and yet very close to them; the keen intelligence goes on thinking, taking in ever wider circles; from the green, fresh, living vale the tempest of fate has raised you up to the high mountains, where the view is infinite, man far but God near." These words, no matter how flattering they sounded to her, nor how honestly they were meant, nevertheless meant to Rahel the final breach of solidarity; they exiled her once again all alone to a place where nothing could reach her, where she was cut off from all human things, from everything that men have the right to claim. The "wider circles," the "high mountains" where man was far but God near—this whole metaphorical circumlocution of the abstractness of her existence was not rendered any more bearable by being ascribed to her "greatly gifted" soul rather than to her fate.

So, for answer, she actually had recourse to her "soul" again, to the little she knew about herself, about the way she was and had been, about her wishes and hopes. For she wanted to show him and prove to him that she had not landed voluntarily on the mountain, that she had been "pushed" and thrust there; he might be justified in placing her there, but she would not do so herself. How glad she would have been if she had had only the first part of his reply to read. "What elevating things you say to me, plaudits that fill me with the most pleasurable pride; how it gratifies me to be praised by you, accorded your recognition as one marked out from others! Not a word escaped the greedily listening, vain self; the heart, craving nourishment, drank it all in before these words came. The keen intelligence (so your tribute ends) goes on thinking, taking in ever wider circles." How good everything might have been; how gladly she would have adjusted to being outside the world, so long as she shared his rank. But: "'From the green, fresh, living vale the tempest of fate has raised you up to the high mountains.' . . . That is unhappiness; if my friends are true, then they must say the dreadful words to me. Am I to be banished from the green, living, fresh vale and yet go on living? I who—I wish you to know me fully!—who knows the God to whom you refer me only in Time, through the mind and the senses; where there is nothing, I cannot think anything. He shows, he reveals himself to us in the earth, colors, forms, the heartbreak of joy or sorrow; he has especially opened up to me consciousness of this knowledge; I worship the whole of nature as I know it, and think nothing base but low, narrow, mendacious minds. Shall I be exiled without being dead? You have spoken, Friend. The best of friends can only moderately alleviate unhappiness by his words of comfort. You are right; specify it; I shall do it, too, and do it again; because it is true I will take it as it is and press it to my heart."

Exile was no distinction, and unhappiness no merit. Yet exile and unhappiness had made her what she was. It was possible to live without complete consciousness, and perhaps she would have been able to dispense with such truths—she would have been glad to—if her friend had not voiced them. As it was, however, there could be heard in these lines a subtle, unmistakable note of parting and farewell. How could she fail to realize, since she heard it from the lips of this man who was closest to her, and whom she considered the best she knew, that fate alone, exile and unhappiness, would remain her realities, and that she would have to accept them as she had always done, press them to her heart because they were true, the grand and unique truths of her life.

He offered a comforting reply: "The mountain is also a part of the earth; it, too, partakes of the vigorous joys of life, only in a more muted, milder, less personal fashion, with constant awareness of the greatest perceptions of the spirit." She did not answer. If she now once again stood where she had stood in the past—and she no longer had any alternative—she knew better than he, from her experiences in the past, what was reality for her. She knew it was senseless to be superior to life because everything "personal," and the personal alone, stood for something more than itself.

She was done with Marwitz, then. He was not willing to take her along with him; he would do nothing for her. It was better to become an anecdote, to live in solitude with someone who loved her, than to be doomed to such Platonic admiration. "And he also loves me—as one loves the sea, a swirl of clouds, a rocky gorge. That is *not* enough for me! *No longer.* The man I love must want to live with me, stay with me. . . . *My* friends all think I can love and live on air. They enjoy watching such a game of hearts as mine is, and I am supposed to live without love! It is *over*, it is too much." She was sick of grandeur, great gifts, sublimity and superhuman qualities— and in 1814 she married Varnhagen.

11

CIVIL BETTERMENT
STORY OF A CAREER

(1811–1814)

LIFE passes, and before you know it youth is gone and age is at hand. Rahel had meanwhile arrived at her fortieth year, and she had succeeded in nothing. She had wanted to escape Judaism and had remained in it. She had wanted to marry and no one would have her. She had wanted to be rich and grew poorer. She had wanted to be something in the world, to count for something, and had lost the few opportunities that had come her way in her youth. Society had been for her "half of life," and the only thing she had almost succeeded in achieving was a legitimate disgust with society.

At the same time she had nothing for which to blame herself. She had not begun at the wrong end, and she had not foolishly shut herself away. She had constantly been convinced of the importance of becoming "outwardly another person"; she had never deceived herself about her unfortunate situation. She had always been ready for a crucial change, had been prepared to make all imaginable sacrifices. She had never hoped for miracles and never believed that she would be able to enter good society unless she were pulled into it— dragged in or carried in by some rescuer. And she, of all persons, who had been without illusions, without principles and without moral scruples, had been neither pulled nor rescued; she had simply been jilted, left where she was.

All her women friends, who had come from the same background and who had wanted to escape from Judaism, had succeeded. Frau von Grotthus and Frau von Eibenberg, Dorothea Schlegel and Henriette Herz, her sister Rose and Rebecca Friedländer—all of them, all of them had married. If

Germans, their husbands had usually been noblemen; if Jews, rich businessmen who had a vital part to play in the world and hence were assured a place in it, even if that place were often challenged.

She alone had failed in everything. She alone, now that she was old, was left with nothing but the memory of a few unhappy love affairs and many insults, the memory of nothing but unsuccessful attempts. And at her elbow, so very close and yet already almost as distant as a memory, stood Marwitz who had taught her much more than he dreamed—above all, that her rejection was really final and that there remained for her no alternative but to try another tack. Never intending to, Marwitz had taught her to look upon Varnhagen as her last chance.

There was no doubt that assimilation by marriage could succeed. But not when a woman acted as Rahel did again and again, though with no conscious will: by transmuting the attempt to assimilate, the effort to climb and to set one's house in order, into a love affair. Not when a woman intensified the already existent insecurity of the Jewish situation by deliberately adding the insecurity of a life dedicated to self-exposure.

The world and reality had, for Rahel, always been represented by society. "Real" meant to her the world of those who were socially acknowledged, the parvenus as well as the people of rank and name who represented something lasting and legitimate. This world, this society, this reality, had rejected her. She never saw the other possibility, of joining those who had not arrived, of throwing in her lot with those who like herself were dependent upon some sort of future which would be more favorable to them. Her passion for generalizing, for making apparently absolute privacies communicable to all, experienceable by all, for feeling out the general human lot in the most personal details—her whole gift for abstraction had, characteristically, never led her to the point of regarding her fate as a Jew as anything more than a wholly personal misfortune. She had never been able to fit her private ill luck into a scheme of general social relationships; she had never ventured into criticism of the society, or even to solidarity with those who for other reasons were likewise excluded from the ranks of the privileged.

This blind spot seems incomprehensible when we examine the biographies of the generations of Jews who came after her. After Heinrich Heine and Ludwig Börne, the best among the assimilated Jews never lost their awareness of necessary solidarity with the underprivileged in general; they inevitably shared the fate of certain movements, took part in certain revolts. But to Rahel, with her still unblemished Enlightened concept of the certainty of progress from which would come reform and a reshaping of society, all struggle was alien. The important thing was to get into this society which was already progressing. For, as she saw it, only in this society was it possible for one to be historically effectual.

That economic security, if not wealth, was the first and indispensable prerequisite for assimilation, was something every Jew knew; but scarcely any expressed it as clearly and courageously as Rahel. That the price of poverty was solitude had been demonstrated to her with cruel clarity. In this respect, too, she had always lacked "the courage to throw myself into wretched situations." Economic security formed the sole basis of her entire harried life. Until the death of her mother she had had a sufficiency. However, her mother died intestate. Thenceforward, Rahel was dependent upon the good will of her brothers; she never knew what she possessed, and received an allowance whose amount was not even fixed but was governed by the state of business. Her bare living was always secure, but after 1807 its standard had dropped below the level of her associates. At the very time, therefore, when normal affluence no longer sufficed and it became necessary to be wealthy in order to maintain a position in society, Rahel had had to live more economically than ever before. The days when she could see everyone in the tiny attic room on Jägerstrasse because everybody thought it fun to come and the lack of convention was itself one of the attractions—those days were definitely gone. More and more wealth was demanded as an alternative to rank. Without it, nothing could be done. Rahel now had to creep secretly into what little society remained open to her; she had to live constantly beyond her means, appear constantly something she no longer was. "If one does not have rank, name, talent, beauty, one must have opulence. Was I opulent? Ever? That was one of the reasons why I saw so few people after Mama's death [in 1809]; these have *already* been lost, and I feel the want of them only now that I cannot have them. Yes, I feel the want of everything I love, *except* personal freedom and comfort (which often is limited by my limited circumstances)—and I love *a great many things.*" Lacking money, she was once again thrown back upon the narrow circle of the family and her brothers' business friends. The change is immediately noticeable in her correspondence. She now corresponded almost exclusively with Jews—Varnhagen and Marwitz were the sole exceptions.

Assimilation existed exclusively for well-to-do Jews. The rest entered the European public's field of vision only when they too rose into the affluent class and assimilated to the already assimilated Jews. Otherwise they were known only as comic sheet figures, caricatures, objects of the most vulgar kind of anti-Semitism. In the eyes of their prosperous co-religionists, the mass of poor Jews were already no more than an object of philanthropy, at best of reformist endeavors whose ultimate goal remained the elimination through reform of these dangerous and regrettable provokers of anti-Semitism.

Rahel could not realize that every effort toward assimilation was possible only for an already privileged class. In her environment she was acquainted only with a relatively uniform degree of affluence; the sole exceptions were the very rich, there were none of the very poor in her circle. She knew members of the Jewish merchant class, but neither Jewish workmen nor declassed Jews, not destitute Jews. Rahel often took pride in calling herself a subject of Frederick the Second; she probably had scarcely any inkling of the extent to which she really belonged to the Jews of the Prussian monarchy. For her total insulation from destitution, struggle, slow betterment, and all that was connected with these things, was due to the Jewish policy of the Prussian State. Prussia tolerated only fairly prosperous Jews, only businessmen and no workmen.

The State punished bankruptcy by deportation, prevented overpopulation by a marriage tax and forced emigration, made the Jewish communities responsible as a body for the tax debts of every individual member. By all these measures, the State created an atmosphere of economic security and made the rich, privileged Jews—especially by the rule of collective responsibility—its allies against the poor immigrant members of their own people. The Jewish question was, in Berlin and in all of Prussia, the problem of the rich Jews, and assimilation was the solution this propertied class hoped for. They seemed, indeed, predestined to merge with the prosperous middle-class stratum of society.

The Jews had, however, no direct social and personal relationships with the bourgeoisie. Their ties were with the nobility, whose financiers they had been, as moneylenders, for a long time. This explains the curious and extremely brief transition period in which we find Jews everywhere entering the society of the nobility, while the houses of the bourgeoisie remained closed to them for a long while. The impoverished junkers suddenly saw the moneylender of the *Judengasse* as the father of a daughter with a large dowry.

Rahel belonged to the first generation of the period of assimilation, a generation to which the nobility temporarily accorded social recognition for a variety of reasons—a belated social legalization of centuries-long economic relationships. After the death of her mother she lost her last chance of a marriage befitting her station, for she was without a dowry. Varnhagen, as she reported with great pride, had taken her "without a single sou." Up to the time of this loss she had always wanted to enter only the society of those who had already arrived, the society in which the standard of living was the same as hers. In that society alone, as far as she was concerned, history was made.

Mixed sociality of Jews and nobles was only a transitional state, although vestiges of it lingered down to the twentieth century. With the establishment of a regulated system of credit, the Jews became superfluous to the nobility, and personal relations lost their point. The nobles shut themselves off once more and scrapped their broad tolerance; they became a caste again. The feudal lord was transformed into the virtually absolute ruler of the soil and master of the grain supply.

The social position of the Jews, meanwhile, had taken such definite shape that no one doubted any longer their economic membership in the bourgeoisie, even though the bourgeois did not recognize them socially. Consequently, all the prejudices the nobles harbored toward the bourgeoisie were applied with redoubled force against the Jews, who were considered with some justice to be the pacemakers and prototypes of the capitalistic bourgeoisie, which was making dangerous incursions upon landed property. Thus the Jews forfeited their social neutrality, which for a short time had permitted them to live socially far beyond their means—forfeited this neutrality in favor of economic security. Moreover, the nobility, in Germany especially, set the standards for bourgeois society; the habits, customs and values of the nobles dominated a bourgeois society rapidly rising in economic power. A paradoxical situation resulted: the bourgeoisie added to its own anti-Semitism that of the nobility which at bottom—insofar as the nobles were reactionary and conservative—was as antibourgeois as it was anti-Jewish. And on the other hand the Jews, to the degree that they took on the attributes of the bourgeoisie—that is, became assimilated and emancipated—were plunged into isolation. The bourgeoisie did not accept them, and the nobility drew away from them. This new rejection was becoming evident before and during the war of 1813–14; after 1815 it was manifested quite openly. Not until social isolation was a *fait accompli* did the Jewish intelligentsia ally itself with revolutionary movements. In Rahel's present situation such solidarity was out of the question. Now she had no choice but to consider the possibility of her finding an individual way out. Abandoned and disillusioned, aware that everything had changed for the worse, she was fundamentally unable to comprehend the altered climate of the times. The only way out was Varnhagen.

The more insecure Rahel's economic situation became, the more inclined she was to seize this last chance. The need for a quick solution opened her eyes to possibilities which she had hitherto overlooked, possibilities for reaching out to new people and new opportunities. She did not now and never would renounce her desire to be included in the society of parvenus; but she began to employ different means. Instead of looking to be raised up by someone who was already on top, she tried now to let herself be carried along by someone who was still below, but on his way up.

Varnhagen was the first person in her life who was altogether poor, unknown, without a name and without rank. If she now decided to throw in her lot with him, she must have realized that for the present he had nothing to offer her; poor and young as he was, he was at present worse off than she. Too bad, but perhaps that situation could be changed. At least he really wanted her; she could be completely sure of him and know that in this respect she could be secure—after all, why should she again risk mortal hurt? She had persuaded neither herself nor him that she loved him. The only question was whether he would succeed. That was indeed questionable, and a real gamble, because she could no longer turn back; she had already become far too involved with him.

Not that she had had to become involved. But compromising herself was the sole return she could make him, who was so ready to do anything for her. And it was not out of generosity that she was acting, but because for the first time in her life she had grown poorer, had to reckon, had to give up a great deal, above all much of her social life. Because she felt, with terror, that the narrow basis still remaining to her was slipping away. In such a plight it was easier to feel drawn to a person who also had nothing and had to begin at the beginning. She had no legal claim upon the funds her brothers provided. "By rights I cannot demand a sou from my brothers. What Moritz gives me is pure generosity." This did not, of course, mean that she had any real pecuniary cares; it was unthinkable that her brothers would not take care of her needs. Nevertheless, this situation fundamentally changed her social position. From a person of private means whose daily outlays were covered by the interest on her capital, who knew that she had back of her a fortune, she became a poor relation who had to be supported by the family. As a woman of means she would have been independent of the family and therefore without ties to the milieu of her origins. But in her present situation she remained involuntarily imprisoned within it, involved with it forever, without any possibility of free choice. On a wholly primitive stratum of everyday life her interests were the same as those of her most immediate Jewish circle, and these interests were by no means coincident with those of her wider environment. "You see," she wrote to Varnhagen, "this is my greatest grief: if only I could be divorced from these interests some time. But God will grant this to me! Just as he granted you to me so late!" Thus, another argument for marriage at all costs was the desire and the necessity for getting away from her family—to which in fact she would always feel that she belonged.

Because she was now poorer, it was easier to feel solidarity with someone who had nothing. Because she had lost all chances to be saved from above, there remained nothing for her but to try to rise together with someone who also had nothing—not yet. Once she had made up her mind, she was not held back by any understanding of how difficult it was to rise when both time and money were lacking. She was too old to be able to wait. All the differences between her and Varnhagen during those years before the marriage derived from his having no clear idea of how he could manage to move on, how he could speedily acquire a position in the world, and from her utter incomprehension of this fact. She blamed everything on his indecisiveness, which kept her "on the seesaw." She simply did not know how scant the chances for him were.

Presumably she was already too old and too "used up" to learn anything more from this experience. It seemed to her merely one more blow of fate, since she had already abjured all her demands, all her pretensions to happiness. "This making a fool of me is going on too long, even if it does come from fate. To me people are nothing but fate." They had never been anything but fate to her, with the single exception of Marwitz, with whom she had been able to speak and from whom she had learned so much. Except for Varnhagen also, one would think, since he was able to understand her and was blessed with the tremendous gift of rationality. All others were mute, did not react, could not be moved by arguments, could not even be bothered: they were nothing but fate, "like an axe that cuts off a great man's head." And for that very reason she had taken Varnhagen, because she was tired of being at the mercy of fate, because everything was over. "I am out of that sphere; my lot has been drawn out of the lotto." And because life was nevertheless quite lovely and worth being lived right down to the end.

Later, when her marriage with Varnhagen had already become so much a matter of course that she could only think to assign the name of love to it, she actually believed that passion required muteness and lack of understanding in order to come into being: "No sort of attachment, no well-wishing, no amount of perception, can ever become heart's pain, inner rending, called passion—not when the object of choice . . . is so sensible that one can *talk* with him, so rational that one can tell him everything!" The less she desired or was able to become entangled in passion, the more determined she was to have her peace. And Varnhagen was not so wrong when, in the end, he resisted her demands upon him, when he declared these to be neither sensible nor fair: "If Marwitz or any other of these fine fellows suddenly had to earn their livings by a definite choice of work, he would be just as unhappy as I." That was true and not true. For what Rahel objected to in Varnhagen, what she chided him for in ever-varied phrases, was something more; it was above all his inability to get on well with people, his tactlessness, his lack of bearing. She was right to be concerned. That concern disappeared later on, after he had made a career for himself. For the present, however, although he "solemnly proposed to Rahel," he knew at the same time that: "You see me neither loved by the world nor distinguished by it."

"But now nothing counts but to advance against the foe. I must fall or rise, give way or gain ground. In peace there is no advancement; that comes only through loss in battle. . . ."

The outbreak of the new war between Austria and France in 1809 called to the colors not only the German patriots, who were in despair at Prussia's passivity. Also attracted were the youth of a state impoverished, reduced in size and politically ruined, who saw no further chance for advancement in Prussia. For them the war was the one lottery which still offered a certain chance of gain. After the victorious battle of Aspern they succumbed easily and willingly to Austria's efforts at recruitment. Among them we find Marwitz and Varnhagen. Marwitz joined up of his own accord; Varnhagen followed him. Marwitz had no need to make a career. He was impelled by a curious mixture of boredom, which led him to seek adventure, and the realization that as a nobleman he could not stand aside, since history is not made only from above. Varnhagen went along (not merely in imitation, as Rahel charged) because he saw that this was his last opportunity.

Varnhagen joined Colonel Bentheim's infantry regiment. His first experience was the defeat at Wagram, which put a rapid end to all dreams of military glory. The troops were sent home, and after the conclusion of peace in October the Prussian soldiers also returned for good. The whole business seemed to have been a senseless undertaking for Varnhagen, a pure loss of time.

But Varnhagen was lucky. By chance he struck up a closer acquaintanceship with his colonel—thanks to his smattering of medicine, he treated the colonel during a severe illness. He thereby entered into a relationship with the colonel which is difficult to define precisely, characteristic though it was, and of such importance for his whole later career. For a time he remained in the colonel's entourage, something between a confidant and a private secretary. He went back to Prague with him, then to the colonel's Westphalian home to help put the Bentheim family affairs in order and finally was taken along to Paris. At the Austrian Embassy in Paris Varnhagen for the first time in his life made the acquaintance of men of influence, obtained the necessary connections with Metternich, who later proved useful to him, and Tettenborn, under whom he served in the war of 1813–14. He even had vague prospects of some small diplomatic position in the Austrian service. These prospects evaporated, however. He remained tied to Bentheim, who returned to Westphalia a totally ruined man, and it was only in response to Rahel's vigorous hectoring that Varnhagen finally resolved to drop this life of an adventurer, which made sense only in wartime. "I advise you not to fetter yourself to your deranged count," Rahel warned him. "A hero, a great man, must have money, means. No fraudulent dealings, like Prince Louis! Otherwise his comrades are unhappy and may even steal from him. So take your leave and come for me at once!"

Varnhagen did not obey immediately. He could not make up his mind to throw away the little patch of reality that three months of war had put into his hands. Nor did he have any idea what he would live on. His position had gradually become solidified by custom; he was now more or less the count's adjutant, wrote his letters and ran his affairs for him. And he was now beginning to set down those recollections which he later published under the name of *Memorabilia* and which, for all that they have been often challenged and do indeed contain some highly dubious statements, remain a valuable historical source. The association with the count profited him in another and really important way. His experiences of recent years had repeatedly and emphatically shown him how pleasant and useful it was to be a nobleman, how right Rahel was when she declared: "As long as one nobleman exists, one must also be ennobled," since after all one had to "fit into the joints" of the world. Whether it was due to his understanding or perhaps only to his touching obedience, he found a way to fit himself into the joint and actually succeeded in making himself a member of the aristocracy. "In an old history of Westphalia I have found information on my family and my coat of arms, and certain evidence that I stem from an ancient knighted family, von Ense, called Varnhagen. This confirms what I learned in the past from oral tradition, through my father."

For a liberal and a declared hater of the nobility, this was certainly a farcical discovery, and probably he would never have made it but for Rahel's remark. For during the first months of the war he had written: "What business have the nobles in this war? Unfortunately, they look upon it as their war, and unfortunately it may turn out to be that!" He would have to lay this attitude aside for a while, until he had acquired nobility for himself; at any rate, he never forgot it for good. The earnestness with which he now set about appointing himself to the nobility was truly comic. "As far as my nobility is concerned, Bentheim and Stein, whom I consulted about it, are of the opinion that the case is crystal clear. . . . Confirmation from the Emperor is necessary, however, so that I can legally lay claim to bequests and the like; Bentheim will probably be able to obtain the confirmation without difficulty."

After a brief spell at the Prague garrison Varnhagen at last took leave of his "deranged count" and set out for Berlin, enriched by nobility and many valuable connections. He fetched Rahel and went to Teplitz with her. All of society was once again assembled in Teplitz, and for the first time Rahel appeared in public with Varnhagen. She felt at ease here amid the typically Berlinese mingling of nobles, actors and artists.

Their staying together was probably a kind of trial balloon on both sides; certainly so on Rahel's. Apparently it was not a complete success, since Rahel terminated the stay by going to Dresden, where she was expecting to meet Marwitz. Thereafter she returned to Berlin and Varnhagen to Prague.

In Prague Varnhagen actually did nothing but see people. He still went on talking about how wonderful Rahel was, but not quite so wildly as in the past. The period spent in Teplitz had probably given him the right to consider himself allied with her, to appear as her fiancé; but on the other hand he was determined to get on in the world and had realized that a Jewess, no matter how well known she was, was not the most useful of appendages. He went far in his betrayals. Having passed on to Clemens von Brentano some deprecatory remarks Rahel had made about him, he did not stop Brentano from sending Rahel a vengeful letter full of the most malicious insults—although Brentano made a point of reading the letter to him beforehand, in order to provoke him. This incident

brought down upon his head the worst and gravest quarrel
Rahel ever had with him, and upon Brentano not Rahel's but
Varnhagen's eternal enmity. This enmity unfortunately led
Varnhagen to destroy many crucial passages from Brentano's
posthumous papers (which were entrusted to him by Bettina),
including all reference in letters to himself or to Rahel.

Amid all this ridiculous and trivial gossip Varnhagen per-
formed so great a service for Rahel that it alone would have
sufficed to bind her to him forever. He used his time and his
inability to keep anything to himself to good purpose, and
began to collate everything that Rahel had ever written to him
about Goethe and Goethe's works. He gathered everything
together, added answers from himself, and offered the whole
thing to the publisher Cotta as a small volume. Cotta sent the
manuscript to Goethe who at first (already suspecting that it
was a correspondence between a man and a woman) thought
the initials which stood for Varnhagen represented the woman,
and those denoting Rahel the man. Varnhagen himself re-
counts the gentle irony with which Goethe treated his own
statements or the passages from his own letters. And he simultaneously quotes Goethe's handsome comment on Rahel:
"The woman does not actually judge; she *has* the subject, and
insofar as she does not possess it, it does not concern her."

A letter from Goethe was something more than a personal
joy. It was unquestionably a step forward toward fame, toward
having arrived. Goethe became another of Varnhagen's connections; thus Varnhagen achieved all that Rahel had not
all her life, because she had not wanted to. "Goethe's letter
lies before me. It has come over me like a flood; it is all like
a sea; and it will take time for things to shape gradually out
of it. Whether I am grateful to you? You know I am; I shall
show you. You know whether I vainly seek applause I would
not accord myself; whether I go to any great trouble to be
praised. But to be able some time to lay my really boundless
love and reverent admiration at the feet of the most glorious
of men and human beings—that has been the silent, secret
wish of my whole life, measured by its duration and its intensity. In one respect I have obeyed an impulse that comes

from my innermost self, to keep a humble distance from Goethe." Nor would she exploit this triumph; Goethe's recognition remained entirely without consequences for the course of her life. He was, one might say, the sole person whom she never wanted to know, nor ever made the slightest attempt to know. For the casual encounter of the young girl in Karlsbad with the already famous man can scarcely be called knowing, or even a meeting. A few years after Varnhagen had obtained this letter for her, she saw Goethe for the second and last time. By chance she learned that he was visiting Frankfurt at the same time as she and wrote him a brief note. He responded by coming to visit her without previous announcement. When word of the visitor was brought in to her, she was not dressed. "I had him admitted and made him wait only the time it took me to button on a skirt; it was a black padded skirt; and in this costume I appeared before him. Sacrificing myself in order not to make him wait a moment longer. . . . On the whole he was like a most distinguished prince, but also like an extremely good man, full of *aisance*, but refraining from anything personal. . . . He left very soon . . . I was content. I feel that on the whole I behaved as I had that time in Karlsbad. . . . But when one sees a man, after so many years of love and life and worshipping, only for a moment, that is the way it is. . . . After he was gone, I dressed up very fine, as though I wanted to make up for it all. A lovely white dress with high collar, a lace coif and veil, the Moscow shawl. . . ." A greater tribute, and a greater display of modesty, than not to dress in order not to make the man "wait a moment longer," could scarcely be offered by a woman to a man.

Varnhagen, however, showed the Goethe letter around everywhere, as though it were a trophy and a proof of something. Yet to him it meant both far more and far less than to Rahel. For he knew quite well that he owed the glory to the letter G., which stood for Rahel, and not to his own comments. "I won this victory with you; I wielded you as an invincible weapon. . . . This I have accomplished: that now we possess, from the wisest of poets, the noblest testimonials to your brilliance; that you are beckoning to each other like spirits in the gloomy mist." This fanfare seems all the more crass in view of the moderate tone in which Goethe couched his appreciation. But more important for Varnhagen—and ultimately for Rahel, since she was now committed to him—was "the tremendous advantage of seeing rise upon the horizon the star of a friendly relationship with the wisest headmaster of our literature; even if that star should set again soon, it would still leave behind a gleam of itself upon my orbit!"

Prague was, during those years, a kind of center of the literary as well as the political world. Stein, who had been expelled from Prussia by Napoleon, had settled down there and gathered the Prussian patriots around himself. Varnhagen, too, met him and for a long time kept hoping to obtain through him a post in the Prussian government or diplomatic service. When the war between France and Russia broke out in 1812, the circle scattered; its members had in any case looked upon Prague only as a temporary refuge. Stein went to Russia. Neither Austria nor Prussia joined Russia, and many patriots therefore decided to leave the Austrian or Prussian service in order to fight Napoleon under the Russian command. Several of Varnhagen's friends had already taken this course, and it seemed the obvious choice for him, too. But in spite of his good experiences with the opportunities of wartime, he had no great desire to expose himself once more to the incalculabilities of chance—not right now, when he had already won something. Bearing recommendations from Humboldt and Metternich, he tried first to ingratiate himself with Hardenberg, the Prussian chancellor. He was probably acting in accordance with Rahel's wish that he go off to the war only if it could not be avoided. For war did not mean to her, as it did to everyone around her, a new beginning and a liberation; rather she saw it as "the world being turned topsy-turvy." And so Varnhagen betook himself to Berlin, but did not obtain a post; he received nothing but promises everywhere and remained in precisely the same vague situation as before.

Not until Berlin was occupied by the Russians at the beginning of 1813 did Varnhagen join the Russian forces. Thanks to his connections, he promptly obtained a post as an Imperial Russian captain in Colonel von Tettenborn's regiment. Before he finally committed himself, he made certain that the Prussian and the Russian causes were officially acknowledged to be identical. For this would naturally be a prime factor if any personal good were to accrue from his action. Then he accompanied Tettenborn to Hamburg, again becoming liaison man and secretary for this colonel. Not only was his position the same as that he had held under Bentheim in 1809, but he even used the same expressions in speaking about both. The absurdly exaggerated praises of the generosity, amiability, bravery, leniency, enlightened intelligence, etc., of the two men are so similar that the letters could easily be interchanged, and the names substituted for each other, without altering anything essential.

But one factor had changed: Varnhagen had grown more patriotic. He became aware much later than his associates, but a good deal earlier than Rahel, that patriotism was indispensable. He wrote "intoxicated by the jubilation I have experienced, by the strength I see before me, by the happy outcome of our undertaking, which cannot fail." He knew that it would be necessary "to be personally and particularly involved," kept a sharp lookout for opportunities for personal advantage—reviewing, for example, in terms of extravagant praise the pitiful war poems of Privy State Councilor Stägemann, and gloating at "having put Stägemann very much in my debt"; he put off Rahel's objections (for she showed far less instinct in such matters than he) with the remark that "what may harm on the one hand always brings advantages on the other hand."

In Rahel this adaptation took place far more slowly. She did not cease to admonish him: "Do not forget that after this period there will come another for those who remain alive, in which everything will return to the old rotten order, and the possessors will laugh at the others." She insisted that he promptly have confirmed, on a civilian and legalistic basis, all his wartime achievements, including the title of Imperial

Captain. "Human beings are mortal; doubly so in wartime." In spite of all these years of preparation, patriotism as such was still as foreign to her as it had been at the beginning. She was once again living entirely within her family—not one of her brothers volunteered!—in utter naïveté, because she had no idea of all that was involved, she did not conceal her true mind—though shortly afterwards, but only for the duration of the war, she yielded at last to the pressure of public opinion and hastily revised it. That opinion was: "That we are called and are Germans is a matter of chance, and the inflated making-much-of-this will end with a bursting of the whole folly."

Rahel could not be won over to the war so easily. As long as it lay within the initiative of individuals to enlist out of patriotism in one unit or another, she would not be prevailed upon to ask any other question than: is it or is it not opportune? Only when the war took on the appearance of a revolt of the entire people against the government, against the policies of the cabinets and against the nobility, did she begin to discover in herself a measure of sympathy for the new movement. Varnhagen wrote: "Nowhere is there talk any longer about nobility, birth and rank; but superior education or true efficiency count for a great deal, and are readily acknowledged. In this respect, too, this war offers us our best hope, and the mental climate that will develop out of it is probably far more important than all changes in states and their boundaries." This, of course, sounded to Rahel like the fulfillment of Fichte's predictions in his *Addresses to the German Nation*, which had first led her to discover her patriotism, and which she later adduced as the basis for it. At this point she actually became interested. Other possibilities seemed to be dawning than the mere "rise and fall" of individuals, than the advancement of a few of the declassés. This actually seemed to be the beginning of the event that Fichte had prophesied for a much later generation: the abolition of all rankings in a general advance of the whole people.

Thus Rahel's patriotism began with enthusiastic admiration for all proclamations which did not wrong the French people, in which the authors "know how to honor the enemy, spare the nation and do not revile." What for others was at most only incidental—justice even in wartime—was to her the main point; indeed, if she could have had her will, the whole war would take place simply to show that the greatest virtue of enlightened humanity—fairness—could win out always and everywhere. She identified the German people with this virtue, in order to arrive by this curiously roundabout route (which, after her, was followed in one way or another by almost all official spokesmen of German Judaism) at identification with German patriotism.

Varnhagen's patriotism carried her along—that is to say, his manner of interpreting the war enabled her to take a sympathetic interest. How right she had been to throw in her lot with a man who still had to rise, and who therefore in many respects had the same starting point as she, whose judgments necessarily sprang from the same point of view as hers. For Varnhagen viewed this entire campaign as a kind of continuation of the French Revolution. That Revolution, he believed, had "degenerated," but its fruits were now going to be reaped by the Prussians as the result of this War of Liberation, with its uprising of the people. "I will not tolerate hearing the French Revolution condemned," he wrote. This war seemed to him the great chance for the middle class, its goal to elevate the epithet burgher to a title of honor. Thus he wrote in an article published in the army newspaper he edited, on the occasion of the nomination of General Tettenborn as an honorary burgher of the city of Bremen: "That men of the highest rank and occupying the highest offices in the state should find it an honor to be named burghers, and to belong to a class which in the past days of folly and arrogance was little respected by them and their fellows, is an irrefutable indication that those days are gone, and that reconciliation of the classes has begun in the most glorious fashion. Thus there is taking place among us, by calm and peaceful means, by gradual evolution, what the less-fortunate French in the past, with noble ambition but by harsh violence, had to force from their stubborn brethren for a time."

For the Prussian Jews, who had just been made citizens of

the state by the edict of 1812, the war was the first opportunity to prove that they belonged, and that they had a legitimate right to be called citizens. Rahel began to do what all the women in her sphere were doing: organize help, collect money and clothing for the wounded, and so on. "If only the Christians gave as generously as the Jews," she wrote, "here at least there would be no distress." For all the Jews tried to make the largest sacrifices in the most conspicuous ways— thereby clearly demonstrating how insecure they felt in spite of the edict. Thousands volunteered for the war—the first war in which Jews fought on the German side—and the women were incessantly active. They contributed money and goods, more than other women, and were gladly accepted, permitted to lend their services.

All this patriotic bustle did not stop Rahel from fleeing Berlin as the war came closer and closer. She went to Austria and to Prague, which had not yet joined the allied forces. In doing so she was not so much fleeing the war as using the war as a pretext for escaping at last from her family. For when the war finally sucked in Austria also, and swarms of soldiers and wounded men flooded Prague, she was by no means unhappy; she remained there, growing more enthusiastic for the cause of Prussia every day.

Flight from the family: "However, I have decided that I shall not go home again without some new commanding reason. There my former existence must be *entirely* forgotten by brothers, friends, enemies, acquaintances, authorities and everybody, and especially by myself! It was simply too shabby!" Flight, then, from her whole former existence, flight, all in all, to Varnhagen. He, for the first time, was earning his livelihood, could for the first time assure her of the wherewithal to live; he gave her travel money, obtained rooms for her in overcrowded Prague, thanks to his connections with Bentheim. There in Prague she felt good again, at last, after so long a time —better than ever before, perhaps. She was living in a foreign city, but among old friends. Marwitz, wounded, had come for a while to be nursed by her; Gentz was concerned again and wrote her little notes every day. Being in a foreign place, being involved in the war, engaged in practical activity, had decided social advantages. Having fled her native place, her alienness was given acceptable form; she was caught up in the general misfortune which, because of its universality, had titles and names and was therefore a stroke of luck for her.

"If in this foreign place I cannot receive people in my own house, cannot communicate, I at least have the title and rank of foreigner. And naturally, the result is that *I* am accepted, and all dislocation, all that painful regretting the past, has dropped away." Her old "mood of wit and jest" returned; she revived, for she could feel "free" in this exile which was not hers alone but affected all, to which anyone could be condemned; free "especially from the old, so very wrong and hated and *long* burdens." Foreignness, exile, was not a dire fate in Prague, was not something to be hidden with difficulty and great effort, like unhappiness and shame. On the contrary, it was a social phenomenon here. In these circumstances, moreover, she had the advantage of having been accustomed to such a life; being foreign was not foreign to her, and in exile there was nothing strange about her lack of ties to others.

Being a Jewess was only a situation for her, an unfortunate situation in the world, but nothing more. Nowhere was that more evident than here in Prague. As soon as all were in her situation—foreigners—her situation was no longer identical with herself. She compared her present situation with the good old days before 1806 when she had lived better, socially speaking, unmolested and unhandicapped. And it seemed to her now that she was once more becoming what she had been then: "But I believe it is this way with my mood: it is always there, only suppressed; since I really have no relationships here but new ones which are not oppressive and obsolete and since I am free of great anxiety, although I feel, think and fear no differently for our country, and the affairs of both of us; but since all this is *suspendu* and I hear and see and can do nothing about it, the whole of the old existence is bobbing up out of the depths in me. In particular I feel this bobbing up as if there were some kind of spring within me; I was *too* depressed for *too* long: I always said so. Now, since I have not died, my being is not killed within me, it lives like one saved from burial alive. Life is sometimes wonderfully obstinate, you know."

In other words, continuing to live—which had been so hard a decision for her to make—had proved worthwhile after all. She was really able to perceive, now that things were going well with her for a brief time, how fine and lovable beyond everything life still was, after all. The "bobbing up as if there were some spring within," was nothing more nor less than her war career; it was something she owed to the war. And she also owed to it a highly temporary evaporation of social distinctions.

The insults had lasted too long, her solitude had been too desperate and too utterly without foreseeable end, and her future was even now too insecure, for her to feel any un-clouded sense of well-being. She thought she had to prove to herself and all others once and for all that she was like every-one else; she had to exaggerate, so that everyone would remark it; she had to be bustling, thorough, possessed of that kind of thoroughness which we have had the amplest opportunity to study in Germany for a hundred years. It is really curious to see her behaving just as abominably as all philanthropic ladies after her time—organizing everything on the slightest pretext, bursting into tears at every benefaction, worshipping all the heroes in every single soldier; and like all such ladies con-cocting the same infantile pacifist programs, born of overesti-mation of her own experience and underestimation, in fact ignorance, of all the objective factors that make history. "I have *such* a plan in my heart to call upon all European women to refuse ever to go along with war; and jointly to help all sufferers; then, at least, we could be *tranquil* on *one* side; we women, I mean. Wouldn't something like that *work?*"

She became thoroughly stupid and commonplace out of sheer wild delight that she was graciously being allowed to help, that she had something to do, that waiting and being a spectator had ceased. "I rejoice, banished as I was by those near and dear to me, without fortune, rank, youth, name, talents, to see that I can nevertheless find my place in the world." Of significance for all that came later was the fact that Varnhagen had made her stay in Prague possible, that he sent her money, and more and more became her supporter.

Varnhagen had meanwhile actually amounted to something; not only had he won the Order of the Sword and a captaincy in the Russian army, but he had become a kind of political journalist. His position with Tettenborn and his personal participation in one of the important and dangerous aspects of the campaign afforded him the opportunity to obtain news at first hand, to be the first to form opinions. He made good use of this chance. He published several war newspapers, and although these soon expired, since they served only the most topical needs, they made his name known. He went to Paris with Tettenborn, witnessed Napoleon's unsuccessful attempt at a breakthrough, which Tettenborn managed to cut off, and then, in Paris, obtained a close-up view of history really taking place. His financial situation was good; Rahel ceased to be dependent upon her family and now belonged wholly to him, without any equivocation.

Varnhagen had no grandiose ambitions; he never snatched at the chance to intervene actively in history, to take responsibility. But he had found his proper place. All events poured toward him, the "beggar by the wayside." All his life henceforth he would walk alongside events, in order to note them down, without ever again feeling the shameful consciousness of emptiness and expulsion. For never again would history be for him the history of individual persons with whom he had to compare himself—in Rahel he had enough of this. Although apparently nothing but individual persons occur in his notes and his "inside-story" narratives, these persons scarcely appear as themselves; they are merely the medium through which history takes its course. "The acts of princes, statesmen and generals are wholly unimportant, mere reflections of the intentions and the deeds of fate; fate uses these human beings as it uses floods, blizzards, tempests and earth tremors, to accomplish its purposes—uses dead things to accomplish living ends, to arouse sympathy and attention. Destiny itself is the sole acting person; only the conscious, shared knowledge of a few free spirits releases them from the spell which makes most human beings into blind instruments. I should like to be one of these spirits. . . ." In these sentences, with this insight and with this formulation of his task, Varnhagen had at last turned away from his own wretched person and had, with an altogether grand élan, fitted himself into the ranks of those "free spirits" who were all more talented than he, but who in the final analysis had no different desire. Schlegel's "participating in thought" and Humboldt's restless thirst to know everything, Gentz's conceit at "being in the know," and Hegel's self-liberation of Reason in history—these sentences of Varnhagen's echo all the tendencies of the age. Precisely in his renunciation of action—"destiny itself is the sole acting person"—he found his place in the age.

Varnhagen had got somewhere and had taken his leave of the class of would-be changers of the world who cannot admit, because change is their aim, that the world was made, is being made and will be made by anything but other human beings. He carried Rahel along with him; she "arrived" at last as the wife of a writer who was on his way up and saw a good career ahead of him. But it must also be considered that she was going to become the wife of a "free spirit" who had no more need to do anything but bear witness to events, who could observe without participating, who needed no longer to be involved in care, anxiety and rebellion, nor be one of those maniacs who want to turn the whole world upside down merely to make a place for his own small person.

12

BETWEEN PARIAH AND PARVENU
(1815–1819)

"I HAVE an impulse I cannot control: to honor myself in my superiors, and to track down their good qualities in order to love them." Thus Varnhagen speaks of himself, and these words clearly suggest a man with the finest prospects for making a good career. Certainly it was not his fault that, in the end, he did not rise very high in government service. At any rate he had opportunities enough to cultivate and perfect all that he had learned in working for Bentheim and Tettenborn.

All parvenus are familiar with Varnhagen's impulse, all those who must climb by fraud into a society, a rank, a class, not theirs by birthright. Making a strenuous effort to love, where there is no alternative but obedience, is more productive of good results than simple and undisguised servility. In "tracking down the good qualities" of superiors they hope to purge themselves of inevitable but intolerable resentment. Those who are resolutely determined to rise, to "arrive," must early accustom themselves to anticipating the stage they hope to attain by simulating voluntary appreciation; must early set their sights higher than the blind obedience, which is all that is demanded of them; must always act as if they were performing freely, and as their own masters, the things that are in any case expected of hirelings and subordinates. This fraud seldom has any direct influence upon their careers, but it is of the greatest value for social successes and for positions in society. By this fraud the pariah prepares society to accept his career as a parvenu.

Varnhagen, too, was recompensed for his love and veneration. For in the end he rescued, out of a career destroyed through no fault of his own, a considerable social influence, a degree of acknowledgment remarkable for his position and his talents and free entry into all social spheres.

He began as secretary at the Congress of Vienna, charged with the task of drawing up from the innumerable "memoranda, petitions, demands, etc., a synopsis and an annotated list, so that the Chancellor [Hardenberg] might make use of them at the Congress" (Varnhagen). After the end of the Congress and the final defeat of Napoleon, Hardenberg appointed him Prussian chargé d'affaires in Baden and entrusted him with representing Prussia at the Karlsruhe Court. The year 1819, which marked the assassination of Kotzebue, the subsequent Karlsbad Decrees and the beginning of the "Persecution of the Demagogues"—meaning all liberals—cost him his position and his whole political career. For he had never repudiated moderate liberalism—although he had also never, as was slanderously said of him, taken sides with the opposition in Baden. At the age of thirty-five he was accorded the title of Privy Legation Councilor and placed "on reserve" for his lifetime by the Prussian government. There is nothing worth recording about his three years of political activity in Baden. On the other hand, his last diplomatic action casts a significant light on the nature of his political interests and abilities. Ten years after his recall, in 1829, he was suddenly sent for by the Court and commissioned to persuade the Electoral Prince of Hesse to break with his mistress and effect a reconciliation with his son; the Prussian Court felt that it could no longer tolerate this public scandal in a neighboring and friendly German state. Varnhagen took this assignment in highborn meddling with deadly earnestness; full of self-importance and high hopes, he departed for Hesse, associated—obeying his old impulse—with love and "unconstraint" with both the opposed parties and of course achieved nothing at all except a decoration for himself. That satisfied him completely, which is to say, socially. He had no true political ambitions; both politics and literature were instruments for social advancement to him; he never complained about having nothing to do. His cup of contentment was full so long as he was received cordially in high and the highest circles. As a private person living on a Prussian pension, right down to the end of his life and in spite of all his openly proclaimed liberalism, he found ample opportunity to give way to his "impulse." For with the fearfully splintered state of Germany, there were several dozen crowned heads at his disposal to whom he could display love and veneration and a solicitous concern for their personal destinies.

"I hear . . . that Varnhagen has now married the little Levy woman. So now at last she can become an Excellency and Ambassador's wife. There is nothing the Jews cannot achieve." Here, as elsewhere, Wilhelm von Humboldt was the best, keenest and most malicious gossip of his age. He hit the nail on the head—even though he did put the matter more crudely and more spitefully than was absolutely necessary. Nineteenth-century Jews, if they wanted to play a part in society, had no choice but to become parvenus par excellence, and certainly in those decades of reaction they were the choicest examples of parvenus. All that was now left for Rahel to do was to play this part to the full; only thus could she really become an example of all the "trivialities." And for a person who wanted to represent life itself, life in both its most deeply stirring sublimity and its inescapable vulgar banality, that could well be more satisfying than feeling herself an exception.

Varnhagen became a parvenu only through Rahel. He never refined his parvenu-ism to perfection—in this, as in so many other things, copying her. Thus the intolerable cheek of his "love" for his superiors actually derived from her. His natural Prussian subordinate's temperament would not, of its own accord, have spawned such repulsive closeness and audacity; without Rahel, his ambition would rather have remained that of the petty official. Rahel, however, wanted decidedly more; she wanted to be esteemed as a peer; indeed, she ought to have been a "princess." And since she was not that, after all, she conceived how she would act if she were—and then used Varnhagen to enthrone her. Like all parvenus, she never dreamed of a radical alteration of bad conditions but rather of a shift of personnel that would work out in her favor, so that the situation would improve as if by the stroke of a magic wand. The parvenu's overestimation of himself, which often seems

quite mad, arises out of the tremendous effort, and the strain-
ing of all his forces and talents, which are incumbent upon
him if he is to climb only a few steps up the social ladder. The
smallest success, so hard-won, necessarily dazzles him with an
illusory: everything is possible; the smallest failure instantly
sends him hurtling back into the depths of his social nullity,
misleads him into the shabbiest kind of worship of success.

"There is nothing the Jews cannot achieve" was true because
they stood outside of society, because there existed no prescribed ladder for them to climb from birth on up and because
no one will of his own free will stay on the lowest rung. It was
not Rahel's fault that her justified yearning to have some rank,
to become a normal person, to possess social equality, should
have ended in reverence for "virtuous monarchs" and princes
with literary interests, in "respect for the sovereign and loyalty" toward the "father of all Hessians, all Prussians, etc.," in
admiration for "clement and paternal royal mercy" (Varnhagen), in breadth of vision consisting in the praise of human
qualities even in princesses and in intense solicitude over roy-
alty's catching a cold. Nor was it her fault to feel these senti-
ments with innocent sincerity: "If only we had seen our Prince
together. . . . He produced in me the feelings of a brother.
Only brothers and sisters can gladden or irk one another in
this manner. . . . Since seeing him our King is twice as dear
to me." Though she herself was only vaguely conscious of it,
there was an excellent basis for her old and new gratitude
toward the monarchs ("only understanding despots can help
us"), toward the rulers of enlightened absolutism. For such
rulers had ultimately, at the end of the most evil times, found
a use for those who had never been used before or only been
used as victims of robbery. Out of need for money they had
helped the outcasts of history enter history, and those outcasts
included Rahel and all her kith and kin. "You know, I worship
Frederick the Great, our great Electoral Prince; I could still
kiss the hem of his coat with pounding heart. Lovely, glorious
feeling: gratitude! Respect!" It was, in fact, a reassurance to
her, in spite of all fantasied familiarity, to know that she could

never rise so high and therefore need not strain quite so hard; that restless ambition to attain the greatest possible height, in order to have attained anything at all, did have limits set to it somewhere; that there was something she could legitimately admire with calm spirit. "Oh, how one would have to *deify* sovereigns and great men if they understood their places, their toilsome, lovely duties and governorships; it would be impossible to think of the good ones as anything but gods. And they are indeed gods upon earth." She only had to attain what fortunate persons of no "infamous birth" already possessed and did not have to attain. Such fortunate ones did not have to prove to themselves, at every new rung they climbed: "People like us cannot be *Jews.*"

The nobility still set the tone in society. Hence, the bourgeois as well as the Jews who became parvenus reacted to the privilege of birth by demonstrating that they were able to obtain the same privileges for themselves by their own powers. They all went to enormous trouble to reach the position already held by the few who had it by birth; they had, as a body, a mania for acquiring titles and nobility. Consequently they too "loved" the monarchs to the point of deification, inasmuch as under the sovereign's "paternal mercy" all were equal. Their supreme hope was that in his grace he would raise them up, elevate them to the nobility. In the bourgeois nineteenth century the absolutistic king became the king of the parvenus. In order to win status in his eyes some sought riches, others strove for literary distinction. It was only in the nineteenth century, post-Goethe, as it were, that literature became a means for attaining equality with princes. Goethe remained the symbol of how the great writer could be a friend of kings (the King of Bavaria paid a birthday visit to Goethe), how decorations, titles and nobility could be received on sheer "merit." The Varnhagens, husband and wife, threw themselves avidly into literature after the failure of Varnhagen's diplomatic career. They formed the center of the Goethe cult in Berlin. In the Varnhagen salon that cult took on a meaning quite different from what it had been in Rahel's garret room thirty years before. The extent to which the Berlin Goethe cult concealed parvenu manners was suspected by no one, save young Heine.

For the present both members of the pair seemed to be doing well. In Baden, a "foreign" state, Rahel won Prussian citizenship. No trace of her "infamous birth" was left; she was simply the wife of the Prussian chargé d'affaires. It had been necessary to run away from home in order to cast off her origins and all those who knew about these origins. It was glorious to associate with princesses and be entitled to their society, rather than be dependent upon their generosity. Glorious to be able to quit her native land when she had been, so to speak, dispatched by that native land as an emissary and could "honor it abroad." It was the greatest satisfaction to have rank, title and acknowledgment and to do, for everybody to see, the sort of thing she could not in any case bear to give up doing. "What I did, I did as a Prussian woman; and I was modest, helpful, good, gentle—and popular—and that was credited to all Prussian women; I had *the* great satisfaction of not being at home—where I should still have had to *prove* that I had the right to be noble, and where every *pebble* would remind me of how it used to be and that I ought to be displaying my old self. And I had the absolutely infinite satisfaction that at last I stood on such a pedestal that the *good* I did *also* counted for something. I call this satisfaction infinite because the difference between having it and not having it is infinite."

For the parvenu, being innocently liked is a triumph, being innocently disliked an offense. Bathing with the Duchess of Sagan—"if only Gentz knew of this! This was his greatest *terreur* in Prague. He always thought he had to plump me underground, bury me alive, out of sheer desperate need to deny he knew me, just on account of the Duchess of Sagan." And on the other hand, not receiving an invitation from Councilor of State Stägemann, when Varnhagen himself had been invited, produced the reaction: "Deadly, nameless annoyance from persons whom I otherwise would not have wished to see." The "great poison of all insight and outlook"[1] which the

[1] From her diary, December 29, 1819, unprinted.

parvenu could never admit to himself in any circumstances was this: that he was gnawed by a multitude of things which he did not even really want, but which he could not bear to be refused; that he had to adapt his tastes, his life, his desires to these things; that in nothing and not for a single minute did he dare to be himself any longer. He had to be something, anything else, had to want to attain everything, had heroically "to tolerate" what he had "not made" and even "despised."

Rahel had striven for everything with the same sincerity with which she had also, simultaneously, questioned everything. Her past, with its experiences, had been so dearly bought and paid for in such hard cash that she could not have "wholly abandoned" her past life, even though she demanded that of herself. It was true that in practice she could not now "arrange my present life according to my past, that is, more according to the wishes of that past than to the actual life I lived in it." But neither could she (and this was both her misfortune and the secret of her remarkable vivacity until her old age) forget the insights she had had, nor emancipate herself inwardly from them. She could not give up experiences so much more extensive than the little she had achieved in reality; could not extinguish a past which had passionately anticipated, pierced to the heart of, judged and rejected everything possible—everything possible in her world—so thoroughly that no amount of "civil improvement" could compare with it. In the blackest, most harried despair, she had already known, as she wrote in 1810 to Pauline, that: "We have been created to live the truth in this world. . . . We are *alongside* of human society. For us no place, no office, no empty title exists! *All* lies have some place; eternal truth, proper living and feeling . . . has no place! And thus we are excluded from society. You because you offended it. . . . I because I cannot sin and lie along with it." One had to pay for becoming a parvenu by abandoning truth, and this Rahel was not prepared to do.

Immediately after her marriage and shortly before Varnhagen's recall from Baden, Rahel began busily adopting precautions to protect her own truth. The first and most important of these precautions was her request to Varnhagen, who was attending the peace conferences in Paris, to locate the most compromised of the friends of her youth, Pauline Wiesel. This former mistress of Prince Louis Ferdinand had in the meantime run through a number of men and an amount of money extraordinary even in those extremely liberal-minded times. She was considered a person of the worst reputation. In earlier days she had been much loved, because of her great beauty and amazing, dismaying naturalness. She was the only woman Rahel had ever thought her equal: "One who knows nature and the world as do we . . ., who knows everything in advance as do we . . ., who is surprised at nothing unusual and who is eternally preoccupied with the mysteriousness of the usual; who has loved and been loved like us; who can no longer endure loneliness and cannot do without it . . ., who has had the absurdly wonderful fortune to encounter one other person who sees things the same way and who is alike, though her talents are so different—which only makes it all the more amusing . . ., who thinks possible all those natural events which appear nonsensical to our rational faculties. . . . "[2] she wrote in 1816 to her friend.

Varnhagen, thoroughly browbeaten, found Pauline in Paris in a snarl of financial disasters, debts and true or invented love affairs. But at first his account of her was obediently enthusiastic. Later, however, after Rahel's death, he took a thoroughgoing revenge for having been forced to know such a person. He left the entire correspondence between Pauline and Rahel unpublished (with the exception of a few extracts which he published without using her name or under the incomprehensible initials Fr. v. V.), although these letters are the only documents which cast a light undistorted by conventionalities upon Rahel's old age.

Pauline was well aware of the way she was being erased from Rahel's life. Almost a decade after the publication of the *Buch des Andenkens,* Varnhagen appealed to her to turn Rahel's letters over to him. She made use of the occasion to ask

[2] Unpublished passage from a letter dated June 26, 1816, an extract of which was published as a diary entry in the *Buch des Andenkens,* II, 407.

in her simple direct manner why "he deleted every passage that refers to me," and commented that others were also wondering "why Herr von Varnhagen had made so many alterations in the letters." Varnhagen, who of course considered it beneath his dignity even to reply to such a question, was familiar with Pauline's circumstances. He knew that she was impoverished, old and sick, and that helping her financially meant acting in accordance with Rahel's wishes. And he did so after his fashion: he offered her a deal, a ducat for every letter. Pauline disdained to reply, but she sent him the letters and accepted the money.

For the benefit of any inquisitive members of posterity who might someday poke among his papers, Varnhagen left a vigorous warning in his own hand: "This woman friend, so longed for and hailed, was to depart for home a few months afterwards, thoroughly exposed as the repulsive, unworthy and insignificant creature she was." [3] This exposure allegedly took place a year before Rahel's death, on the occasion of Pauline's last visit, when she had "for a time estranged Rahel completely [from Varnhagen], turned her cold and rude, and stirred up everyone against everyone else." If this description of Pauline Wiesel's conduct was based on truth—which is quite likely— it did not in the least shake Rahel's fondness for Pauline—as is indicated by one of Rahel's last letters, written a few weeks before her death, which Varnhagen did not destroy. In this letter she still addressed Pauline as "the *first* and *only* person to whom I write."

Pauline Wiesel was the only person whom Varnhagen objected to fiercely and with good reason during Rahel's lifetime. Varnhagen's virtuous soul was particularly outraged after he became the object of her seductive arts while he was in Paris. Rahel, unlike Varnhagen, was not in the least incensed; Pauline wanted, she commented, to "taste Rahel's husband— like iced punch." Rahel vainly tried to explain to Varnhagen that this attempt at seduction was proof of the liveliest interest in Rahel's own fate. Varnhagen retorted that he could "not help" himself and thought "her flight all too often too low,

[3] Unpublished.

her manners worse than her morals," and a variety of other incontrovertible clichés. Rahel was never for a moment offended by such trivialities. All her life she had admired this extraordinary woman; she had forgotten and almost lost her only during the years of her most violent mania for social climbing. The moment she had really "arrived" and was, in her mind, over the hill—married, baptized, and with a husband about to make a career: at the most unsuitable moment, in other words—she had hunted up Pauline and begun anew a regular relationship with her, the one continuous correspondence that lasted until her death. For, Rahel believed, "there is only one difference between us: you *live* everything because you have the courage and have had the luck; I *think* most things because I have had no luck and have acquired no courage." She believed they belonged together because Pauline, like herself, was "bankrupt, although in an opposite way and with the greatest courage." Or, to put this in other words: Pauline exercised utter freedom in placing herself outside the pale of respectable society because her temperamental and untamable nature would submit to no conventions. Her courage was her naturalness, which was supported and strengthened by all those who fled from society to her, and made a free life possible for her. Mendacity—Pauline's conception of it was, at most, the conventional and hypocritical denial of nature within society. As a Jew Rahel had always stood outside, had been a pariah, and discovered at last, most unwillingly and unhappily, that entrance into society was possible only at the price of lying, of a far more generalized lie than simply hypocrisy. She discovered that it was necessary for the parvenu—but for him alone—to sacrifice every natural impulse, to conceal all truth, to misuse all love, not only to suppress all passion, but worse still, to convert it into a means for social climbing. Courage could not be hers, the courage to take a position outside of society, because the pariah does not voluntarily renounce; he can only assume acquired heroic poses after renunciation has been forced on him. A woman, moreover, could afford social courage only if she were beautiful and had not been humiliated. It was also possible to have courage as, essentially, a highest degree of understanding and rationality, an identification with general ideas, without regard to personal qualities. Rahel, however, was vouchsafed her understanding slowly, a fragment at a time; not until the end of her life did she understand the whole thing and admit to herself the cause of her own "bankruptcy." It had been her privilege to have preserved a "soft heart, of flesh and blood," to have remained eternally vulnerable, to have admitted each weakness to herself, and thus, only thus, to have acquired experience. "I can swear to Almighty God that never in my life have I overcome a weakness!"

The pariah who wants to reach parvenu status strives to attain everything, in empty general terms, to the very degree that he is excluded from everything. Specific desires are a luxury beyond his means. The parvenu will always discover that what he has become is something he basically did not want to become, for he could not have wished it. The only goal he can possibly have is to rise, to get out of his present status; he cannot possibly see where this striving will ultimately land him. He remains subject to the same adverse law that he revolted against when he was a pariah: having to acquiesce in everything. No career, no matter how brilliant, can change that. Because of the inevitable indefiniteness of his wishes he must be proud of anything he achieves. If he does not want this sort of imposed pride, if he thinks of this, too, as acquiescence, he will not manage to make parvenu status. Instead, like Rahel, he will remain a "rebel" when he has apparently reached his goal; otherwise he must swallow the humiliation of having to be content with status bought so dearly, so painfully. Rahel had never been able to reconcile herself to having "to seek with effort" what she felt ought to have "dropped into [her] lap"; she had always gone on hoping that she would be "too proud . . . to take a step for it." And yet she went on seeking with a great deal of effort and took many steps.

An honest parvenu who admits to himself that he only vaguely desired what everybody has, and honestly discovers that he never did want anything specific, is a kind of paradox. "And everything that I wished to purchase with such effort *really* has *never* existed for me." A parvenu who longs to return to his pariah existence is, in respectable society, a fool. Rahel found it intolerable that "now I have to behave toward people as if I were nothing more than *my husband;* in the past I was *nothing,* and that is a great deal." But officially she wanted to be neither a fool nor a paradox, and therefore she needed Varnhagen to make her in reality Frau Friederike Varnhagen von Ense, to annihilate her whole existence, even including her given name. Secretly, in opposition to him, in conscious revolt against such a condition, she conjured up scraps of her old life, lived her own life "*altogether* inwardly." The witness of these unofficial machinations was Pauline Wiesel, with whom she had more in common than character traits, for she shared with Pauline the deeply humane love of all outcasts from society for the "true realities"—"a bridge, a tree, a ride, a smell, a smile."

This tendency to undo what she had achieved gathered strength as she became aware that her rise was only a semblance, that a pariah remained, in truly good society, nothing but a parvenu, that she could not escape her intolerably exposed position, any more than she could escape insults. The first and crucial experience of this sort was her meeting with Caroline von Humboldt again. This encounter took place in Frankfurt shortly after the conclusion of the Congress of Vienna. Caroline was one of the few non-Jews with whom Rahel had been friendly since her youth. She had no way of knowing that this friend, whose husband had been officially considered one of the great defenders of the Jews, had become openly anti-Jewish and had been trying to influence Humboldt to share her views. Rahel's first intimation of this occurred when, in the presence of a large company, Caroline used the *Sie,* the polite form of address, to her—a very simple way to wipe out an old, now embarrassing friendship. In Frankfurt, where Rahel awaited Varnhagen's return from Paris, it was emphatically impressed upon her that she was tolerated only with her husband, not at all when she was alone nowadays, not even though she was married. "Like a turkey in a strange yard, I ran around, and cowered in a chancy corner." She did not share the dubious good fortune of her sister-in-law whom Herr Stägemann liked particularly (and Varnhagen's future was dependent upon Stägemann) because she "has nothing of the Jewess about her" (Varnhagen). Right after Rahel's marriage and even before the actual beginning of the reaction in Prussia, Rahel was forced to realize how little the marriage had profited her and yet how indispensable it had been because it at any rate provided her with a social minimum. But that minimum also represented the absolute maximum she could achieve.

The three years in Karlsruhe were the happiest she had known, the period of fewest insults. Later, she always thought back upon them as the happiest years of her life. But when she returned to Berlin again in 1819, in despair beforehand at having to "go home" where she was known to all and would therefore not be treated solely as her husband's wife, her old complaints began again. "I like *nothing* here . . . *nothing* gives me pleasure here. . . . No one should return to his native place when he had been long away! . . . All such are mournful revenants. Those who want to have me and use me and regard me as they did in the past—those, that is, who are still left here . . . are Furies out of the past." Nevertheless her "rank, marriage, change of name," remained some sort of refuge, a straw to grasp at, the illusion of a native place. For the sake of this straw she accepted what came.

Since, however, she had never—and certainly not after the return to Berlin—achieved that virtuoso capacity for self-deception which would make life bearable to her, a veritable panic erupted under the calm and superficially happy connubial life: "Can one entirely get away from what one truly is; away, far away, like a feeble little ship driven far off on a vast ocean by wind and tempest! The one thing that in truth still concerns me personally, that has sunk deep into my heart and lies down at the bottom, dark and heavy as granite—that far down, I cannot see; I let it lie; like a poor worker who loses himself in the operations of life all week long and perhaps on Sunday can come close to its real essence." That is the way it is for the person who is required to appear to be what she does not wish to be. She had at last rid herself of Rahel Levin, but she did not want to become Friederike Varnhagen, *née* Robert. The former was not socially acceptable; the latter could not summon up the resolution to make a fraudulent self-identification. For "all my life I considered myself Rahel and nothing else."

This passionate protest, this furious attempt to undo everything again, to repudiate all she had achieved as something never desired, preserved an odd youthfulness in her. The older she grew, the more rigidly she clung to the conviction "that we still wish, want and mean the same things" as in the past. "So I find myself in the same relation to myself as at fourteen or sixteen. All that age has contributed are a few annihilating, murderous blows."

Remaining youthful, not changing, being untrammeled at least in opinions, continuing to cherish only her old "comrades of youth," "carrying on in a larger sphere . . . the garret room," at fifty-six still believing in the "passion of love" as the "uniquely beautiful, Eden-like phenomenon on earth" —all this meant continuing to desire the impossible after the possible had been attained. Her defiant insistence that nothing had changed was senseless. She was no longer young, she had acquired name, rank and fortune, was married, the wife of a government official, no longer without ties, had to act with caution, dissimulate—what more could there be in the way of change? She was not living with the old "comrades of her youth," but sitting in Varnhagen's salon; she was becoming less and less known as Rahel. Love was over for good also, for she had never loved the man she was living with. But although at first glance such nostalgia seemed senseless, such continuance of a life buried decades before seemed irrational and obstinate, it had its points: secretly, beneath the surface, all this was preparing the ground for those few important perceptions which she had to have before she died, for to die without them would have constituted real bankruptcy; those few insights which, for her generation and in her milieu, were so hair-raisingly heretical that without bourgeois security she would never have found the boldness to face them. For "I always lacked the courage to plunge into wretched situations; that is why I endured what I . . . despised; that is why I am sick." She had had to pay, in the coin of "true realities," the glories which no society could ever strike from a person's hand; she had had to sacrifice the freer life of the pariah and "green things, children, love, weather." Certainly "one is not free when one has to represent something in respectable society, a married woman, an official's wife, etc." If one had freedom one was, in the eyes of that society, always in "wretched situations," and Rahel had encountered too many of these, knew them too intimately, not to fear them more than any loss of freedom. After all, the much-praised freedom of the outcast as against society was rarely more than complete freedom to feel despair over being "nothing . . . not a sister, not a sweetheart, not a wife, not even a citizen."

She had to despair or admit bankruptcy in any case. The price demanded of the pariah if he wishes to become a parvenu is always too high and always strikes at those most human elements which alone made 'up his life. Was it not cause for grief to have no children, no husband her own age, no natural aging and growing gradually weary? What aroused her profoundest indignation was the diabolic dilemma to which her life had been confined: on the one hand she had been deprived of everything by general social conditions, and on the other hand she had been able to purchase a social existence only by sacrificing nature. "I should really like to present myself as just as old as I am; I cannot do that . . . because I have a young husband who loves me dearly. There is nothing more comical. The upside-down crown upon my fate; still I am *grateful*."

The levees were high enough to ensure that the streams of rebellion and freedom did not burst their banks. Gratitude helped hold everything in check even more than the "upside-down crown upon my fate," which had, in fact, been conferred upon her by her own gratitude. "Qualities which one cannot govern are faults"; gratitude, excessive attachment, is the typical vice of the pariah, who feels obligated even by a casual word, an almost unintentional gesture of friendliness, because he expected nothing of the sort from the world. "I am too grateful because I was too miserable so that I always think of how to reciprocate . . . And this inclination to reciprocate has become passionate and mechanical at the same time." "Qualities which one can not govern" have the compulsory force of addiction; gratitude as a "vice," the urge for kindness, gentleness, being welcome; "mechanical and passionate reciprocating" the futile attempt at bribing people, forcing them to love you; the lack of self-restraint of the outcast who has to obligate people, to use all means to draw their attention, cannot bear their indifference and thus deceives himself in producing an artificial atmosphere of friendship, warmth and familiarity.

This longing to be grateful would be only a fault if it were not accompanied by another trait equally characteristic of the pariah: what Rahel called "too much consideration for a human face. I rather can hurt my own heart than hurt somebody else's and watch his vulnerability." This sensitivity is a morbid, exaggerated understanding of the dignity of every human being, a passionate comprehension unknown to the privileged. It is this passionate empathy which constitutes the humaneness of the pariah. In a society based upon privilege, pride of birth and arrogance of title, the pariah instinctively discovers human dignity in general long before Reason has made it the foundation of morality.

These traits—and Rahel calls them her twin "unspeakable faults"—the parvenu must discard. He dare not be grateful because he owes everything to his own powers; he must not be considerate to others because he must esteem himself a kind of superman of efficiency, an especially good and strong and intelligent specimen of humanity, a model for his poor pariah brethren to follow. The parvenu pays for the loss of his pariah qualities by becoming ultimately incapable of grasping generalities, recognizing relationships or taking an interest in anything but his own person.

Rahel never rid herself of her "faults." They kept her from becoming a real parvenu, from feeling happy as a parvenu. Her relationship with Varnhagen, which in the end rested upon nothing more than gratitude, and was expressed as gratitude, had originally been intended as a means for securing a parvenu existence. But in the course of the marriage it became a refuge, an offered and gratefully accepted asylum, in which the "fugitive from Egypt and Palestine" found "help, love and tender care." That she succeeded in salvaging her pariah qualities when she entered her parvenu existence opened up a loophole for her, marked out a road toward aging and dying. It was the very loophole through which the pariah, precisely because he is an outcast, can see life as a whole, and the very road upon which the pariah can attain to his *"great* love for free existence." It is offered to the pariah if, though unable to revolt as an individual against the whole of society, he disdains the alternative of becoming a parvenu and is recompensed for his "wretched situations" by a "view of the whole." That is his sole dignified hope: "that everything is related; and in truth, everything is good enough. This is the salvage from the *great* bankruptcy of life."

13

ONE DOES NOT ESCAPE
JEWISHNESS
(1820–1833)

As a young girl Rahel had made her first journey to Breslau—
to those inescapable provincial Jewish relations through whom,
at the time, every assimilated Jew with a European cultural
background was connected to the Jewish people and the old
manners and customs he had discarded. Rahel, who at this
time had scarcely any command of the German language—
her early letters to her family were written in the Jewish-
German of the time, with Hebrew letters—records how she
watched "out of curiosity" a marriage according to the Jewish
rites. She was welcomed to the affair "as if the Grand Sultan
were entering a long-neglected seraglio." And she added
promptly: "This made me ashamed." The central desire of
her life had been escape from Jewishness, and this desire
proved unfulfillable because of the anti-Semitism of her
milieu, because of the ban, imposed from outside, against a
Jew's becoming a normal human being. If there were still
another reason, it was this shame. Every Berlin Jew felt like a
Grand Sultan in contrast to his poor, backward co-religionists.
From their degradation, from the great gap that separated him
from them, he drew his consciousness of being an exception,
his pride in having come so gloriously far, and his resistance
to the incessant insults, humiliations and setbacks which, ultimately, every Jew experienced. This gap, this dark stage-set of
poverty, misery, ignorance of Europe's cultural goods and utter
foreignness, repeatedly assured him of the grandeur of progress, gave him new hope for a better future, for continuous
improvement. He felt certain of it; now that the first giant
steps obviously lay behind him, it could not fail. That dark
stage-set, virtually unknown to the non-Jews among whom he

lived, transformed the shaming feeling of being one of the "last in society" into the elevating feeling of belonging to it after all and of being able to fight within it, rather than outside of it, for progressively better conditions, progressively higher steps. The Berlin Jew who looked upon his origins, which at that time were still present in living form, and geographically close by, became convinced that he was not one of the last but one of the first.

To be ashamed of such feelings of condescension, which after all still expressed a sense of affiliation, meant cutting oneself off altogether from all origins, all consolations, all compensations. In expressing her shame, in thrusting from her her sense of affiliation, Rahel was giving up far more than she guessed: not only affiliation to the dark mass of the people, but also the far more necessary solidarity with the tiny group of Prussian "exception Jews" from whom she sprang and whose destiny she shared. No baptism, no assimilation, no marriage into wealth and nobility, could have had so radical an effect as this shame of hers.

Without a stage-set, man cannot live. The world, society, is only too ready to provide another one if a person dares to toss the natural one, given him at birth, into the lumber room. If Rahel dared to expose herself to society as a Jew without being sustained by pride or vanity in what Jews had already achieved, she would lack self-assurance, would lack, as it were, feet with which to walk. "Every step I want to take and cannot does not remind me of the general woes of humanity, which I want to oppose; instead I feel my special misfortune still, and doubly, and tenfold, and the one always makes the other worse for me." Since in her eyes belonging to Judaism represented no part of the "general woes" which she might seek to remove from the world or, in solidarity with other Jews, manage to endure as the destiny of her people, since she saw it as her own "special misfortune," it could not help striking her "doubly and tenfold." The evil of being a Jew seemed specialized, concentrated entirely upon herself; it became her individual fate, as inescapable as a hump on the back or a clubfoot. "How ugly it makes me seem. Is the world wise, do people say: 'The poor fellow is lame; let us carry this to the poor fellow; oh, you can see how hard every step must be for him'? No, people pay no attention to his steps, because they are not doing the walking; they find it ugly to watch and do not carry anything to him because his struggle seems as nothing to them, while any struggle on their part is horrible to them. And how can you expect the lame man, who is forced to walk, not to be unhappy?" Judaism could not be cast off by separating oneself from the other Jews; it merely became converted from a historical destiny, from a shared social condition, from an impersonal "general woe" into a character trait, a personal defect in character. Judaism was as innate in Rahel as the lame man's too-short leg.

Judaism could be converted into a defect in character or, at times, a characteristic advantage: for example, in the salon during the brief period when Jews counted for so much because of their naturally unbiased views; when Rahel boasted of having told Louis Ferdinand a few "garret truths" and emphasized her differentness from those other baptized Jews who had thrown away their advantage—which had consisted, precisely, in being exempt from the world's prejudices. Perhaps it was for the Jews themselves to make a virtue of necessity. When you are all alone it is hard to decide whether being different is a blemish or a distinction. When you have nothing at all to cling to, you choose in the end to cling to the thing that sets you off from others. "So the Jews are badly off here? It is their own fault, for I assure you I *tell* everybody here that I am one; *eh bien, le même empressement.* But only a Berlin Jew can have the proper loftiness and manners in himself; can—I don't say, has. I assure you, it really gives one a kind of *contenance* here to be from Berlin and a Jew; at least it does me; I could tell you anecdotes about that." But she had thought this way only so long as she had been tempest-tossed to a foreign place by luck and chance, was living in Paris; she had thought this way only because she personally wanted nothing from anyone at the moment, had no pretensions, did not want to achieve anything she could not get.

For otherwise, in all everyday surroundings, in all ordinary milieus, it was no fun going about as an exception—especially not when she had separated herself from the dark mass of the people, was ashamed of her condescension and despised the cheap vanity of the "enlightened" Jews as against their "backward co-religionists." To enter society all alone, marked with the blemish and condemned to be one of the last, was far worse than waiting outside and hoping for better conditions. Always having to represent oneself as something special, and having to do it all alone, in order to justify her bare existence, was so strenuous that it nearly consumed all her strength. "How loathsome it is always having to establish one's identity first. That alone is enough to make it so repulsive to be a Jew." Legitimation, moreover, was not even possible most of the time; only in rare, isolated situations did the kindness of the others give her a chance, leave a crack through which she could put her head and proclaim her uniqueness. In all ordinary converse, at all ordinary times and in every unexpected encounter with people, that was ruled out; as a Jew the world attributed to her what it considered to be the Jewish qualities. From this situation arose her constant longing for foreign places, "to be away from the place where I am who I am; and at some place where no vulgar person knows me"—in other words, in a situation where the exceptional chance to make new acquaintances was offered, where known identity no longer existed. The flight abroad had been a desperate attempt at rebirth. "Man," she declared, "is *himself* only abroad; at home he must represent his past, and in the present that becomes a mask, heavy to carry and obscuring the face." Abroad, her place of origin was called Berlin; in Berlin it was called Judengasse (Jew Street). In order to become a Berliner, therefore, a "citizeness," a Prussian, she had to go away from Berlin, leave everything behind—as she had done in Paris, then in Prague, finally in Karlsruhe with Varnhagen. Unfortunately, such attempts at flight had only tided her over for a very short time—not only because a person cannot easily shed his skin, but because being a Jew was not a problem that pertained specially to Berlin; because there were likewise Jews in Paris, Prague and Karlsruhe who clearly enough reminded others, if not herself, of her true origins. It was not possible to be born a second time.

Out of the secret knowledge that Judaism was inescapable because of the existence of other Jews, of the internationality of the people, there arose the hope and the desire that nothing at all would happen to Judaism as a whole, that there would be no civil improvement, no emancipation, above all no reform. For then alone could a few individuals prove that they were exceptions; then they would be—what a paradoxical, though logical wish—would be, by exception, declared normal. "But I really do not understand *at all* what can be done for and with Jews—except very much in general, as a well-organized mind *must* understand everything. . . . Except that I would like you to serve them and yourself at the same time. Hitherto it has not been possible to do anything for this scattered, neglected, and more than all that, deservedly despised nation." Sharing the opinion her hostile milieu held in regard to her own origins from this "deservedly despised nation," having assimilated to her enemies without being accepted by them, without being received to the point where her past was forgotten, there could remain, for her, only the hope that by a miracle her appeal, "I am not like them," would be heard. And the bitter experience was that it never would be heard.

The world became peopled with evil demons who shouted from every corner, at every opportunity, the thing she wished she could conceal forever. Life was transformed into an unending succession of insults because she had not wanted to accept herself, wanted to deny herself. The spite of others always held up to her the grinning caricature of herself that these others had fashioned. Having denied her origin at all costs, "even at the cost of life itself"; having broken of her own accord, and all alone, with the natural social ground which, even as a pariah, she had from birth; having believed that Judaism was an unfortunate personal quality which had to be "extirpated"; having renounced utterly the aid of other Jews, the existence and the historical actuality of the entire people, she could be for a moment an individual, possessing power because of her "heart's strength and what my mind shows me." She could rest for a while in the "sphere indicated for me by nature; in that sphere *I* am powerful and the others insignificant." But very soon she tumbled from these sublime heights into the hands of enemies who rejoiced in having for once caught a wholly isolated Jew, a Jew as such, as it were, an abstract Jew without social or historical relationships. They could treat this Jew as the very essence of Jewishness, as though there were only this one Jew in the whole wide world, and they would show her the meaning of being a Jew in society. The insults that rained down upon her had compelled Rahel to accept as a fate for which she was fully responsible the circumstance which she might otherwise have been able to dismiss as an unimportant incidental for which she was not to blame. This she could have done if she had not centered her whole life around her "disgrace," her "infamous birth." But for her to negate Jewishness fully and without ambiguity would have had the same effect as an unequivocal affirmation. Being a Jew could develop from a politico-social circumstance into a personal, individual problem only for persons who for whatever reason equivocally wanted "to be Jews and at the same time to not be Jews" (as the contemporary liberal theologian H. E. G. Paulus once brilliantly phrased it). As a personal problem the Jewish question was insoluble, and for that reason everything Rahel undertook always ended in the "madness of gloom, fright and despair winding up like snakes for all eternity—despair over my position, my situation." In some circumstances the existence of walls can only be demonstrated by the existence of broken heads.

"The misfortunes that come directly from Heaven I always endure with entire tranquility of soul. But where injuries proceeding from people have threatened me, my soul loses its composure, and this I cannot endure at all. Also I have discovered that I can calmly get along without the most essential, most natural vital nourishment, and that to which I am most entitled; no one I have ever seen can compare with me in this; but my demands among and upon people must not be fraudulently withheld from me, or taken away from me. Where I feel entitled to things by right and custom, they *must* be offered to me; I don't mind surrendering them to manifest force, but I cannot bear having them stolen from me by hypocritical words and deeds—and have the state and society conniving in this theft. My ambition counts for more than anything to me; *this* anger, I deem my ambition. For it has never occurred to me to want to be more than others, or not to do them justice." Rahel could not help thinking that Jews like herself had been lured into society by fraud and deception, "by hypocritical words and deeds," allured, in fact, by the very lack of "manifest force." It seemed to her that she had been robbed and cheated by a secret, spiteful alliance between state and society which combined to withhold from Jews first civil rights and then social equality. Deceptively, the Jews had been lured out of their two-thousand-year-old badger-hole. Their lives had been poisoned when they were inoculated with the poison of ambition, which in the end led them desperately to want to attain everything because they did not receive the simplest rights such as "peasant women and beggar women have"—and were not even permitted to say so. Rahel had fought for this stolen "natural existence," without ever being able to rest; she had demanded it of everyone who chanced her way, snatched at it with all the means at her command— and attained "the upside-down crown upon my destiny." She had let herself be driven by the winds, had stubbornly insisted upon her rights, upon human rights, had resolutely refused to share the general fate of the Jews, to place her hopes in political measures which would benefit all. And the more she did these things, the more typically Jewish her fate turned out to be, the more illuminatingly she demonstrated to the observer —and finally to herself as well—all that a Jew could undertake without ceasing to be a Jew. She had walked down all the roads that could lead her into the alien world, and upon all these roads she had left her track, had converted them into Jewish roads, pariah roads; ultimately her whole life had become a segment of Jewish history in Germany. Thus in the end she understood her *"whole* fate [as] an historical, inexorable, Old Testamentarian fate, indeed [as] the *curse* which the children of its adherents vainly try to flee in all quarters of the globe."

Never did she imagine that any part of it could have been foreseen or averted. Only by acting in good faith and exposing herself to all consequences could she prove the hypocrisy of society, which pretended to treat assimilated Jews as if they were not Jews. It was essential to try each successive step. The change of name was of crucial importance; it made her, she thought, "outwardly another person." After that came baptism, since the change of name had proved insufficient and "no reason exists to want to remain in the semblance of the religion of [her] birth." What counted was to "adhere in external matters as well to the class" whose customs, opinions, culture and convictions she wished to identify with. The most important thing, she believed, was "to baptize the children as well. They . . . must learn to think of that crazy episode of history as no different from other aspects of history in general."

But was Rahel really prepared to take all the consequences and radically extirpate her own identity? After having recommended all these measures to her friend—measures which could arise only out of shame—she suddenly warned her "not to be ashamed of Jewish birth and of the nation whose misfortunes and defects you know all the better because of it; you must not abandon them for fear of people's saying that you still have some Jewishness about you!" Yet what strange logic here, that after having made such concessions to the prejudices of society that one had virtually extinguished oneself by radical change, one was nevertheless forbidden to take part in that invigorating sport of good society, the "modern hatred of Jews"; that, though one had left no lingering mark of Jewishness upon one's own person, one was forever to be obligated "always to aid the wretched survivals (I should like to say, dreadful warnings for founders of states) of a great, gifted nation that went far in the knowledge of God." All her efforts to rid herself entirely of Jewishness were ruined by this contradiction, by this equivocation. For the person who really wanted to assimilate could not pick and choose among the elements to which she would be willing to assimilate, could not decide what she liked and disliked. If one accepted Christianity, one had to accept the time's hatred of the Jews along with it. Both Christianity and anti-Semitism were integrating components of the historical past of European man and living elements in the society of Rahel's day. No assimilation could be achieved merely by surrendering one's own past but ignoring the alien past. In a society on the whole hostile to the Jews—and that situation obtained in all countries in which Jews lived, down to the twentieth century—it is possible to assimilate only by assimilating to anti-Semitism also. If one wishes to be a normal person precisely like everybody else, there is scarcely any alternative to exchanging old prejudices for new ones. If that is not done, one involuntarily becomes a rebel—"But I am a rebel after all!"—and remains a Jew. And if one really assimilates, taking all the consequences of denial of one's own origin and cutting oneself off from those who have not or have not yet done it, one becomes a scoundrel.

"I was a Jew, not pretty, ignorant, without *grâce, sans talents et sans instruction; ah ma soeur, c'est fini; c'est fini avant la fin réelle.* I could not have done anything differently." With this insight into the vanity of all efforts, Rahel entered old age. She had done nothing wrong, had left no stone unturned. "And so one grows old and life falls away behind one like old dreams." The amount of real adjustment life had produced was only semblance, and even the fulfillment of wishes remained illusory. Personal achievement could become glorious, overwhelming, blissful reality only when it accorded with the general direction in which the world moved. In a progressive world (a world in which, as Rahel had hoped, "hatred of Jews and pride of nobility, now fading, are blazing up one last time") she might have grown old proudly and happily, in spite of all failures, because her personal solution would not have been sham, her having arrived would not have been a masquerade. But as it was: "The world is going backward so fast that if one does not die soon one will end up making the acquaintance of Cardinal Richelieu, of the serpent, of Adam, and the whole *first* society." Rescued by Varnhagen, respectably established, she found herself in an "unknown" existence, "almost without connection with my old Being." Where and with whom could she live? "One would think Berlin consisted of nothing but guilds. The court and the ministers, the diplomatic corps, the civil servants, the businessmen, the officers, etc.—all give their own balls, to which only persons belonging to their circle appear. . . . All the balls of the people of quality aspire, with more or less success, to imitate the court affairs or princely balls" (Heine). Exclusive as these "guilds" were toward one another individually, they were exclusive *in toto* toward the Jews. The provinces did not differ from Berlin: the "Christian middle class dull and uninspired, with unusual wealth; the higher class the same to a higher degree . . ." (Heine).

Since, then, the world was very badly arranged, since the cry of "down with the Jews" rang out at every hand (in 1819 a wave of pogroms swept over all of Prussia), the old, unreal, desperate existence suddenly seemed to Rahel far more real, more true, more suitable than the new. It turned out that the pariah was capable not only of preserving more feeling for the "true realities," but that in some circumstances he also possessed more reality than the parvenu. For the latter, being condemned to lead a sham existence, could seize possession of all the objects of a world not arranged for him only with the pseudoreality of a masquerade. He was masked, and consequently everything that he touched appeared to be masked; he concealed his true nature wherever he went, and through every hole in his costume his old pariah existence could be detected. In the Berlin of the 1820s, which had returned to convention and had forgotten the great upsurge around the turn of the century, everything had resumed its assigned place. It became transparently clear that no one could wantonly step out of his place, that it was not possible to step into someone else's place, that one was "swimming with the stream after all, no matter with how much of a sidewise drift." The current always recaptured one, and "the banks only seem to be there." It became apparent that the fate of the Jews was not so accidental and out of the way, that on the contrary it precisely limned the state of society, outlined the ugly reality of the gaps in the social structure. Consequently there was no escape, unless it were to the moon. "I am no proper daughter of the earth, though a true child of the earth. . . . So I remain a kind of observer of her, not a daughter who takes on her qualities, and receives a dowry and presents of all sorts."

How easily age can mislead one in seeking a place for oneself on another planet, since, after all, "every heart desires a home." How easily weariness can deceive and represent the monotonous similarity of events as inexorability, always the same for two thousand years: "Our history is nothing but the case history of our illness." How strong the longing for death must have become, how consoling the thought that everything would end sooner or later: "Just imagine, we *here* were told by the domestics that two Jews had poisoned the wells *here*. . . . I want peace at last, I tell you," she wrote to her brother at the time of the great Berlin cholera epidemic of 1831. How hard it must have been, having no children and not being part of any continuing line, to realize that such disgust and such hopes for death were false, that death was never any kind of solution for human beings. "The greatest miracle is always this, that after our death the objects of the world continue to exist as they did during our lives; and that life, to that extent, was not pure fantasy."

The greatest miracle was the greatest comfort. After all was said and done, she had found the thing that guaranteed her her reality. With this insight she liquidated her personal bankruptcy. The July Revolution found the old woman regarding the *Globe as pain quotidien* and coming to the illusory, but for her correct perception that: "One thing is certain. Europe no longer desires to conquer pieces of ground, but something more serious: pieces of *equality*. . . . The talk is of rights and no longer of origins." She became a Saint-Simonist, enthusiastic over "this great newly invented instrument which is at last probing that great old wound, the history of man upon earth." She became "entirely interested only in what improvements the *earth* can make for us: it and our actions upon it." She had realized that the "diseased matter" which had to "get out of us" was not contained in the Jews alone; that the pox only broke out on the Jews, infecting them by contagion; that everything she herself had undertaken to fight it, all her life, was nothing but a "cosmetic" which did not "help, even if it were slapped on with housepainter's brushes." And so, at the end of her life, she unconcernedly wrote whole paragraphs in her letters to her brother in Hebrew characters, just as she had done in her girlhood. Freedom and equality were not going to be conjured into existence by individuals' capturing them by fraud as privileges for themselves.

Rahel had remained a Jew and pariah. Only because she clung to both conditions did she find a place in the history of European humanity. In her old age she could observe what came of "honest inquiry" when pursued by an "injured and healed soul," such as Ludwig Börne. She hailed young Heine with enthusiasm and great friendship—"only galley slaves know one another." (Few of her letters addressed expressly to him have come down to us; the greater part of Heine's letters and early manuscripts were destroyed in a great fire in Hamburg.) Heine's affirmation of Jewishness, the first and last resolute affirmation which was to be heard from an assimilated Jew for a long time, derived from the same reasons and the same feeling for truth as Rahel's negation. Both had never been able to accept their destiny serenely; both had never attempted to hide it behind big words or boastful phrases; both had always demanded an accounting and had never gone in for "prudent silence and patient Christian suffering" (Heine). Rahel had not suffered alone, nor in vain, had not erred in vain, since Heine could masterfully and unabashedly sum up for her: "If stealing silver spoons had been within the law, I would not have had myself baptized." Neither Marwitz nor Varnhagen had, in a serious historical sense, saved "the image of her soul," but only Heine who promised to be "enthusiastic for the cause of the Jews and their attainment of equality before the law. In bad times, which are inevitable, the Germanic rabble will hear my voice ring resoundingly in German beer halls and palaces."

With this promise spoken, Rahel could die with peaceful

heart. She left behind her an heir on whom she had much to bestow: the history of a bankruptcy and a rebellious spirit. "No philanthropic list, no cheers, no condescension, no mixed society, no new hymn book, no bourgeois star, nothing, nothing could ever placate me. . . . *You* will say this gloriously, elegiacally, fantastically, incisively, extremely jestingly, always musically, provokingly, often charmingly; you will say it all very soon. But as you do, the text from my old, offended heart will still have to remain yours."

CHRONOLOGY

1771 May 19. Rahel born in Berlin, eldest child of well-to-do merchant Markus Levin. Younger brothers and sisters: Markus (1772), Ludwig (1778), Rose (1781), Moritz (1785).
The parental household is still orthodox, uneducated in German culture, probably almost equally ignorant of Jewish learning. Rahel's early letters to her family are written in Yiddish, i.e., in Hebrew characters.

1780s. Friendship with David Veit, a Jewish boy her own age. Regular correspondence with him from 1793 through 1796.

circa 1790. Father's death. Brother Markus gradually assumes direction of the family business.

1794. First travels, visit to relatives in Breslau.

circa 1790–1806. Rahel's salon in the attic room on Jägerstrasse, to which almost all the important intellectuals of Berlin come: the Humboldt brothers, Friedrich Schlegel, Friedrich Gentz, Schleiermacher, Prince Louis Ferdinand of Prussia and his mistress, Pauline Wiesel, the classical philologist Friedrich August Wolf, Jean Paul, Brentano, the Tieck brothers, Chamisso, Fouqué, etc.

1790s. Beginning of friendship with the Swedish ambassador, Karl Gustav von Brinckmann.

1795 summer. Rahel meets Wilhelm von Burgsdorff.
She accompanies the actress Unzelmann to Teplitz, there lives in the home of Countess Josephine von Pachta. Goes to Karlsbad for a few days, meets Goethe there.

1795–96 winter. Rahel meets Count Karl von Finckenstein. Engagement. The affair is protracted until 1800.

1796 summer. In Teplitz and Karlsbad. Burgsdorff there also.

circa 1800. Baptism of brother Ludwig, who assumes the name Robert, under which name he became known as a writer.

1800 July to 1801 May. Rahel accompanies Countess Karoline von Schlabrendorff to Paris, where she meets Caroline and Wilhelm von Humboldt and Wilhelm Bokelmann, a Hamburg businessman.

1801. Sister Rose marries Asser, a petty official from Amsterdam. In May Rahel goes to Amsterdam to bring her mother back to Berlin.

1801 end. Rahel meets Friedrich Gentz.

1801–02. She meets the secretary of the Spanish Legation, Don Raphael d'Urquijo, and becomes engaged to him.

1804. Break with Urquijo.

1806 October 27. Napoleon enters Berlin, which then remains under French occupation until 1808. The war produces the break-up of Rahel's circle of friends.

1806–07. Wealth of the family reduced. Retrenchments, disputes with her brothers which continue until 1812.

1807–08 winter. Fichte's *Addresses to the German Nation.*

1808 spring. Beginning of relationship with Varnhagen.

1808 autumn. The tension between Rahel and her mother, arising out of their restricted financial circumstances, reaches its climax when the mother moves out of the home on Jägerstrasse. Rahel cannot maintain the expensive house by herself and moves to Charlottenstrasse, where she lives until 1810. Varnhagen goes to Tuebingen. Rahel's brief visit to Leipzig.

1809 spring. Rahel meets Alexander von der Marwitz.

1809 June. Varnhagen goes to the Austrian theater of war, accompanies Count Bentheim to Paris in 1810 and from there via Westphalia to Vienna in 1811.

1809 October. Death of mother.

1810. She calls herself Rahel Robert.

1811 May 25. Finckenstein's visit to Rahel, who has not seen him since the engagement was broken. He died in September of the same year.

1811 June. Varnhagen takes Rahel form Berlin to Teplitz.

1811 September. Return to Berlin via Dresden, where she sees Alexander von der Marwitz again.

1812. Publication in Cotta's *Morgenblatt* of the passages on Goethe from the correspondence between Varnhagen and Rahel.

1813 May 9. Accompanies her brother Markus's family to Breslau to escape the upheavals of the war. Proceeds from there via Reinerz to Prague (May 30, 1813). Received by the actress Auguste Brede, a friend of Count Bentheim's. Sees Gentz and Marwitz again.

1813–14 winter. Severe illness.

1814 summer. Reunion with Varnhagen again in Teplitz.

1814 end of August. Varnhagen precedes her to Berlin.

1814 September 5. Rahel arrives in Berlin, stays with her brother Moritz.

1814 September 27. Baptism and marriage to Varnhagen. Name: Antonie Friederike.

1814 October. Varnhagen attends Congress of Vienna as member of the diplomatic corps. Rahel follows him that same month.

1815 June. Varnhagen leaves Vienna, and Rahel spends several weeks during the summer with the Arnstein family in Baden, near Vienna.

1815 August. Rahel goes to Frankfurt.

1815 September 8. Goethe calls on Rahel in Frankfurt.

1815 November. Varnhagen arrives in Frankfurt.

1816 July. Varnhagen and Rahel move to Karlsruhe, where Varnhagen has become Prussian chargé d'affaires.

1819 July 22. Varnhagen recalled from his post in Karlsruhe.

1819 October. The Varnhagens return to Berlin.

1821 spring. Rahel meets the twenty-three-year-old Heinrich Heine, who becomes a close friend until her death. Though she was on more or less intimate terms with a number of Jewish women, he was the first Jewish close male friend since her youthful friendship with David Veit.

1821–32. The Berlin salon of the Varnhagens. The most prominent guests were: Bettina von Arnim, Heine, Prince Pückler-Muskau, Hegel, Ranke, Eduard Gans.

1826 end. Brother Markus dies.

1829 summer. Vacation trip to Baden, where she sees Pauline Wiesel again.

1831 end of August. Cholera breaks out in Berlin.

1832 July 5. Brother Ludwig dies.

1832 December. Gentz dies.

1833 March 7. Rahel dies, is laid to rest in a vault at Trinity Church near the Hallesche Tor in Berlin and thirty years later buried there together with Varnhagen.

BIBLIOGRAPHY

Sections II through IV list all published letters by and to Rahel, arranged chronologically.

I THE VARNHAGEN MANUSCRIPT COLLECTION

Stern, Ludwig, *Die Varnhagen von Ensesche Sammlung in der Königlichen Bibliothek zu Berlin*. Berlin, 1911.

II RAHEL: CORRESPONDENCE

Rahel. Ein Buch des Andenkens für ihre Freunde. Herausg. und eingeleitet von K. A. Varnhagen von Ense. 3 Bde., Berlin, 1834.
Briefwechsel zwischen Rahel und David Veit. Aus dem Nachlaß Varnhagens von Ense. Herausg. von Ludmilla Assing. 2 Bde., Leipzig, 1861.
Briefwechsel zwischen Varnhagen und Rahel. Herausg. von Ludmilla Assing. 6 Bde., Leipzig, 1874–75.
Aus Rahels Herzensleben. Briefe und Tagebuchblätter. Herausg. von Ludmilla Assing. Leipzig, 1877.
Briefwechsel zwischen Karoline von Humboldt, Rahel und Varnhagen. Herausg. von Albert Leitzmann. Weimar, 1896.
Rahel und ihre Zeit. Briefe und Zeugnisse. Ausgewählt von Bertha Badt. München, 1912.
Rahel Varnhagen. Ein Frauenleben in Briefen. Ausgewählt und eingeleitet von Augusta Weldler-Steinberg. Weimar, 1917.
Rahel und Alexander von der Marwitz in ihren Briefen. Herausg. von Heinrich Meissner. Gotha, 1925.
Pauline Wiesel. Herausg. von Carl Atzenbeck. Leipzig, o.J.
Rahel Varnhagen, Briefwechsel mit Alexander von der Marwitz; Rahel Varnhagen, Briefwechsel mit August Varnhagen von Ense; Rahel Varnhagen im Umgang mit ihren Freunden (Briefe 1793–1893); *Rahel Varnhagen und ihre Zeit* (Briefe 1800–33). Herausg. von Friedhelm Kemp. München, 1966–68.

III LETTERS AND DIARIES BY RAHEL PUBLISHED DURING HER LIFETIME

Cottas *Morgenblatt für gebildete Stände*. Nr. 161, 162, 166, 169, 176, 1812.
"Bruchstücke aus Briefen und Denkblättern." Herausg. von K. A. Varn-

hagen von Ense (nach Rahels Briefen, 1793–1816), *Schweizerisches Museum.* Herausg. von Ignaz P. V. Troxler, 2./3. Heft, Aarau, 1816. "Briefe." *Die Wage.* Eine Zeitschrift für Bürgerleben, Wissenschaft und Kunst. Herausg. Ludwig Börne. 2 Bde., 5. Heft, Tuebingen, 1821. "Briefe und Gespräche über Wilhelm Meister." Herausg. von K. A. Varnhagen von Ense, *Der Gesellschafter oder Blätter für Geist und Herz.* Herausg. Friedrich Wilhelm Gubitz. Nr. 131–38, Berlin, 1821. "Aus Denkblättern einer Berlinerin." *Berlinische Blätter für deutsche Frauen.* Herausg. von Friedrich de la Motte Fouqué. 3./4. Heft, Berlin, 1828.

IV SINGLE LETTERS BY AND TO RAHEL

Galerie von Bildnissen aus Rahel's Umgang und Briefwechsel. Herausg. von K. A. Varnhagen von Ense. Leipzig, 1836.
Schriften von Friedrich von Gentz. Ein Denkmal. Herausg. von Gustav Schlesier. Bd. 5, Mannheim, 1838–40.
Dorow, Wilhelm, *Reminiszensen,* 1842.
Denkwürdigkeiten und vermischte Schriften von K. A. Varnhagen von Ense. Bd. 8, Leipzig, 1859.
Briefe an Ludwig Tieck. Ausgewählt und herausg. von Karl Holtei. Bd. 4, Breslau, 1864.
Briefe von Stägemann, Metternich, Heine, Bettina von Arnim. Herausg. von Ludmilla Assing. Leipzig, 1865.
Briefe des Prinzen Louis Ferdinand von Preußen an Pauline Wiesel. Nebst Briefen von A. v. Humboldt, Rahel, Varnhagen, Gentz und Marie von Meris. Herausg. von Alexander Büchner. Leipzig, 1865.
Briefwechsel zwischen Varnhagen von Ense und Oelsner nebst Briefen von Rahel. Herausg. von Ludmilla Assing. 3 Bde., Stuttgart, 1865.
Briefe von Chamisso, Gneisenau, Haugwitz, W. von Humboldt, Prinz Louis Ferdinand, Rahel, Rückert, Tieck u.a. Herausg. von Ludmilla Assing. Leipzig, 1867.
Lettres du Marquis A. de Custine à Varnhagen d'Ense et Rahel Varnhagen d'Ense. Edité par Ludmilla Assing. Bruxelles, 1870.
Biographische Portraits von Varnhagen von Ense. Nebst Briefen von Koreff, Clemens Brentano, Frau von Fouqué, Henri Campan und Scholz. Herausg. von Ludmilla Assing. Leipzig, 1871.
Briefwechsel und Tagebücher des Fürsten Hermann von Pückler-Muskau, 3. Band, *Briefwechsel zwischen Pückler und Varnhagen von Ense* nebst einigen Briefen von Rahel und der Fürstin von Pückler-Muskau. Herausg. von Ludmilla Assing. Berlin, 1874.
Geiger, Ludwig, "Aus dem Varnhagen-Chamissoschen Kreise." *Goethe-Jahrbuch.* Bd. 24, 1903.
Wilhelm von Burgsdorff, Briefe an Brinkman, Henriette von Finckenstein, Wilhelm von Humboldt, Rahel, Friedrich Tieck, Ludwig Tieck und Wiesel. Herausg. von Alfons F. Cohn. Berlin, 1907.
Briefe von und an Friedrich von Gentz. Herausg. von Friedrich Carl Wittichen und Ernst Salzer. 3 Bde., München und Berlin, 1909–13.
"Briefe von Rahel an Clemens Brentano." Herausg. von Agnes Harnack, *Zeitschrift für Bücherfreunde.* Neue Folge III, Leipzig, 1911–12.
Geiger, Ludwig, "Eine unbekannte Charakteristik der Bettina von Arnim." *Frankfurter Zeitung.* 61. Jahrgang, Nr. 13, 14, Januar 1917.
Behrend, Fritz, "Rahel Varnhagen an Schleiermacher." *Zeitschrift für Bücherfreunde.* Neue Folge IX, Leipzig, 1918.

Geiger, Ludwig, "Ludwig Börne und Rahel Varnhagen. Mit zwei unge-druckten Briefen." *Archiv für das Studium der neueren Sprachen und Literatur.* Bd. 139, Braunschweig, 1919.

Berend, Eduard, "Ein ungedruckter Brief Rahels an Jean Paul (Paris, 16. Dezember 1800)." *Zeitschrift für Bücherfreunde.* Jahrgang 1920.

Arendt, Hannah, "Ein Brief Rahels an Pauline Wiesel." *Deutscher Almanach,* 1932.

Misch, Carl, "Die wirkliche Rahel. Zum 100. Todestage (7. März)." *Sonntagsblatt der Vossischen Zeitung.* Nr. 63, 4. März 1933.

Auf frischen, kleinen, abstrakten Wegen. Unbekanntes und Unveröffent-lichtes aus Rahels Freundeskreis, Nachrichten aus dem Kösel-Verlag. München, Dezember 1967.

V CONTEMPORARY BACKGROUND MATERIAL

Anonym, "Der Salon der Frau von Varnhagen. Berlin, im März 1830." *Denkwürdigkeiten und vermischte Schriften von K. A. Varnhagen von Ense.* Bd. 8, Leipzig, 1859.

Brinckmann, August von, "Rahel." Brief an Varnhagen von Ense, *Denk-würdigkeiten und vermischte Schriften von K. A. Varnhagen von Ense.* Bd. 8, Leipzig, 1859.

"Brief von Karl Gustav von Brinckmann an Friedrich Schleiermacher." *Mitteilungen aus dem Literaturarchiv in Berlin.* Neue Folge, 1912.

Caroline. Briefe aus der Frühromantik. Nach G. Waitz vermehrt. Herausg. von Erich Schmidt. 2 Bde., Leipzig, 1913.

Chézy, Helmina von, *Unvergessenes.* Denkwürdigkeiten aus dem Leben der Helmina von Chézy. Herausg. von Bertha Borngräber. Leipzig, 1858.

Custine, Marquis de, "Madame de Varnhagen." *Denkwürdigkeiten und vermischte Schriften von K. A. Varnhagen von Ense.* Bd. 8, Leipzig, 1859.

Geiger, Ludwig, "Eine literarische Verspottung Varnhagens durch Clemens Brentano." *Zeitschift für Bücherfreunde.* Neue Folge, 10, Jahrgang 1919.

Gentz, Friedrich von, *Tagebücher.* Aus dem Nachlass Varnhagens von Ense. Herausg. von Ludmilla Assing. 4 Bde., Leipzig, 1873–74.

Herz, Henriette, *Ihr Leben und ihre Erinnerungen.* Herausg. von J. Fürst. Berlin, 1850.

"Jugenderinnerungen von Henriette Herz." *Mitteilungen aus dem Litera-turarchiv in Berlin,* 1896.

Henriette Herz, ihr Leben und ihre Zeit. Herausg. von Hans Landsberg. Weimar, 1913.

Wilhelm und Karoline von Humboldt in ihren Briefen. Herausg. von Anna von Sydow. 7 Bde, Berlin, 1906–16.

Wilhelm von Humboldts Briefe an eine Freundin. Herausg. von Albert Leitzmann. 2 Bde., Leipzig, 1910.

Pückler-Muskau, Fürst Hermann von, *Briefwechsel und Tagebücher.* Herausg. von Ludmilla Assing-Grimelli. Bd. 1–2, Hamburg, 1873; Bd. 3–9, Berlin, 1874–75.

"Leopold von Ranke und Varnhagen von Ense. Ungedruckter Briefwech-sel." Herausg. von Theodor Wiedemann. *Deutsche Revue.* 3 Bd., 20. Jahrgang.

Robert-Tornow, Walter, "Ferdinand Robert-Tornow, der Sammler und die Seinigen." *Deutsche Rundschau.* Bd. 65, 1890.

Rogge, Helmuth, "Kleist und Rahel." *Jahrbuch der Kleistgesellschaft,* 1923–24.

Caroline und Dorothea Schlegel in Briefen. Herausg. von Ernst Wieneke. Weimar, 1914.
Briefe von und an Friedrich und Dorothea Schlegel. Herausg. von Josef Körner. Berlin, 1926.
"Briefe von Dorothea Schlegel an Friedrich Schleiermacher." *Mitteilungen aus dem Literaturarchiv.* Neue Folge 7 und 8, Berlin, 1913.
Dorothea von Schlegel geb. Mendelssohn und deren Söhne Johannes und Philipp Veit. Briefwechsel. Herausg. von J. M. Raich. 2 Bde., Mainz, 1881.
Aus Schleiermachers Leben. In Briefen. 4 Bde., Berlin, 1858–63.
"Briefwechsel Varnhagens mit J. P. V. Troxler 1815–1818." *Mitteilungen aus dem Literaturarchiv in Berlin,* 1900.

VI GENERAL

Börne, Ludwig, *Der ewige Jude,* 1821; *Für die Juden,* 1819; *Brief aus Paris,* 1832–34.
Brentano, Clemens, *Der Philister vor, in und nach der Geschichte.* Heidelberg, 1811.
Buchholz, Friedrich, *Untersuchungen über den Geburtsadel.* Berlin, 1807.
Dohm, Christian Wilhelm, *Über die bürgerliche Verbesserung der Juden.* Berlin, 1781–83; *Denkwürdigkeiten meines Lebens.* Lemgo, 1814–19.
Fichte, Johann Gottlieb, *Die Grundzüge des gegenwärtigen Zeitalters, in Vorlesungen, gehalten im Winter 1804/05.* Berlin, 1806; *Reden an die deutsche Nation.* Berlin, 1808.
Friedländer, David, *Sendschreiben an Seine Hochwürden, Herrn Oberconsistorialrath Probst Teller zu Berlin von einigen Hausvätern jüdischer Religion.* Berlin, 1799.
Geiger, Ludwig, "Vom Wiener Kongress." *Die Zeit.* 29. Sept.–4. Okt. 1917.
Grattenauer, Carl, *Über die physische und moralische Verfassung der heutigen Juden. Stimme eines Kosmopoliten.* Berlin, 1791. Rezensiert in *Allgemeine Deutsche Bibliothek.* Bd. 112, 1792; *Wider die Juden.* Berlin, 1802.
Herder, Johann Gottfried, *Briefe zur Beförderung der Humanität,* 1793–97; "Über die politische Bekehrung der Juden." *Adrastea und das 18. Jahrhundert,* 1801–03.
Humboldt, Wilhelm von, "Über die männliche und weibliche Form," 1795. *Gesammelte Schriften.* Herausg. von Albert Leitzmann. Bd. 1., Berlin, 1903–36; "Gutachten," 1809. J. Freund, *Die Emanzipation der Juden in Preussen.* Berlin, 1912; "Tagebücher." *Gesammelte Schriften.* Bd. XIV u. XV.
Jost, J. M., *Neuere Geschichte der Israeliten. 1815–1845.* Berlin, 1846.
Marwitz, Friedrich August Ludwig von der, "Letzte Vorstellung der Stände des Lebusischen Kreises an den König," 1811. *Werke.* Herausg. von Meusel. Berlin, 1908; "Über eine Reform des Adels," 1812, ibid.; "Von den Ursachen des Verfalls der preussischen Staaten," ibid.
Mendelssohn, Moses, "Schreiben an Lavater," 1769. *Gesammelte Schriften.* Bd. 7, Berlin, 1930; "Vorrede zur Übersetzung von Menasseh ben Israel. Rettung der Juden," 1782. *Gesammelte Schriften.* Bd. 3, Leipzig, 1843–45.
Mirabeau, H. G. R. de, *Sur Moses Mendelssohn.* London, 1788.
Paulus, Heinrich E. G., *Beiträge von jüdischen und christlichen Gelehrten zur Verbesserung der Bekenner des jüdischen Glaubens.* Frankfurt, 1817; *Die jüdische Nationalabsonderung nach Ursprung, Folgen und Besserungsmitteln,* 1831.

Rousseau, Jean Jacques, "Confessions." *Oeuvres complètes.* vols. 23–26, Paris, 1788–93.

Ruehs, Christian Friedrich, "Über die Ansprüche der Juden auf das deutsche Bürgerrecht." *Zeitschrift für neuere Geschichte der Völker und Staatenkunde.* Berlin, 1815; *Die Rechte des Christentums und des deutschen Volkes verteidigt gegen die Ansprüche der Juden und ihrer Verfechter,* 1815.

Briefwechsel zwischen Schiller und Wilhelm von Humboldt. Dritte vermehrte Ausgabe, mit Anmerkungen von Albert Leitzmann. Stuttgart, 1900.

Schlegel, August Wilhelm und Friedrich, *Athenäum.* Berlin, 1798.

Schlegel, Friedrich, *Lucinde.* Berlin, 1799; "Charakteristik des Wilhelm Meister." *Charakteristiken und Kritiken.* I. Bd., Königsberg, 1801.

Schleiermacher, Friedrich, *Briefe bei Gelegenheit der politischen theologischen Aufgabe und des Sendschreibens jüdischer Hausväter,* 1799. *Werke.* Abt. I, Bd. 5, 1846; "J. G. Fichte. Die Grundzüge des gegenwärtigen Zeitalters" (Rezension in der Jenaer Literaturzeitung, 1807). *Aus Schleiermachers Leben.* Herausg. von Wilhelm Dilthey. Bd. 4, Berlin, 1858–63.

Wahl, Hans, *Prinz Louis Ferdinand von Preussen,* 1925.

Zimmer, Heinrich W. B., *Johann Georg Zimmer und die Romantiker.* Frankfurt, 1888.

OTHER NEW YORK REVIEW CLASSICS

For a complete list of titles, visit www.nyrb.com.